641.555   Lagasse, Emeril.
LAG
          Sizzling skillets and
          other one-pot
          wonders.

ADN
0277

GP

T0642227

Sizzling Skillets
and Other One-Pot Wonders

Also by Emeril Lagasse

Farm to Fork

Emeril 20-40-60

Emeril at the Grill

Emeril's Creole Christmas

Emeril's Delmonico: A Restaurant with a Past

Emeril's New New Orleans Cooking

Emeril's Potluck: Comfort Food
with a Kicked-Up Attitude

Emeril's There's a Chef in My Family!:
Recipes to Get Everybody Cooking

Emeril's There's a Chef in My World!:
Recipes That Take You Places

Emeril's TV Dinners: Kickin' It Up a Notch with
Recipes From *Emeril Live* and *Essence of Emeril*

Every Day's a Party: Louisiana Recipes for
Celebrating with Family and Friends

From Emeril's Kitchens: Favorite Recipes
from Emeril's Restaurants

Louisiana Real and Rustic

Prime Time Emeril: More TV Dinners
From America's Favorite Chef

Emeril's Chef in My Soup!: Recipes for the Kid in Everyone

Sizzling Skillets

and Other One-Pot Wonders

Emeril Lagasse

With Photography by Steven Freeman

WILLIAM MORROW

An Imprint of HarperCollins*Publishers*

SIZZLING SKILLETS AND OTHER ONE-POT WONDERS. Copyright © 2011 by Emeril/
MSLO Acquisitions Sub, LLC. All rights reserved. Printed in the United States of
America. No part of this book may be used or reproduced in any manner whatsoever without written permission except in the case of brief quotations embodied in
critical articles and reviews. For information address HarperCollins Publishers,
10 East 53rd Street, New York, NY 10022.

HarperCollins books may be purchased for educational, business, or sales promo-
tional use. For information please write: Special Markets Department, Harper-
Collins Publishers, 10 East 53rd Street, New York, NY 10022.

FIRST EDITION

Designed by Leah Carlson-Stanisic

Library of Congress Cataloging-in-Publication Data

Lagasse, Emeril.
  Sizzling skillets and other one-pot wonders / Emeril Lagasse ; with photography by
Steven Freeman.—1st ed.
    p. cm.
  Includes index.
  ISBN 978-0-06-174296-5
  1. One-dish meals. 2. Quick and easy cooking. I. Title.
  TX840.O53L35 2011
  641.5'55—dc22

                                        2011005121

11 12 13 14 15   DESKTOP/RRD   10 9 8 7 6 5 4 3 2 1

I'd like to dedicate this book to everyone who
has helped make Emeril's Restaurant what it is today, twenty-one
years later——a place where great food and incredible service come
together to create an atmosphere that folks never want to leave.
Both my dedicated staff and loyal customers alike
have shown me the true value of the family table.

Meat and Veggie Lover's
Deep-Dish Pizza, page 61

Contents

Acknowledgments

My family—Alden, EJ, Meril, Jessie, Jillian, Mom, Dad, Mark, Wendi, Katti Lynn, Dolores, Jason, Jude, and Steven.

Emeril's Culinary Team: Charlotte Martory, Alain Joseph, Stacey Meyer, Angela Sagabaen, and Kamili Hemphill.

My Homebase team: Eric Linquest, Tony Cruz, Dave McCelvey, Marti Dalton, Chef Chris Wilson, Chef Bernard Carmouche, Tony Lott, Scott Farber, Doug Doran, George Ditta, Maggie McCabe, and Jeff Hinson. And all of the Homebase and Emeril's restaurant employees.

Photographer Steven Freeman, assistant Kevin Guiler, and prop stylist Jen Lover.

My Martha Stewart Living Omnimedia associates—Martha Stewart, Charles Koppleman, Lisa Gersh, Lucinda Scala Quinn, and Lesley Levenson.

Michelle Terrebonne and Paige Capossela Green.

HarperCollins: Liate Stehlik, Lynn Grady, Cassie Jones, Jessica Deputato, Tavia Kowalchuk, Michael Brennan, Andrea Rosen, Mary Schuck, Leah Carlson-Stanisic, Kim Lewis, Ann Cahn, Christine Benton, and Karen Lumley.

Carrie Bachman.

Partners: All-Clad/T-Fal, Allen Brothers, American Home Foods 2, B&G Foods, CM International, Inc., Lehrhoff/Sterling, Lenox/Gorham, New Orleans Fish House, Timothy's, Viking Range Corporation, and Zak Design.

Friends: Jim Griffin and Mark Stein.

Our generous and gracious friends at Lucullus and Wirthmore Antiques in New Orleans.

INTRODUCTION

For many of us, the term *one-pot cooking* calls to mind simmering stews and vast cauldrons of hearty, homemade soup. But if you really think about it, you can find all sorts of surprisingly exciting and unique one-pot meals that span the culinary globe. From the regional posoles of Mexico to the stir-fries of China to the paellas of Spain (to name only a few), one-pot cooking is a universal practice. Not only is it the key to speedy kitchen cleanup, but once assembled, many of these dishes can cook mostly unattended, giving the cook time to tend to other things. It was this realization that inspired me to write a book based on dishes that come together in just one pot.

It's not uncommon for cooks to have one go-to pan that they prefer above all others: restaurant chefs swear by their sauté pans, while many home cooks instinctively throw together complete meals in casserole dishes or slow cookers. Others love their Dutch ovens almost as much as members of the family. And some of us couldn't live without the wok, the quintessential one-pot wonder tool. Then there's the "big pot," a simple soup pot or stockpot used to make just about anything the mind can imagine: think chicken-'n'-dumplings, bean stews, and rich chowders. I started out writing a book about my beloved pan, the ubiquitous skillet, but quickly realized that we couldn't leave out these other wonderful one-pot vessels.

Minestrone page 248

After searching for intense flavor combinations and international takes on familiar dishes that cook in one pot, we've arrived at more than 130 delicious recipes with worldly flavors and easily accessible ingredients. From elegant soups to hearty meat-and-potato kinds of fare, it's all here. We did our best to include recipes that form the basis of a complete meal, though some dishes are easily rounded out with steamed rice, mashed potatoes, or a loaf of crusty bread. No matter the degree to which your kitchen is outfitted, if you have any kind of pot or pan, there is something here for you.

So dig in! Put a dish together, watch it simmer, and serve it up. Here's to home cooking at its best.

SKILLETS AND
Sauté Pans

SKILLET, frying pan, or sauté pan— by any name, it's the mainstay of any chef's kitchen.

FETTUCCINE WITH A CRAWFISH CREAM SAUCE

Crawfish pasta is a hugely popular dish in New Orleans, especially in the spring, when crawfish is inexpensive and abundant. Cooked and peeled crawfish tails come packaged in 1-pound bags and can be found both fresh and frozen in almost all of our local grocery stores and fish markets, or they can be found online. Make sure to use Louisiana crawfish; they are far superior in taste and texture to the imported Chinese variety.

3 tablespoons unsalted butter

1 cup finely chopped yellow onion

1/2 cup minced red bell pepper

1 tablespoon minced garlic

1/4 cup minced smoked ham

2 cups heavy cream

2 teaspoons freshly squeezed lemon juice

1 1/2 teaspoons salt

1/2 teaspoon freshly ground black pepper

1 pound peeled cooked Louisiana crawfish tails, with fat

1 1/2 teaspoons Emeril's Original Essence or Creole Seasoning (recipe follows)

1/4 cup finely chopped green onion

1/2 cup finely grated Parmigiano-Reggiano cheese

2 tablespoons minced fresh parsley leaves

1 pound fettuccine or linguine, cooked until al dente and drained

Crushed red pepper (optional)

1. In a large skillet, melt the butter over medium-high heat. Add the onion, bell pepper, and garlic and sauté for 3 to 4 minutes, stirring occasionally. Add the ham and cook, stirring, for 1 minute. Stir in the cream, lemon juice, salt, and pepper.

2. Bring to a boil and cook until the cream has thickened and reduced by almost half in volume, about 4 minutes. (The sauce should be thick enough to coat the back of a spoon.)

3. Season the crawfish with the Essence. Add the crawfish to the pan and cook, stirring, until the crawfish are firm and warmed through, about 2 minutes. (Do not overcook or the crawfish will become tough.) Stir in the green onion, cheese, and parsley and toss to combine. Add the cooked pasta and toss until coated with the sauce and warmed through. Remove from the heat. Taste and adjust the seasoning if necessary.

4.   Serve immediately, garnished with crushed red pepper if desired.

4 to 6 servings

CREOLE SEASONING

---

2 ½ tablespoons paprika

2 tablespoons salt

2 tablespoons garlic powder

1 tablespoon freshly ground black pepper

1 tablespoon onion powder

1 tablespoon cayenne

1 tablespoon dried oregano

1 tablespoon dried thyme

Combine all the ingredients thoroughly and store in an airtight container for up to 1 year.

2/3 cup

RIGATONI WITH A BEEFY MUSHROOM GORGONZOLA SAUCE

This is a rich and indulgent dish with assertive flavors. Blue cheese is a classic complement to beef. Keep in mind that the flavor of the sauce will vary based on the specific type of blue cheese you use because blue cheese can range from mild to pungent. It's easy: choose a blue cheese that *you* like.

3 tablespoons vegetable oil

1 tablespoon unsalted butter

1 rib-eye or sirloin steak, about 1 1/4 inches thick (1 1/2 pounds)

1 teaspoon kosher salt

3/4 teaspoon freshly ground black pepper

1 pound cremini mushrooms, stems trimmed, sliced 1/4 inch thick

1/3 cup minced shallot

1 1/2 teaspoons minced garlic

1/2 teaspoon minced fresh rosemary leaves

1/2 teaspoon minced fresh thyme leaves

1/2 cup dry white wine

1 tablespoon all-purpose flour

1 cup canned low-sodium beef broth, plus more if needed

5 ounces crumbled Gorgonzola or other creamy blue cheese

2/3 cup heavy cream

1 pound rigatoni, cooked until al dente, drained, and 1/2 cup cooking liquid reserved

1 tablespoon chopped fresh parsley leaves

1 tablespoon snipped fresh chives

1.   In a large skillet, heat 1 tablespoon of the vegetable oil over medium-high heat. When hot, add the butter. Season the steak with the kosher salt and 1/2 teaspoon of the pepper. Add the steak to the pan and cook, undisturbed, until nicely browned on one side, about 4 1/2 minutes. Turn the steak over and cook for another 4 1/2 minutes. Remove from the pan, transfer to a paper towel–lined plate, and tent with foil. Set aside.

2.   Add the mushrooms, the remaining oil, and the remaining black pepper and cook, stirring occasionally, until the mushrooms are softened and their liquid has evaporated, about 4 minutes (if the bottom of the pan begins to get too brown, add a little water and stir to release any browned bits). Add the shallot, garlic, rosemary, and thyme and cook, stirring, for 2 minutes.

3. Pour in the wine and cook until the liquid is almost completely evaporated, 1 to 2 minutes. Sprinkle with the flour and stir to combine. Cook for 1 minute. Add the cup of broth and cook, stirring to release any browned bits on the bottom of the pan, until reduced by half, about 5 minutes. Add the cheese and cream to the pan and cook until the cheese is melted and the sauce is creamy, 2 to 3 minutes.

4. Add the rigatoni and stir to combine. If necessary, add some of the reserved pasta-cooking water or a bit more beef broth to achieve the desired sauce consistency. Cook just until the sauce is heated through and creamy. Thinly slice the beef, return to the pan, and stir to combine.

5. Serve immediately, garnished with the parsley and chives.

4 to 6 servings

CHICKEN POT PIE WITH A BISCUIT TOP

This homespun classic comes to the table in the skillet it is cooked in, topped with herbed buttermilk biscuits that kick its comfort level up to new heights. Don't hesitate to make the filling in advance if you like; then simply reheat and top with the biscuits before popping it in the oven.

2 pounds boneless, skinless chicken thighs, cut into 1-inch pieces

1 ½ teaspoons salt

¾ teaspoon freshly ground black pepper

1 tablespoon olive oil

3 tablespoons unsalted butter, plus 3 tablespoons melted

1 pound button mushrooms, stemmed and quartered

1 ½ cups small-diced onion

¾ cup small-diced carrot

¾ cup small-diced celery

1 tablespoon minced garlic

¼ cup all-purpose flour

4 cups chicken stock or canned low-sodium chicken broth

8 ounces Yukon Gold potatoes, scrubbed and diced

1 tablespoon fresh thyme leaves

½ cup fresh or frozen green peas

1 recipe Tarragon Biscuits (recipe follows)

1. Set a 12-inch cast-iron skillet over medium-high heat.

2. In a large bowl, combine the chicken thighs with 1 teaspoon of the salt, ½ teaspoon of the pepper, and the olive oil. Place half the chicken in the pan and sear, stirring occasionally, until the chicken begins to brown, 3 to 4 minutes. Remove the chicken and set aside in a separate bowl while you cook the remaining chicken. Place that cooked chicken in the bowl as well.

3. Add the unmelted butter to the pan and, when melted, add the mushrooms and the remaining salt and pepper. Cook until the mushrooms are well caramelized, 3 to 4 minutes, then add the onion, carrot, celery, and garlic and cook, stirring occasionally, until lightly caramelized, 4 to 5 minutes. Add the flour and cook, stirring, for 1 minute. Add the stock, browned chicken, potatoes, and thyme.

4. Preheat the oven to 475°F.

5. Bring the liquid to a boil, reduce the heat so that the sauce just simmers, and cook, stirring occasionally, until the chicken and potatoes are tender, about 35 minutes. Gently stir in the peas and then remove the pan from the heat. Place the biscuits on top of the chicken and gravy, with 8 biscuits around the

edge of the pan and the remaining 4 biscuits in the center. Be sure the biscuits do not touch. Brush the tops of the biscuits with the melted butter and bake until the biscuits are golden brown and flaky, 14 to 15 minutes. Allow the pot pie to cool briefly before serving.

About 6 servings

TARRAGON BISCUITS

---

1 ½ cups all-purpose flour, plus more for dusting
1 cup cake flour
1 ¼ teaspoons baking powder
½ teaspoon baking soda
2 teaspoons sugar
1 ½ teaspoons salt
5 tablespoons cold unsalted butter, cubed
1 tablespoon chopped fresh tarragon leaves
1 ½ cups buttermilk

1. Sift the all-purpose flour, cake flour, baking powder, baking soda, sugar, and salt into a large bowl.

2. Using your fingers or a pastry cutter, work the cold butter into the flour until the pieces of butter are pea sized. Add the tarragon and buttermilk and, with your hands or a rubber spatula, stir just until the milk and flour come together to form a dough.

3. Sprinkle some of the extra all-purpose flour on a work surface and place the dough on top of the flour. Use your hands to press the dough into a ½-inch-thick disk about 9 inches in diameter. Using a 2-inch round cutter dusted with flour, cut out 12 dough rounds. Be sure to press straight down when cutting the dough—a twisting motion will prevent the dough from rising.

4. Place the biscuits on top of the pot pie and bake as directed (see Note).

12 biscuits, 6 servings

Note: Should you desire to make the biscuits on their own, brush the tops with 3 tablespoons of melted butter and bake at 475°F on a large ungreased baking sheet, with the biscuits spaced evenly apart, for about 15 minutes.

VEAL MARSALA

This classic pairing goes way back, and, boy, lemme tell you, it's one not to be tampered with. Marsala wine is of Sicilian origin and can range from sweet to very dry. Keep in mind that the type of Marsala you use here will directly impact the flavor of the sauce. If you can find only dry Marsala, you may not need the full amount of lemon juice to balance the sauce.

1 tablespoon olive oil

4 tablespoons ($\frac{1}{2}$ stick) unsalted butter

1 pound veal cutlets (4 to 5 pieces), pounded to $\frac{1}{4}$-inch thickness

$\frac{3}{4}$ teaspoon salt

$\frac{1}{2}$ teaspoon freshly ground black pepper

2 tablespoons all-purpose flour

1 pound button mushrooms, stems trimmed, sliced

2 tablespoons minced shallot

1 teaspoon minced garlic

$\frac{2}{3}$ cup sweet Marsala wine

1 tablespoon freshly squeezed lemon juice

1 cup dark chicken stock, beef stock, or mushroom stock or canned low-sodium chicken, beef, or vegetable broth

2 teaspoons chopped fresh parsley

Buttered egg noodles or mashed potatoes, for serving

1. Preheat the oven to 200°F.

2. Set a 12-inch sauté pan over medium-high heat. Add the olive oil and 1 tablespoon of the butter to the pan. Season the veal with $\frac{1}{2}$ teaspoon of the salt and $\frac{1}{4}$ teaspoon of the pepper. Dust with the flour, shaking to remove any excess, then add the veal to the sauté pan. Sear for 1 minute per side, then transfer the veal to a baking sheet and place in the oven while you prepare the sauce.

3. Add the mushrooms, shallot, garlic, and 2 tablespoons of the remaining butter to the pan and sauté, stirring often, until the mushrooms are well caramelized and have given off most of their liquid, about 5 minutes. Deglaze the pan with the wine and lemon juice and cook until nearly evaporated, 2 to 4 minutes. Add the stock and cook until reduced by half, 4 to 5 minutes. Add the parsley and the final tablespoon of butter to the pan and swirl to combine.

4. Remove the veal from the oven and add back to the pan with the sauce. Baste the veal with the sauce and then serve immediately over buttered egg noodles or mashed potatoes.

About 4 servings

PORK SCHNITZEL WITH CREAMY
SHIITAKE MUSHROOM SAUCE

Wiener schnitzel is a traditional Austrian dish using veal cutlets, but lean pork loin cutlets work just as well and are more economical. Schnitzel is a surprisingly simple yet comforting dish. Simple buttered egg noodles would be the perfect accompaniment.

3 eggs

¼ cup milk

1 cup fine dry breadcrumbs

1 pound pork loin cutlets, pounded to ⅛-inch thickness

1 ½ teaspoons salt

1 teaspoon freshly ground white pepper

¼ cup olive oil

5 tablespoons cold unsalted butter

8 ounces shiitake mushrooms, stemmed and sliced

1 cup finely chopped leek, white part only

2 cloves garlic, thinly sliced

⅔ cup white wine

¾ cup heavy cream

½ cup chicken stock or canned low-sodium chicken broth

2 teaspoons chopped fresh thyme leaves

½ teaspoon freshly ground black pepper

1 ½ tablespoons chopped fresh parsley leaves

4 lemon wedges

1.   Preheat the oven to 200°F.

2.   Combine the eggs and milk in a shallow dish and whisk to combine. Place the breadcrumbs in a separate shallow dish. Season the pork cutlets with 1 teaspoon of the salt and the white pepper. Working one at a time, dip the cutlets in the egg and milk mixture, letting any excess drip off, and then dredge in the breadcrumbs. Set the cutlets aside.

3.   Heat the oil in a 14-inch sauté pan over medium-high heat. Add 1 tablespoon of the butter and heat until the foam subsides. Add half the breaded cutlets (taking care not to overcrowd the pan) and cook until the cutlets are browned on both sides, about 1½ minutes per side. Briefly transfer to a plate lined with paper towels to drain, then place the cutlets on a baking sheet in the oven while you cook the remaining cutlets. Repeat with an additional tablespoon of butter and the remaining cutlets.

4. When you've finished cooking the cutlets, discard any oil remaining in the skillet and wipe the skillet with paper towels to remove any browned bits. Add the remaining 3 tablespoons butter to the pan. When the foam subsides, add the mushrooms and cook for 3 to 4 minutes, or until the mushrooms are golden brown and their liquid has evaporated.

5. Add the leek and garlic and cook for 2 minutes. Pour in the wine and cook until it has reduced by half. Add the cream, stock, and thyme and cook until the sauce reduces slightly and is thick enough to coat the back of a spoon, 2 to 3 minutes. Season with the remaining ½ teaspoon salt and the black pepper.

6. Divide the schnitzel among four plates and spoon some of the mushroom sauce over each portion. Garnish with the chopped parsley and a lemon wedge and serve immediately.

4 servings

EMERIL'S CHICKEN BRAISED WITH
APPLES AND CABBAGE

You know I love cabbage. Here's a favorite one-dish meal I whip up all the time at home. You'll be bowled over by the combination of apples and cabbage with the chicken. Go ahead: knock 'em dead.

1 cup apple juice or cider

½ cup vegetable oil

2 ½ cups chopped onion

2 tablespoons honey

2 tablespoons fresh thyme leaves

¼ teaspoon cayenne

3 pounds chicken thighs, trimmed of excess fat

2 ¼ teaspoons salt

1 teaspoon freshly ground black pepper

1 ½ tablespoons unsalted butter

2 teaspoons minced garlic

3 pounds cabbage, cored and chopped into large pieces

1 cup dry white wine

2 cups chicken stock or canned low-sodium chicken broth

3 sprigs fresh thyme

1 sweet apple, unpeeled, such as Fuji or Gala

1. To make the marinade, add the apple juice, vegetable oil, ½ cup of the chopped onion, the honey, thyme leaves, and ⅛ teaspoon of the cayenne to a blender and blend on high for 1 minute. Transfer the marinade to a resealable 1-gallon plastic food storage bag. Add the chicken pieces to the bag, seal, and refrigerate for 8 hours or up to overnight.

2. Remove the chicken from the marinade and pat lightly with paper towels to remove any excess liquid. (Discard the marinade.) Season the chicken with 1½ teaspoons of the salt and ½ teaspoon of the pepper and set aside.

3. Melt the butter in a 12-inch (or larger) skillet set over medium heat. Increase the heat to medium-high, add the chicken pieces to the pan skin side down, in batches if necessary, and cook until nicely browned, 1 to 2 minutes per side. Remove the chicken pieces and set aside.

4. Add the remaining 2 cups chopped onion to the pan and cook, stirring frequently, until translucent, about 2 minutes. Add the garlic and the remaining ¾ teaspoon salt, ½ teaspoon pepper, and ⅛ teaspoon cayenne and cook for 1 minute longer. Add half the cabbage and cook, stirring, until slightly softened, about 5 minutes. Add the rest of the cabbage and cook

for 5 minutes longer. Return the chicken to the pan, nestling it in the cabbage. Add the wine, stock, and thyme sprigs. Bring to a boil, reduce the heat to low, and cover. Simmer the chicken until it is very tender, 50 to 60 minutes.

5.   Core and chop the apple into ½-inch dice and add to the pan. Continue to cook until the apple is just tender, about 10 minutes longer. Serve in shallow bowls.

4 to 6 servings

SEARED SCALLOPS WITH SAVOY CABBAGE, FINGERLING POTATOES, PINK LADIES, AND SULTANAS

Scallops are incredibly easy to cook if you remember one thing: the pan needs to be screaming hot. They cook very quickly, and with a hot pan and the right amount of oil the scallops will turn a beautiful golden brown. Just resist the urge to move the scallops around as they sear. The cabbage, potatoes, apples, and raisins turn this dish into a delicious fall harvest.

½ pound Ruby Crescent or other fingerling potatoes

1 sprig fresh thyme

2 bay leaves

5 black peppercorns

3 ½ teaspoons salt

2 tablespoons sultanas (golden raisins)

⅓ cup apple cider

12 large (U-10) sea scallops

1 teaspoon freshly ground white pepper

3 tablespoons grapeseed or olive oil

3 cups Savoy cabbage cut into 1-inch squares

⅓ cup white wine

⅓ cup chicken stock or canned low-sodium chicken broth

6 tablespoons (¾ stick) cold unsalted butter, cut into cubes

1 teaspoon chopped fresh thyme leaves

½ cup cored and julienned apple, preferably Pink Lady or Honeycrisp

1 tablespoon toasted pine nuts, for garnish

1. In a medium saucepan, combine the potatoes, thyme sprig, bay leaves, peppercorns, 2 teaspoons of the salt, and enough cold water to cover the potatoes by 1 inch. Bring the potatoes to a boil over high heat and then reduce the heat to a simmer. Cook the potatoes until fork-tender, about 20 minutes. Cool the potatoes in the cooking liquid to reduce the risk that they will crumble or break when sliced. Then slice them crosswise into ¼-inch rounds and set aside. This may be done up to several days in advance.

2. Combine the raisins and cider in a small bowl and let stand until the raisins are plumped, about 15 minutes.

3. Season the scallops on both sides with 1 teaspoon of the remaining salt and ½ teaspoon of the white

pepper. Heat 2 tablespoons of the oil in a large sauté pan over high heat. When hot, add half of the scallops and cook until deep golden brown on the first side, about 3 minutes. Turn the scallops and cook until browned on the second side, about 3 minutes longer. Transfer the scallops from the pan to a paper towel–lined plate and repeat with the remaining scallops. Once all of the scallops have cooked, tent them with a piece of aluminum foil to keep them warm.

4. Add the remaining tablespoon of oil to the pan and reduce the heat to medium-high. Add the cabbage and cook until it begins to wilt, 2 to 3 minutes. Add the wine and cook until reduced by half, 2 to 3 minutes. Add the potatoes, the raisins and cider, and the stock. Bring the liquid to a boil, occasionally swirling the pan. As the sauce begins to thicken, whisk in the butter little by little, working quickly and fully incorporating each addition before adding more. Do not allow the sauce to boil after you begin adding the butter or the sauce will break. Add the chopped thyme and julienned apple and season with the remaining ½ teaspoon salt and ½ teaspoon white pepper.

5. To serve, spoon one-quarter of the cabbage and potato mixture along with some of the sauce onto each of four plates, then top each plate with 3 scallops. Sprinkle the toasted pine nuts around the scallops and serve immediately.

4 main-course or 6 appetizer servings

EMERIL'S PAELLA

There are many regional variations of this well-known Spanish dish, but some things always remain the same: using short-grain rice, a flavorful broth, and saffron and cooking the rice just right for the perfect texture. Although we give a suggested cooking time, stoves and ovens do vary, so take the time to practice and perfect your paella. Be patient and have fun. Of course, a paella pan is ideal, but if you don't have one, not to worry; simply use a 14-inch ovenproof sauté pan.

---

3 tablespoons Spanish olive oil

1 pound head-on jumbo shrimp, deheaded, peeled, and deveined, or 1/2 pound jumbo shrimp without heads, peeled and deveined

2 1/2 teaspoons sweet pimentón (smoked Spanish paprika)

2 teaspoons salt

4 ounces firm Spanish chorizo, sliced into 1/4-inch half-moons

1 cup small-diced onion

1 cup small-diced red bell pepper

1 cup small-diced green bell pepper

2 tablespoons minced garlic

2 teaspoons saffron threads, crumbled between your fingers

2 cups short-grain rice, such as Valenciano or California Pearl

5 cups Shrimp Stock (page 26), clam juice, or fish stock

1 pound manila clams, well scrubbed and purged (see page 32)

1/2 cup fresh or frozen green peas

1 pound mussels, well scrubbed and debearded

3 tablespoons chopped fresh parsley

1. Preheat the oven to 375°F.

2. Set a 14-inch paella pan or a 14-inch ovenproof sauté pan over medium-high heat and add 2 tablespoons of the olive oil. Season the shrimp with 2 teaspoons of the pimentón and 1/2 teaspoon of the salt. When the oil is hot, sear the shrimp, about 1 minute per side. Remove the shrimp from the pan and set aside. Add the remaining olive oil and the chorizo to the pan and sear, stirring occasionally, until the sausage is nicely browned, 1 to 3 minutes.

3. Add the onion, bell peppers, garlic, and saffron to the pan and sauté, stirring often, until lightly caramelized, 6 to 7 minutes. Add the rice to the pan and cook, stirring, for 3 minutes. Season with the remaining 1 1/2 teaspoons salt and 1/2 teaspoon pimentón. Add the stock to the pan, bring to a boil, reduce the heat to a simmer, and cook, undisturbed, until the rice is no longer soupy but some liquid remains, 5 to 6 min-

utes. Give the rice a quick stir, then add the clams, with the opening-edge facing up. Reduce the heat to low and continue to simmer for 5 minutes. Add the peas, mussels (again, opening-edge facing up), and shrimp to the pan and cook, undisturbed, for 10 minutes.

4. Transfer to the oven and cook until the clams and mussels have opened up, the liquid is mostly absorbed, and the rice is almost cooked through, about 10 minutes.

5. Remove the paella from the oven and cover with foil. Let it sit for another 10 minutes before serving. (The rice will continue to cook and absorb liquid as it sits.) Serve garnished with the chopped parsley.

6 to 8 servings

CHICKEN PAPRIKASH

Here's a delicious old-fashioned chicken dish from Hungary. Try it for yourself; it'll be a family favorite in no time. If it's too spicy for you, serve it with additional sour cream—it'll still be authentic.

3 pounds chicken thighs, trimmed of excess fat

2 tablespoons Hungarian sweet paprika

2 ½ teaspoons salt

½ teaspoon freshly ground black pepper

½ cup all-purpose flour

3 tablespoons vegetable oil

1 onion, thinly sliced (about 2 cups)

1 green bell pepper, cut into ¼-inch strips (about 1 ½ cups)

1 red bell pepper, cut into ¼-inch strips (about 1 ½ cups)

½ teaspoon cayenne

3 sprigs fresh marjoram, plus 2 tablespoons chopped

2 teaspoons minced garlic

1 cup dry white wine

1 cup canned diced tomatoes, with juice

1 cup chicken stock or canned low-sodium chicken broth

8 ounces egg noodles, cooked and tossed with 2 tablespoons butter, for serving

½ cup sour cream, plus more for serving if desired

2 tablespoons chopped fresh parsley

1.   Place the chicken in a medium bowl and season with 1 tablespoon of the paprika, 1 teaspoon of the salt, and the black pepper. Mix well to combine. Add the flour and toss until evenly coated. Shake the chicken to remove any excess flour, then set it aside on a plate.

2.   Heat the oil in a 12-inch skillet over medium-high heat until hot but not smoking. Add the chicken pieces to the pan, skin side down and in batches if necessary, and cook until nicely browned, 3 to 4 minutes per side. Remove the chicken pieces and set aside.

3.   Add the onion, bell peppers, cayenne, marjoram sprigs, and remaining 1 tablespoon paprika and 1½ teaspoons salt and cook, stirring as needed, until softened, about 10 minutes. Add the garlic and cook for 1 minute longer. Pour the wine, tomatoes and juice, and stock into the pan. Return the chicken to the pan, nestle the pieces in the sauce, and bring to a boil. Reduce the heat to low, cover, and simmer the chicken until fork-tender, about 1 hour.

4. To serve, remove the chicken from the pan and set aside on top of the egg noodles in a warm place. Add the sour cream to a small bowl. Whisk 1 cup of the sauce from the pan into the sour cream, then carefully whisk the sour cream mixture into the hot sauce remaining in the pan. Stir in the chopped marjoram and parsley and remove from the heat. Spoon the sauce over the chicken and noodles and serve immediately.

4 to 6 servings

CHORIZO AND POTATO QUESADILLAS WITH CILANTRO-CHILE CREMA

Well, you know how much I love chorizo. I couldn't help putting it in these quesadillas with some diced potatoes for one knockout meal. Don't skip the cilantro-chile crema; it is super-easy to put together and really *is* the icing on this cake!

1 ½ pounds Idaho potatoes, peeled and cut into ½-inch cubes

Kosher salt

1 ¼ cups sour cream

2 tablespoons sliced green onion, green part only

1 serrano or jalapeño chile, seeded if desired and minced

½ teaspoon minced garlic

⅛ teaspoon cayenne

¾ cup lightly packed fresh cilantro leaves

1 pound fresh chorizo sausage, removed from casings and crumbled

1 ½ cups minced red onion

Freshly ground black pepper to taste

6 large burrito-size flour tortillas (10-inch diameter)

¾ cup chopped red bell pepper

3 cups grated Colby Jack cheese (12 ounces)

3 tablespoons vegetable oil

1. Place the potatoes and 2 teaspoons of salt in a small saucepan and add enough cool water to cover the potatoes by ½ inch. Bring to a brisk simmer over high heat and cook until the potatoes are fork-tender, 5 to 7 minutes. Drain the potatoes in a colander and set aside.

2. Combine the sour cream, green onion, serrano, garlic, cayenne, ¼ cup of the cilantro leaves, and ½ teaspoon salt in a blender and process until smooth. Transfer to a small bowl and set the crema aside.

3. Heat a 10- or 12-inch nonstick skillet over medium-high heat and add the chorizo. Cook until browned, stirring to break up any clumps, about 4 minutes. Add the red onion and cook until soft, about 4 minutes. Add the potatoes, stir to combine, and season with salt and pepper to taste. Transfer the meat-potato mixture to a heatproof bowl and set aside.

4. Carefully wipe the skillet with a paper towel and then return it to the stove. Working one at a time, place ¾ cup of the chorizo-potato filling onto one side of a tortilla, then top with 2 tablespoons of the bell pepper and ½ cup of the grated cheese. Fold the empty side of the tortilla over the filling ingredients.

5. Heat 1½ teaspoons of the oil in the hot skillet and then transfer a filled tortilla to the skillet. Cook until the tortilla is crisp and golden brown on the bottom, 2 to 3 minutes. Flip the quesadilla to the other side and cook until crisp and golden brown on the second side and the cheese is melted, about 2 minutes longer. Remove from the skillet and repeat with the remaining quesadillas.

6. Cut the quesadillas into wedges and serve drizzled with the crema. Garnish with the remaining cilantro leaves.

6 servings

FIDEUÀ

Don't let the fancy name scare you ... this is nothing more than small pieces of pasta cooked by the paella method, and for you pasta lovers out there, it'll knock your socks off. It's a great dish to prepare for small gatherings since it serves a bunch and is simple to boot. But take care when sautéing the pasta—once it starts browning it can quickly go from golden to dark brown if you take your eyes away for a second.

2 pounds head-on extra-large shrimp, peeled and deveined, heads and shells reserved for the shrimp stock (see Note 1)

1 ½ teaspoons sweet pimentón (smoked Spanish paprika)

1 tablespoon extra-virgin olive oil

3 ½ teaspoons kosher salt

¾ cup plus 2 tablespoons mild olive oil

1 pound angel hair pasta (capellini), broken into 1-inch pieces (see Note 2)

2 medium onions, finely chopped (3 ½ cups)

½ cup chopped green bell pepper

2 tablespoons minced garlic

1 teaspoon crushed red pepper

1 pound plum tomatoes, finely chopped (2 cups)

¼ cup finely chopped fresh parsley, plus more for garnish

¾ teaspoon loosely packed saffron threads

½ cup dry white wine

6 ½ cups Shrimp Stock (recipe follows) or purchased shrimp or light fish stock

1 recipe Alioli (recipe follows)

1.   In a small bowl, combine the shrimp, pimentón, extra-virgin olive oil, and ¾ teaspoon of the salt and set aside.

2.   Preheat the oven to 400°F. Line a large heatproof bowl with paper towels and have it ready near the stove.

3.   Heat ¾ cup of the mild olive oil in a 14-inch ovenproof skillet over medium-high heat (it should come about ¼ inch up the sides of the pan). When hot, add the pasta pieces and cook, stirring and tossing frequently, until the pasta is toasted and golden brown. Take care not to let the pasta burn; it cooks quickly once it begins to brown. Using a slotted spoon, transfer the pasta pieces to the paper towel–lined bowl and set aside. (You may need to wipe the skillet with a paper towel to remove any stubborn pieces of pasta clinging to the pan.)

4.   Add the remaining 2 tablespoons mild olive oil to the skillet, then add the onions, bell pepper, and garlic.

Season with the crushed red pepper and ¼ teaspoon of the remaining salt and cook until the onions are softened, 4 to 6 minutes. Add the tomatoes, ¼ cup parsley, and saffron and cook for 1 minute. Add the wine and shrimp stock and bring to a gentle boil. Cook for 5 minutes to allow the flavors to come together slightly. Add the remaining 2½ teaspoons salt and taste; the broth should be well seasoned, if not, add more salt to taste.

5.   Add the sautéed pasta to the boiling broth and cook, stirring frequently, until the liquid returns to a boil and the pasta expands and absorbs some of the broth; it should be thickened but still somewhat soupy, 3 to 5 minutes. Add the shrimp and 2 tablespoons of the alioli, stir well to combine, and nestle the shrimp down into the pasta. Transfer the skillet to the oven and cook until the pasta has absorbed almost all of the liquid (it may appear just a bit jiggly in the center) and the surface is crispy, about 10 minutes. Set aside, loosely covered, for 10 minutes before serving.

6.   Serve hot, garnished with the additional parsley and with the remaining alioli passed at the table.

8 to 10 servings

SHRIMP STOCK

1 tablespoon mild olive oil
Shrimp heads and shells reserved from 2 pounds shrimp
    for Fideuà
1 onion, quartered
1 celery stalk, coarsely chopped
1 small carrot, coarsely chopped
1 clove garlic, smashed
¼ teaspoon freshly ground black pepper
½ teaspoon kosher salt
8 cups water

Note 1: If head-on unpeeled shrimp are unavailable, substitute 1 to 1 ½ pounds of peeled and deveined shrimp and purchase 6 ½ cups shrimp or light fish stock. Skip the steps and ingredients for making the shrimp stock with the shells and proceed as directed.

Note 2: Goya makes a product called capelli di angelo (angel hair) that is already broken into ½-inch pieces. It can often be found in the international aisle of supermarkets along with other Latin products. If you can find this product, by all means use it here instead of having to break the pasta yourself.

Heat a large saucepan over high heat and add the oil. Add the shrimp heads and shells and cook, stirring, until toasted and fragrant, about 4 minutes. Add the onion, celery, carrot, garlic, pepper, salt, and water and bring to a boil. Reduce the heat to a simmer and cook, skimming any foam that rises to the surface, until the stock is flavorful, about 20 minutes. Strain the stock through a fine-mesh sieve and discard solids. If necessary, add enough water, clam broth, or chicken stock to bring the volume up to $6\frac{1}{2}$ cups.

about 6 $\frac{1}{2}$ cups

ALIOLI

This Spanish take on aïoli is integral to the success of this dish. Depending on where you are in Spain, it might be called *alioli, allioli,* or *ajoaceite,* but no matter what you call it, garlic bathed in olive oil is never a bad thing. In Catalonia, traditional alioli is made without eggs, but you'll find it creamier, milder, and easier to make if you leave the yolks in as instructed here.

    2 tablespoons minced garlic
    $\frac{3}{4}$ teaspoon kosher salt
    2 egg yolks
    2 teaspoons freshly squeezed lemon juice
    1 cup olive oil

Mash the garlic and salt into a paste using a mortar and pestle or the side of a chef's knife; transfer to a food processor and add the egg yolks and lemon juice. Process to combine. While the motor is running, add the oil, in a thin steady stream, until a smooth mayonnaise is formed. (Should the mayonnaise break slightly, add a bit of water, a teaspoon at a time, and stir to recombine.) Taste and adjust the seasoning if necessary. Transfer to a small bowl and refrigerate for up to 1 day before serving.

About 1¼ cups

TORTILLA ESPAÑOLA

This dish works equally well at breakfast, lunch, or dinner and may be served hot, warm, or at room temperature. A classic Spanish tortilla, though similar to a frittata, is characterized by the use of potatoes and ham and is traditionally served with a garlic mayonnaise known as *aioli, alioli,* or *allioli.*

Flipping the tortilla takes a little practice; we suggest using oven mitts when doing so to help protect your hands and arms.

½ cup plus 1 ½ tablespoons olive oil

6 cups thinly sliced onion

¼ teaspoon sugar

1 ½ teaspoons kosher salt

¾ teaspoon freshly ground black pepper

2 pounds Idaho Russet potatoes, peeled and cut into small dice (about 4 cups)

½ cup fresh chorizo or other spicy sausage, removed from casings (about 4 ounces or 1 sausage link)

9 eggs, beaten until frothy in a medium bowl

½ cup finely diced ham

Alioli, for serving (page 27)

1 tablespoon snipped fresh chives

1. Heat ¼ cup of the oil in a 12-inch nonstick sauté pan over medium heat. When the oil is hot, add the onion, sugar, ¼ teaspoon of the salt, and ¼ teaspoon of the pepper and cook, stirring occasionally, until the onion is very soft and well caramelized, 45 to 50 minutes. Transfer the onion to a small bowl and set aside. Wipe the skillet clean with a paper towel.

2. Add another ¼ cup of the oil to the skillet and heat over medium-high heat. Season with ½ teaspoon of the remaining salt and ¼ teaspoon of the remaining pepper. Add the potatoes to the hot oil and cook, undisturbed, until golden brown, about 8 minutes. Gently turn the potatoes and continue cooking, flipping occasionally, until most of the potatoes are golden brown and tender, 7 to 10 minutes. Transfer the potatoes to a bowl and set aside. Wipe the skillet clean with a paper towel.

3. Return the skillet to medium heat; add the chorizo and cook, breaking it into little pieces, until cooked through, 4 to 5 minutes. Remove the chorizo from the pan and set aside.

4. Add the remaining 1½ tablespoons oil to the skillet and heat over medium heat.

5. Add the remaining ¾ teaspoon salt and ¼ teaspoon pepper to the eggs. Whisk to combine. Fold the onion, potatoes, chorizo, and ham into the eggs. Pour the entire mixture into the hot pan and cook, undisturbed, until the bottom is set and the top is still runny, about 12 minutes. Continue to cook until the bottom is lightly golden, using a rubber spatula to run around the edge of the eggs, lifting slightly to allow the eggs to run to the bottom and cook.

6. When the top of the tortilla begins to set, place a large plate or serving platter on top of the skillet and, working quickly, invert the tortilla onto the plate. Carefully slide the tortilla back into the skillet so that the browned side is now facing up. Cook until the bottom is golden brown, 10 to 12 minutes longer. Remove the tortilla from the skillet and serve hot, warm, or at room temperature. To serve, cut the tortilla into thin wedges and serve with dollops of the alioli. Garnish with fresh chives.

4 to 6 servings

ANCHO-RUBBED FLAP STEAK WITH A WARM CORN AND BLACK BEAN RELISH

Flap steak is an underrated cut of meat. It has been called the butcher's cut because the butcher would take this less expensive cut for himself. It's also known as a *bavette* or the *French bistro steak* because it's the most common cut used for steak frites. Flap steak is similar to hanger, skirt, and flank steak and should be marinated before cooking. Be sure to cook it properly to showcase its beefy flavor and melt-in-your-mouth texture.

1 tablespoon ancho chile powder (see Note)

1 tablespoon light brown sugar

1 teaspoon unsweetened cocoa powder

1/2 teaspoon dried Mexican or regular oregano, crumbled between your fingers

1/4 teaspoon ground coriander

1 tablespoon plus 1/2 teaspoon Mexican chili powder (found in most grocery stores, or use regular chili powder)

3/4 teaspoon ground cumin

1/4 cup olive oil

1 1/2 pounds flap steak (usually two 12-ounce steaks)

2 1/4 teaspoons salt

1 1/2 cups small-diced red onion

1 cup small-diced red bell pepper

1 cup small-diced green bell pepper

One 14.5-ounce can black beans, drained and rinsed

2 cups fresh corn kernels, cut from the cob, or frozen corn

1 cup drained canned petite diced tomatoes

1/4 cup sliced green onion, both green and white parts

1/4 cup freshly squeezed lime juice

1 tablespoon minced jalapeño chile

1 tablespoon minced garlic

Sour cream, for garnish

Avocado slices, for garnish

Chopped fresh cilantro, for garnish

Warmed corn tortillas, for serving

1.   In a small bowl, combine the ancho powder, brown sugar, cocoa powder, oregano, coriander, 1 tablespoon of the chili powder, 1/2 teaspoon of the cumin, and 2 tablespoons of the oil until thoroughly mixed. Rub the paste evenly over both sides of the flap steaks. Cover the meat lightly with aluminum foil or plastic wrap and marinate in the refrigerator for at least 1 hour and up to 4 hours.

2.   Remove the steaks from the refrigerator and set aside at room temperature for 20 minutes. Heat

1 tablespoon of the remaining olive oil in a large sauté pan over medium-high heat. Season the steaks on both sides with 1¼ teaspoons of the salt. Place the steaks in the pan and cook for 4 to 5 minutes per side. Transfer the steaks to a platter and tent with foil.

3. Add the remaining 1 tablespoon olive oil to the sauté pan. Add the red onion and the red and green peppers and cook over medium-high heat for 3 to 4 minutes, or until the vegetables are tender. Add the black beans, corn, tomatoes, green onion, lime juice, jalapeño, garlic, and remaining ½ teaspoon chili powder and ¼ teaspoon cumin and continue to cook over medium-high heat for 10 minutes, stirring occasionally. Season with the remaining 1 teaspoon salt.

4. Return the steaks along with any juices to the pan and cook until just heated through, 4 to 5 minutes.

5. To serve, transfer the steaks from the pan to a cutting board and, using a carving knife, slice the steak across the grain into thin slices. Divide the corn and black bean relish among four plates, lay the steak slices over the relish, and garnish with sour cream, avocado, and cilantro. Serve with a basket of warm corn tortillas.

4 servings

Note: Ancho powder is made from ground ancho chiles, which are dried poblano peppers. It is a dark, smoky-flavored powder with a rich taste but little heat and is commonly used in traditional Mexican cuisine. It can be found in the international aisle at your local grocer, in Latin markets, or online.

SPAGHETTI WITH CLAMS

This dish reminds me of my childhood in Fall River, Massachusetts. Spaghetti and clams was a staple in my house growing up. Along the East Coast, clams are plentiful and inexpensive. If you're lucky enough to find fresh clams, this simple preparation really showcases their wonderful briny flavor.

1 pound spaghetti, cooked in salted water until al dente and drained

¼ cup olive oil

3 tablespoons unsalted butter

2 tablespoons sliced garlic

½ teaspoon crushed red pepper

2 pounds small clams, such as manila, cockles, or littlenecks, scrubbed and purged in salted water, any open or broken clams discarded (see Note)

⅔ cup dry white wine

Juice of ½ lemon

¾ teaspoon salt

2 tablespoons chopped fresh parsley

Lemon wedges, for serving

1. Toss the cooked spaghetti with 1 tablespoon of the olive oil and set aside.

2. Heat a 14-inch skillet over medium-high heat. Add the butter and the remaining 3 tablespoons olive oil to the pan. Once the butter has melted, add the garlic and crushed red pepper and cook, stirring, until the garlic is lightly toasted, 2 to 3 minutes. Add the clams, wine, lemon juice, and salt and cover the pan. Cook, shaking the pan occasionally, until the clams begin to open, 3 to 4 minutes. Remove the lid and add the reserved pasta and the parsley. Cook, stirring, until the pasta is warmed through, 1 to 2 minutes.

3. Divide the pasta among four large, shallow bowls and serve hot, garnished with lemon wedges.

Note: Clams live buried in the sandy bottom of the ocean floor. They accumulate grit, sand, and dirt because they do not fully close their shells. Live clams need to be purged of the sand and grit prior to cooking. To purge clams, they must be submerged in a saltwater solution of ⅓ cup salt mixed with 1 gallon water for 30 minutes, after which the water should be changed. This should be repeated two or three times. Alternatively, the clams can be left in a large amount of water overnight.

4 servings

"BLT" RISOTTO

The classic combination of bacon, lettuce, and tomato is a natural fit for a simple, creamy risotto. This quick dish is a meal in itself and, once the prep work is done, can be on the table in next to no time.

6 cups chicken stock or canned low-sodium chicken broth

6 ounces thick-cut bacon, diced

1 cup chopped yellow onion

3/4 teaspoon kosher salt

1/2 teaspoon freshly ground black pepper

1 teaspoon minced garlic

1 1/2 teaspoons chopped fresh thyme leaves

1 1/2 cups Arborio or Carnaroli rice

3/4 cup dry white wine

1 pound vine-ripened tomatoes, cored, seeded, and diced (about 1 1/2 cups)

5 ounces baby spinach

2 tablespoons unsalted butter

2 ounces Parmigiano-Reggiano cheese, finely grated (about 3/4 cup)

1. Place the stock in a small saucepan and bring to a bare simmer. Keep warm over low heat.

2. In a 12-inch skillet over medium-high heat, cook the bacon until it is crisp and has released most of its fat, 3 to 4 minutes. Add the onions, salt, and pepper and cook for 3 to 4 minutes. Add the garlic, thyme, and rice and cook, stirring, until the rice is opaque, 3 minutes. Pour in the wine and cook, stirring, until evaporated, about 2 minutes.

3. Add 1 cup of the hot stock to the skillet and cook, stirring frequently, until the rice has absorbed the stock, about 3 minutes. Continue adding the stock in 1/2-cup increments, adding more stock only as each previous addition has been absorbed, until the rice is nearly al dente, about 18 minutes from the time you began adding the stock. You should have about 1/2 cup of stock left.

4. Add the tomatoes and cook for 1 1/2 minutes, or until the tomatoes have released some of their liquid and have softened a bit. Add the spinach, the remaining 1/2 cup stock, the butter, and half of the Parmesan and stir until thoroughly combined and the spinach has wilted. Taste and adjust the seasoning if necessary.

5. Serve the risotto hot, in shallow bowls, garnished with the remaining Parmesan.

4 to 6 servings

LAMB PATTIES WITH A MEDITERRANEAN VEGETABLE RAGOUT

These lamb patties are flavored with spices reminiscent of Mediterranean cooking and paired with vegetables that are cooked in the same skillet, making a ratatouille-ish sauce that perfectly complements the lamb. Garnish with a bit of salty feta and enjoy! To do this in one batch, you'll need to use a 14-inch sauté pan. But, hey, if you don't own one this size, you can cook the recipe in two batches in a 10- or 12-inch pan. To have the patties and vegetables finished simultaneously, pay close attention to the timing instructions I've given here.

3 cups diced eggplant

Kosher salt

1 ½ pounds ground lamb
    (90 percent lean)

2 tablespoons Greek-style yogurt

2 teaspoons ground cumin

1 teaspoon ground coriander

½ teaspoon freshly ground black
    pepper

1 tablespoon plus 1 teaspoon
    minced garlic

2 tablespoons chopped fresh mint
    leaves

2 tablespoons chopped fresh
    parsley leaves

2 tablespoons olive oil

1 cup diced onion

1 ½ cups diced zucchini

1 ½ cups diced yellow squash

1 teaspoon ground allspice

½ teaspoon ground cinnamon

2 ½ cups diced seeded tomato

1 tablespoon freshly squeezed lemon juice

Crumbled feta cheese, for garnish

1.   Place the eggplant in a medium mixing bowl and sprinkle with a few pinches of kosher salt. Toss to coat well, then spread the eggplant on a paper towel–lined baking sheet. Let it sit for 30 minutes. Gently pat dry with paper towels before using.

2.   Combine the lamb, yogurt, cumin, coriander, pepper, 1½ teaspoons of the salt, 1 tablespoon of the garlic, 1 tablespoon of the mint, and 1 tablespoon of the parsley in a large mixing bowl and mix gently to combine. Let it sit at room temperature for about 30 minutes for the flavors to come together. Form the meat into four ¾-inch-thick patties.

3.   Add the oil to a 14-inch skillet or sauté pan and heat it over medium-high heat. When hot, add the patties and cook for about 5½ minutes. Push them to

one side of the pan and add the remaining 1 teaspoon garlic to the other side of the pan. Cook until fragrant, about 30 seconds. Add the onion, eggplant, zucchini, and yellow squash to the side of the pan with the garlic, season with the allspice, cinnamon, and a pinch of salt, and cook, stirring the vegetables as needed, for 2 minutes.

4.   The lamb patties should now be browned on one side. Flip the patties and cook until browned on the second side, 7 to 8 minutes longer. During the last 4 minutes of cooking, add the tomatoes and lemon juice to the vegetables and cook until the tomatoes are tender and the vegetables are saucy. Add ½ teaspoon salt and the remaining 1 tablespoon mint and 1 tablespoon parsley to the vegetable mixture.

5.   Divide the patties among four serving plates, top with the vegetables, and garnish with the crumbled feta cheese. Serve immediately.

4 servings

LINGUINE WITH ARTICHOKES, SHRIMP, AND MASCARPONE

This dish is redolent of spring because the flavors are fresh and bright. The tarragon and lemon zest marry nicely with the shrimp and artichokes, and the addition of creamy mascarpone adds a richness that is hard to replicate. We also tested this recipe using fromage blanc and crème fraîche and, while not exactly the same, they would be the best substitutes if you cannot find mascarpone.

2 tablespoons extra-virgin olive oil

¼ cup minced shallot

½ teaspoon freshly ground white pepper

½ cup dry white wine

Two 15-ounce cans artichoke hearts, drained and quartered

1 pound large shrimp, peeled and deveined

1 teaspoon salt

⅛ teaspoon cayenne

1 teaspoon finely grated lemon zest

1 teaspoon chopped fresh tarragon leaves

8 ounces mascarpone cheese

1 pound linguine, cooked in salted water until al dente, drained, and ¼ cup cooking liquid reserved

½ cup freshly grated Parmigiano-Reggiano cheese

1.   In a 14-inch sauté pan, heat the olive oil over medium heat. When hot, add the shallot and pepper and cook until the shallot is soft and translucent, about 1 minute. Add the wine, bring to a brisk simmer, and cook until the wine is almost completely evaporated, 1 to 2 minutes longer.

2.   Add the artichoke hearts, shrimp, salt, and cayenne and cook the shrimp for 1½ minutes per side. Add the lemon zest, tarragon, and mascarpone and cook, stirring, until thoroughly incorporated, 1 to 2 minutes.

3.   Add the pasta and reserved pasta-cooking liquid to the pan and cook, tossing, until the pasta is warmed through, 1 to 2 minutes. Add the Parmesan, toss to combine, and serve immediately.

Note: If you do not have a 14-inch sauté pan, you may want to cook this dish in two batches.

4 to 6 servings

SPICY SIRLOIN STEAK FAJITAS

Sirloin is a tasty cut of beef that needs to be cooked quickly to achieve the best texture. We prefer it medium-rare, and the quick cooking time makes it a perfect match for fajitas. This Tex-Mex favorite is easy to make at home and is a natural for group get-togethers; guests can assemble their own tortillas with any number of accompaniments.

2 tablespoons freshly squeezed lime juice

2 tablespoons roughly chopped fresh cilantro leaves

4 cloves garlic, smashed, plus 1 tablespoon minced garlic

1 tablespoon chipotle sauce (see Note)

2 teaspoons Worcestershire sauce

1 teaspoon dried Mexican or regular oregano, crumbled between your fingers

1 teaspoon crushed red pepper

1 teaspoon ground coriander

2 teaspoons ground cumin

1/4 cup plus 2 tablespoons olive oil

2 pounds grass-fed beef top sirloin, cut into 1/4-inch slices across the grain

1 tablespoon kosher salt

1 teaspoon freshly ground black pepper

6 large flour tortillas

1 red bell pepper, thinly sliced

1 green bell pepper, thinly sliced

1 yellow bell pepper, thinly sliced

1 large white onion, thinly sliced

1/4 cup thinly sliced green onion

1 teaspoon New Mexican chile powder, regular chili powder, or ancho chile powder

Lime wedges, for serving

Sour cream, for serving

Guacamole, for serving

Pico de gallo, for serving

Cold Mexican beer, for serving (optional)

1. In a small bowl, whisk together the lime juice, cilantro, smashed garlic, chipotle sauce, Worcestershire sauce, oregano, crushed red pepper, coriander, 1 teaspoon of the cumin, and 1 tablespoon of the olive oil. Pour into a large resealable plastic food storage bag, add the steak, and seal. Place in a baking dish and refrigerate for 30 minutes to 1 hour, turning the bag over occasionally.

2. Remove the meat from the bag and pat dry. Discard the marinade. Season the meat on both sides with 2 teaspoons of the salt and 1/2 teaspoon of the black pepper.

3. Preheat the oven to 350°F.

4. Wrap the tortillas in foil and place in the oven to warm while you prepare the meat and vegetables.

5. Heat ¼ cup of the remaining olive oil in a 14-inch sauté pan over medium-high heat. When hot, add the steak and cook for 2 minutes per side. Transfer the cooked beef to a platter and set aside, loosely tented with foil to keep it warm.

6. Meanwhile, in the same sauté pan, heat the remaining tablespoon of olive oil over medium-high heat. Add half of the bell peppers, white onion, green onion, and minced garlic and cook, stirring, until soft and slightly caramelized, 6 to 8 minutes. Transfer to the platter next to the beef, then repeat with the remaining vegetables.

7. In a small bowl, combine the chile powder with the remaining 1 teaspoon salt, ½ teaspoon black pepper, and 1 teaspoon cumin. Return the vegetables to the skillet and add the spice mixture. Cook, stirring, until fragrant, 1 to 2 minutes. Return the cooked beef to the pan and cook, tossing, until warmed through, 1 to 2 minutes.

8. Remove the tortillas from the oven and place one onto each plate. Divide the meat and vegetables evenly among the tortillas and serve immediately, with lime wedges, sour cream, guacamole, your favorite pico de gallo, and cold beer if desired.

6 servings

Note: Chipotle sauce is a hot sauce made from chipotle peppers, which have a warm, smoky flavor. This recipe was tested using La Morena Home Made Style Chipotle Sauce, which can be found in the international aisle of your grocery store, in Latin markets, or online. If you cannot find it in your area, substitute an equal amount of smashed and finely chopped canned chipotles in adobo.

PASTA E FAGIOLE

Fagiole translates as beans in Italian. Traditionally pasta e fagiole is a soup, but many people serve it as a pasta dish with a brothy sauce. Here I kicked it up with pancetta, kale, and crushed red pepper. Use the best-quality pancetta that you can find—it makes a difference. To utilize your time best, cook the pasta while the sauce is simmering.

Three 15-ounce cans white beans, drained and rinsed lightly

4 ounces pancetta, cut into small dice

1 cup small-diced onion

2 teaspoons fresh thyme leaves

1 tablespoon minced garlic

1 teaspoon dried basil, crumbled between your fingers

½ teaspoon crushed red pepper

1 cup roughly chopped drained canned San Marzano tomatoes

6 cups chicken stock or canned low-sodium chicken broth

1 ½ teaspoons kosher salt

12 ounces lacinato or regular kale, chopped

12 ounces dried small pasta such as ditalini (about 2 ½ cups), cooked until al dente and drained

⅓ cup grated Parmigiano-Reggiano cheese, plus more for garnish

Extra-virgin olive oil, for drizzling

1. Mash 2 cups of the beans until almost smooth; set aside.

2. Heat a large skillet over medium heat and add the pancetta. Cook until the pancetta is brown and crispy, 6 to 7 minutes. Using a slotted spoon, transfer the pancetta to a paper towel–lined plate to drain. Discard all but 2 tablespoons of the pancetta drippings.

3. Add the onion and thyme to the skillet and cook, stirring occasionally, until the onion is lightly caramelized, about 4 minutes. Add the garlic, basil, and crushed red pepper and cook, stirring constantly, until the garlic is fragrant, 30 seconds.

4. Add the tomatoes and cook until a bit saucy, about 1 minute. Add the stock and 1 teaspoon of the salt. Stir in the mashed beans and kale and bring to a boil. Simmer the sauce for 7 minutes, then add the whole beans. Continue to cook until the sauce thickens, 7 to 8 minutes longer. Add the pasta and the remaining ½ teaspoon salt and cook, stirring occasionally, until heated through, about 2 minutes. Stir in the Parmesan and reserved pancetta. Divide among serving bowls and drizzle lightly with the extra-virgin olive oil. Garnish with additional Parmesan and serve immediately.

6 to 8 servings

SKILLET STRATA

Yes, it can be done! Strata in a skillet. Why, who'd a-thunk it? This skillet casserole rises and browns beautifully on the top and bottom yet stays nice and creamy inside. After cooking, run a rubber spatula around the edges to help loosen it from the pan, then slide it onto a serving plate for a dramatic presentation.

3 cups half-and-half

10 large eggs

$\frac{1}{2}$ teaspoon freshly ground black pepper

$\frac{1}{4}$ teaspoon cayenne

$\frac{1}{4}$ teaspoon paprika

$\frac{1}{4}$ teaspoon freshly grated nutmeg

$\frac{3}{4}$ teaspoon salt

8 cups 1 $\frac{1}{2}$- to 2-inch cubes Italian bread (a 14- to 16-ounce loaf)

Nonstick cooking spray

3 tablespoons unsalted butter

8 ounces Canadian bacon, chopped into $\frac{1}{2}$-inch pieces

1 small onion, chopped

1 teaspoon minced garlic

1 pound spinach, cleaned

8 ounces Gruyère cheese, grated (about 2 cups)

$\frac{1}{2}$ cup finely grated Parmigiano-Reggiano cheese

1.   In a large bowl, whisk together the half-and-half, eggs, pepper, cayenne, paprika, nutmeg, and $\frac{1}{2}$ teaspoon of the salt. Add the bread, cover, and set aside for at least 1 hour at room temperature and up to overnight in the refrigerator.

2.   Preheat the oven to 400°F.

3.   Spray the bottom and sides of a 12-inch ovenproof skillet generously with nonstick cooking spray. Add the butter and melt it over medium-high heat. Add the Canadian bacon, onion, garlic, and the remaining $\frac{1}{4}$ teaspoon salt and cook for 2 minutes. Add the spinach and cook for 1 minute longer, until wilted. Remove half the mixture from the pan and set aside. Reduce the heat to medium.

4. Using a large spoon, add half of the bread mixture to the pan. Sprinkle half of the cheeses over the bread, then top with the remaining half of the spinach mixture. Spoon the remaining bread on top and finish with the remaining cheese. Bake the strata until puffed and golden brown and the center is set, about 30 minutes. Let stand for 5 minutes before serving.

5. To serve, loosen the strata by running a rubber spatula around the sides and bottom of the pan. Tilt the pan, give it a slight shake, and allow the strata to slide onto a serving plate. Alternatively, leave the strata in the pan, cut into slices, and serve.

6 to 8 servings

BAKED EGGS WITH CORNED BEEF HASH

Created especially to use up leftovers and save money, this dish has become a mainstay over the years not just for practical reasons but because it tastes good. You can find corned beef hash and eggs on menus across America, and it's fitting to eat at any time of day.

4 cups diced peeled Idaho potatoes

Kosher salt

3 tablespoons unsalted butter

1 tablespoon vegetable oil

4 cups diced onion

1 cup diced bell pepper (red, green, or a combination)

Freshly ground black pepper

12 ounces corned beef, cut into ¼-inch cubes (2 generous cups)

1 tablespoon minced garlic

4 eggs

1 tablespoon chopped fresh parsley

1. Place the potatoes in a medium saucepan and add just enough cold water to cover. Place over high heat and season with salt, stirring to dissolve. Bring to a boil, then immediately remove from the heat, drain, and set aside.

2. Preheat the oven to 400°F.

3. In a 12-inch ovenproof nonstick skillet, heat the butter and oil over medium-high heat. Add the potatoes and spread out in a single layer. Cook, undisturbed, until golden brown on the bottom, about 8 minutes. Toss the potatoes, spread in a single layer again, and cook, stirring only occasionally, until most of the potatoes are golden brown and tender, about 4 minutes longer. Add the onion, bell pepper, ½ teaspoon salt, and ¼ teaspoon pepper and stir well to combine. Cook until the onions and bell pepper are tender, about 4 minutes. Add the corned beef and garlic, stir again, and cook for another 2 minutes.

4. Remove from the heat and, using a spoon, create 4 small wells in the hash. Crack an egg into each of the wells. Transfer the skillet to the oven and cook until the eggs are set (or cooked to the desired degree of doneness), about 9 minutes. Remove from the oven, season the eggs with a pinch of salt and pepper, garnish with the parsley, and serve immediately.

4 servings

CASSEROLES AND
Baking Dishes

CASSEROLES became an American staple in the 50s and have retained their popularity ever since.

JUMBO SHELLS STUFFED WITH RICOTTA, MUSHROOMS, AND ROASTED RED PEPPERS

Here's a slight twist on an easy classic that is sure to become a family favorite.

1 1/2 teaspoons salt, plus more for cooking the pasta

24 to 30 jumbo shells (about 1 1/2 pounds)

1/4 cup extra-virgin olive oil

6 tablespoons (3/4 stick) unsalted butter

1 cup chopped onion

2 tablespoons minced garlic

1 pound mixed mushrooms, such as button and shiitake, stemmed and thinly sliced

1 teaspoon freshly ground black pepper

1/4 cup sweet Marsala wine

2 1/2 cups whole-milk ricotta cheese

One 16-ounce jar roasted red peppers, well drained and finely chopped

3/4 cup mixed chopped soft fresh herb leaves, such as parsley, basil, oregano, marjoram, and thyme

1 egg, lightly beaten

3 cups homemade marinara sauce or one 25-ounce jar

12 ounces mozzarella cheese, grated (about 3 cups)

1/2 cup grated Parmigiano-Reggiano cheese

1. Set a 4- to 6-quart pot filled with salted water over high heat and bring to a boil. Add the shells and cook until al dente, about 12 minutes. Gently remove the shells with a slotted spoon and transfer to a baking sheet. Drizzle 2 tablespoons of the olive oil over the shells to prevent them from sticking to one another and set aside to cool.

2. Preheat the oven to 350°F.

3. While the shells are cooling, make the stuffing. Melt the butter in a 10-inch skillet set over medium-high heat. Add the onion and cook, stirring, until translucent and soft, about 2 minutes. Add 1 tablespoon of the garlic and cook for 1 minute longer. Increase the heat to high, add the mushrooms, and cook until the mushrooms are nicely browned and the liquid has evaporated, about 4 minutes. Add 1/2 teaspoon of the salt, 1/2 teaspoon of the pepper, and the Marsala. Cook until the liquid is absorbed, about 1 minute more. Remove the pan from the heat and set aside.

4. In a medium bowl, combine the ricotta, red peppers, herbs, mushroom mixture, and egg with the re-

maining 2 tablespoons olive oil, 1 tablespoon garlic, 1 teaspoon salt, and ½ teaspoon pepper. Stir well to combine.

5. Choose the 24 nicest shells (you may have a few that have torn or broken during cooking). Place 2 tablespoons of the stuffing in each shell and place them, open end down, in a 9 × 13-inch casserole dish. Any extra filling may be placed in any extra shells that are available. Pour the marinara sauce evenly over the shells and top with the grated mozzarella and Parmesan. Bake until the cheese is melted and the shells are heated through and lightly browned on top, about 30 minutes. Serve hot.

6 servings

BAKED SEMOLINA GNOCCHI WITH SMOKED HAM AND GREEN BEANS

This dish is based on a beloved Italian side dish called *gnocchi alla Romana*. We decided to take a green bean casserole to the next level by topping it with this luscious gnocchi to turn a side dish into a main course fit for a king. Though this recipe involves a lot of steps, it can be assembled 2 days in advance of baking, making it great for entertaining.

2 teaspoons salt, plus more for cooking the beans

1 pound haricots verts or fresh green beans, stem ends trimmed, halved crosswise

8 tablespoons (1 stick) unsalted butter, plus 5 tablespoons softened

2 eggs

1/2 cup finely grated pecorino Romano cheese

1/2 cup finely grated Parmigiano-Reggiano cheese

4 1/2 cups whole milk

1 teaspoon freshly ground white pepper

1 1/4 cups semolina flour

2 ounces Maytag or other blue cheese

1 cup chopped onion

1/4 cup chopped celery

1 tablespoon minced garlic

8 ounces applewood-smoked or other smoked ham, finely chopped

1/4 cup all-purpose flour

1 1/2 cups chicken stock or canned low-sodium chicken broth

1. Bring a medium pot of salted water to a boil over high heat. Add the beans and cook for 1 minute. Remove the beans with a slotted spoon and transfer them to a bowl of ice water. Once cool, drain the beans and set them aside on a kitchen towel.

2. Grease a 9 × 13-inch casserole dish or other dish 2 to 3 inches deep and around 3 1/2 quarts, with 1 tablespoon of the softened butter. Lay the beans in the dish in an even layer and set aside.

3. Grease the sides and bottom of a rimmed baking sheet (jelly-roll pan) with 1 tablespoon of the remaining softened butter. Cut two pieces of parchment paper the size of the pan and use another tablespoon of the remaining softened butter to grease the papers. Line the pan with one of the pieces of parchment, buttered side up. Reserve the other.

4. Whisk the eggs in a medium bowl and set aside. Combine the grated cheeses in a second small bowl and set aside.

5. Add 4 cups of the milk, 4 tablespoons (½ stick) of the butter, 1½ teaspoons of the salt, and the pepper to a 3-quart or larger heavy-bottomed saucepan and heat over medium-high heat until the liquid begins to bubble. Using a whisk, gradually add the semolina while stirring vigorously. Reduce the heat to medium-low and continue to cook, stirring with a rubber spatula or wooden spoon, for 10 minutes. The mixture will become very thick. Stir in the blue cheese and half the grated cheese mixture and remove from the heat.

6. Add ½ cup of the semolina mixture to the eggs and whisk to combine. Add another ½ cup and whisk in, then whisk in ½ cup more. Return the semolina mixture to the pot and stir until thoroughly combined. Transfer the mixture to the prepared baking sheet and, using a rubber spatula (an offset metal icing spatula works very well too), spread it evenly in the pan. (Since the gnocchi won't be pourable, this will take a little effort.) Lay the buttered side of the reserved parchment on top of the gnocchi. Set another jelly-roll pan on top and weight it with a few cans. Refrigerate until completely cool, at least 30 minutes (this can be done up to 1 day ahead).

7. Preheat the oven to 450°F.

8. While the semolina is cooling, melt the remaining 4 tablespoons (½ stick) butter in a small pot over medium-high heat. Add the onion, celery, garlic, and remaining ½ teaspoon salt and cook, stirring as needed, until the vegetables are soft, about 5 minutes. Add the ham and cook for 2 minutes. Sprinkle in the all-purpose flour, stir to combine, and cook for 1 minute longer. Whisk in the stock and the remaining ½ cup milk and cook, stirring, until no floury taste remains, about 5 minutes. Remove from the heat.

Note: At the point when it's ready to bake, the casserole can be covered and refrigerated for up to 2 days. The baking time may increase slightly.

9. Pour the ham mixture over the green beans and spread in an even layer.

10. Remove the semolina from the refrigerator. Remove the top jelly-roll pan and the top piece of parchment. Invert the gnocchi onto a cutting surface and peel off the last piece of parchment. Using a 1½- to 2-inch round cutter, cut the semolina into circles. Lay the circles in rows on top of the ham mixture, overlapping them like shingles to cover the ham mixture completely. Dot the top with the remaining 2 tablespoons of softened butter and sprinkle the remaining grated cheeses over the top. Bake for 20 minutes, until bubbly and nicely browned. Serve immediately.

6 to 8 servings

ITALIAN SAUSAGE, ZUCCHINI, AND BELL PEPPER BREAD PUDDING

This is my kinda dish, baby. It's perfect for brunch or dinner and can be made in advance, which is a real plus in my book!

1 tablespoon vegetable or olive oil, plus more for greasing the pan

1 pound fresh Italian sausage, removed from casings and crumbled

1 1/2 cups small-diced onion

3/4 cup small-diced red bell pepper

1 pound zucchini, sliced into 1/4-inch half-moons

1 1/2 teaspoons salt

1 tablespoon chopped fresh marjoram leaves

1 tablespoon chopped fresh oregano leaves

1 tablespoon chopped fresh parsley leaves

1 pound seeded Italian bread, cut into 1/2-inch cubes (about 8 cups)

12 ounces fontina cheese, grated

2 ounces Parmigiano-Reggiano cheese (about 3/4 cup), finely grated

10 eggs

2 cups half-and-half

1 cup chicken stock or canned low-sodium chicken broth

1/2 teaspoon freshly ground black pepper

1. Preheat the oven to 350°F. Lightly grease a 9 × 13-inch baking dish with oil and set aside.

2. Heat a 12-inch sauté pan over medium heat. Add the sausage and cook, stirring and breaking the meat into small pieces, until lightly browned, 8 to 9 minutes. Transfer to a paper towel–lined plate to drain.

3. Add 1 tablespoon oil to the same pan and increase the heat to medium-high. Add the onion, bell pepper, zucchini, and 1/4 teaspoon of the salt and cook, stirring occasionally, until the vegetables are just tender, about 4 minutes. Add the herbs and stir to combine. Transfer to a plate to cool.

4. In a medium mixing bowl, combine the cooled sausage and vegetables and stir gently to mix well.

5. Spread 4 cups of the bread cubes in the bottom of the prepared baking dish. Top with half of the sausage-vegetable mixture. Sprinkle with half of the fontina and half of the Parmesan. Repeat with the remaining bread, sausage-vegetable mixture, and cheeses.

6. In a medium mixing bowl, whisk the eggs, half-and-half, stock, pepper, and remaining 1¼ teaspoons salt. Pour the egg mixture evenly over the top of the casserole, making sure you cover as much of the bread as possible.

7. Bake the casserole until cooked through, the cheese has melted, and the top is golden and a nice crust has formed, about 1 hour. Set the casserole aside to rest for about 10 minutes before serving.

10 to 12 servings

Note: The casserole may be assembled and then refrigerated up to overnight before being baked. Allow it to return to room temperature before baking.

BAKED CAVATAPPI WITH CHICKEN IN A PESTO CREAM SAUCE

Ooohhh, this is so herbalicious. Prepare this for your next potluck dinner and watch 'em come running. Feel free to make your pesto a day or two ahead of time and then add it when it's needed. Also, vegetarians can make this dish without the chicken—simply omit the chicken and adjust the seasoning amounts accordingly.

1 pound cavatappi, penne, or other tubular pasta

1 3/4 teaspoons salt, plus more for cooking the pasta

3/4 cup olive oil

1 pound boneless, skinless chicken breasts, thinly sliced

3/4 teaspoon freshly ground black pepper

1 cup small-diced onion

2 teaspoons minced garlic

9 ounces spinach, tough stems removed, roughly chopped

1/2 cup toasted pine nuts

1/4 teaspoon crushed red pepper

1 1/4 teaspoons finely grated lemon zest

1 cup packed fresh basil leaves

3 tablespoons unsalted butter

3 tablespoons all-purpose flour

3 1/2 cups whole milk

8 ounces Parmigiano-Reggiano cheese, finely grated (about 2 1/2 cups)

1. Cook the pasta in a large pot of salted water until just under al dente, 2 to 3 minutes less than the time recommended on the package. Drain, drizzle with 1 tablespoon of the olive oil, and toss to coat. Set aside.

2. Grease a 3-quart ovenproof baking dish with 1 tablespoon of the remaining oil and set aside.

3. Heat 1 tablespoon of the remaining olive oil in a 12-inch sauté pan over medium heat. Add the chicken, 1/4 teaspoon of the salt, and 1/4 teaspoon of the black pepper and cook, stirring, until the chicken is opaque, about 2 minutes. Remove from the pan and set aside.

4. Add another tablespoon of the oil to the hot pan and add the onion. Cook until tender, about 4 minutes. Add 1 teaspoon of the garlic and cook until fragrant, about 20 seconds, then add the spinach and 1/4 teaspoon of the remaining salt and cook until the spinach begins to wilt, 1 to 2 minutes. Remove from the pan and set aside.

5. To make the pesto, combine the pine nuts, crushed red pepper, 1/4 teaspoon of the lemon zest, and the remaining 1 teaspoon garlic in a food processor. Pulse

until blended. Using a rubber spatula, scrape down the sides. Add the basil leaves, ¼ teaspoon of the remaining salt, ¼ teaspoon of the remaining black pepper, and the remaining ½ cup olive oil and pulse until completely blended. Set the pesto aside (see Note).

6. Preheat the oven to broil.

7. Wipe the sauté pan clean with a paper towel. Return the pan to the stove over medium heat. Add the butter and flour and whisk to combine. Cook, whisking constantly, for about 2 minutes. Do not allow the flour to brown. Whisk in the milk, ½ cup at a time, and cook until thickened, 4 to 6 minutes. Remove from the heat and stir in the pesto, three-quarters of the Parmesan, and the remaining 1 teaspoon salt and ¼ teaspoon black pepper.

8. In a large mixing bowl, combine the pasta, chicken, spinach mixture, pesto sauce, and remaining 1 teaspoon lemon zest. Toss to mix well. Pour into the prepared baking dish. Sprinkle the top with the remaining Parmesan and broil until the pasta is heated through and the top is golden brown and bubbly, 4 to 6 minutes.

6 to 8 servings

Note: Pesto made ahead of time should be covered with a thin film of oil to prevent discoloring.

ENGLISH COTTAGE PIE WITH ROOT VEGETABLES

It is commonly understood that shepherd's pie is made with beef, but authentic shepherd's pie is actually made with lamb; hence its name. Here we're calling it what it is—cottage pie, a delicious and comforting casserole of simmered beef, vegetables, and aromatic herbs with a mashed potato crust.

5 tablespoons unsalted butter, plus more for greasing the pan

2 tablespoons vegetable oil

2 pounds lean ground beef

1 1/2 teaspoons salt, plus more for cooking the potatoes

3/4 teaspoon freshly ground black pepper

1 1/2 cups diced onion

1/4 cup (about 12 cloves) minced garlic

1 1/2 cups diced turnip

1 1/2 cups diced parsnip

1 cup diced carrot

2 tablespoons tomato paste

3 tablespoons all-purpose flour

2 teaspoons dried rosemary

1 tablespoon dried thyme

1 tablespoon dried parsley

1 bay leaf

1 tablespoon plus 1 teaspoon dry mustard

1 3/4 cups beef stock or canned low-sodium beef broth

1 tablespoon Worcestershire sauce

3 pounds Idaho potatoes, peeled and quartered

1/4 cup plus 2 tablespoons half-and-half

1/4 teaspoon freshly ground white pepper

1/8 teaspoon freshly grated nutmeg

1 cup shredded sharp yellow cheddar cheese (about 4 ounces)

1. Grease a 3-quart baking dish with a small amount of butter and set aside.

2. Heat 1 tablespoon of the butter and 1 tablespoon of the oil in a deep 5-quart sauté pan over medium-high heat. When hot, add the ground beef, 1/2 teaspoon of the salt, and 1/4 teaspoon of the black pepper. Cook the meat until browned, breaking it into pieces with a wooden spoon, 10 to 12 minutes. Transfer the beef to a plate and set aside.

3. Return the pan to the heat and add 1 tablespoon of the remaining butter and the remaining tablespoon of oil. Add the onion and cook, stirring, until soft and lightly caramelized, about 5 minutes. Add the garlic and cook, stirring, for 30 seconds. Add the turnip, parsnip, carrot, and 1/4 teaspoon of the remain-

ing salt and cook until the vegetables are slightly tender, about 4 minutes. Return the beef to the pan and add the tomato paste. Cook, stirring, for about 1 minute. Add the flour and cook, stirring, for another minute. Add the dried herbs, bay leaf, mustard, stock, and Worcestershire and stir to combine. Bring to a simmer and cook until the sauce is slightly thickened, about 1 minute. Reduce the heat so that the sauce barely simmers, cover, and continue to cook, stirring once midway, for 20 minutes. Remove from the heat, remove the bay leaf, and season with ½ teaspoon of the remaining salt and the remaining ½ teaspoon black pepper. Cover and set aside.

4. Position a rack in the upper third of the oven and preheat the oven to 400°F.

5. Place the potatoes in a saucepan and add enough cold water to cover by at least 1 inch. Bring the water to a gentle boil, season with salt, and cook until the potatoes are fork-tender, 12 to 15 minutes. Immediately drain the potatoes. Pass the potatoes through a ricer into the same pot (or mash until smooth using a potato masher) and return the pot to the stove over low heat. Add the remaining ¼ teaspoon salt and 3 tablespoons of butter, the half-and-half, white pepper, nutmeg, and ½ cup of the cheese. Stir to mix well and cook until heated through.

6. Transfer the meat mixture to the prepared baking dish. Spoon the mashed potatoes over the meat mixture and, using the back of the spoon, smooth the top of the potatoes. Sprinkle the remaining ½ cup cheese over the mashed potatoes. Place the baking dish on a baking sheet and bake until browned and bubbly on top, about 25 minutes. Remove from the oven and serve.

8 to 10 servings

MEAT AND VEGGIE LOVER'S DEEP-DISH PIZZA

Now here is a decadent pie. Want some? We allow the pizza dough to rise twice for a more tender crust. If you're short on time, though, skip the second rise. It'll still be enjoyable. Just shape and bake. Yeah, babe, I said it.

Semolina Pizza Dough (recipe follows)

1/4 cup plus 2 teaspoons olive oil

1 cup chopped onion

1 tablespoon minced garlic

1/2 teaspoon fennel seeds

1 sprig fresh thyme

1 sprig fresh oregano, plus 1/4 cup chopped fresh leaves

1/2 teaspoon salt

1/4 teaspoon freshly ground black pepper

1/4 teaspoon crushed red pepper

One 28-ounce can whole tomatoes, coarsely crushed, with juice

1 tablespoon dry red wine

1 1/2 teaspoons sugar

One 15-ounce can tomato puree

1 pound fresh hot Italian sausage, removed from casings and crumbled

8 ounces mushrooms, stemmed and sliced

All-purpose flour

1 pound good-quality low moisture or part skim mozzarella cheese, grated (about 4 cups)

8 ounces pepperoni, sliced

1 green bell pepper, cut into thin strips (about 1 cup)

1/2 cup sliced pitted Kalamata or other favorite olives

1/2 cup chopped fresh basil leaves

1 pound fresh mozzarella cheese, cut into 1/4-inch-thick slices

4 ounces Parmigiano-Reggiano cheese, finely grated (about 1 1/2 cups)

2 tablespoons extra-virgin olive oil, for garnish (optional)

1. Prepare the pizza dough as instructed.

2. While the dough is rising, make the tomato sauce: Heat 2 tablespoons of the olive oil over medium-high heat. Add the onion, garlic, fennel seeds, thyme, oregano sprig, salt, black pepper, and crushed red pepper and cook, stirring constantly, until the onion is soft, about 2 minutes. Add the crushed tomatoes, wine, and sugar and bring to a boil. Lower the heat and simmer, stirring occasionally, until thickened, about 30 minutes. Stir in the tomato puree, remove from the heat, and allow the sauce to cool completely before

using. (You can speed this up by setting the sauce in the refrigerator for 15 minutes or so.) Remove the herb sprigs.

3. Add 2 teaspoons of the remaining olive oil to a medium skillet over medium heat. When hot, add the sausage and cook until nicely browned and the fat is rendered, about 6 minutes. Using a slotted spoon, remove the sausage from the pan and set aside. Discard all but 1 tablespoon of the fat in the pan. Add the mushrooms to the pan and sauté for 3 minutes to release some of the liquid. Remove the mushrooms from the pan and set aside.

4. Set the oven racks as low in the oven as possible and line with baking sheets. Preheat the oven to 475°F.

5. Oil two 10-inch round cake pans or deep-dish pizza pans with the remaining 2 tablespoons olive oil. Roll out the dough into two 14-inch circles with a floured rolling pin on a lightly floured work surface and place the dough inside the pans, allowing about 2 inches of the dough to fall over the sides of the pans. Let the dough rest for 5 minutes.

6. Sprinkle the grated mozzarella cheese all over the bottom of the pies. Top each pie with half of the pepperoni, mushrooms, bell pepper, olives, and sausage. Ladle the sauce evenly over each pizza and top each with the chopped oregano, basil, mozzarella slices, and Parmesan. Trim excess dough if needed, then fold and pinch it decoratively around the rim.

7. Set the pizzas on the baking sheets and bake until the cheese is golden and bubbly and the crust is nicely browned, about 25 minutes. You may need to tent the edges of the crust with foil for the last 5 minutes of baking. Remove from the oven and allow the pizzas to rest for 10 to 15 minutes before slicing. Serve hot, drizzled with extra-virgin olive oil if desired.

Two 10-inch pizzas, 8 servings

SEMOLINA PIZZA DOUGH

If you're making this dough way ahead of time, divide it into two portions after the first rise, roll each portion into a ball, cover, and refrigerate it until ready to use, up to overnight. If refrigerated, allow the dough to return to room temperature for about 20 minutes before rolling it out.

1 ½ cups warm water (about 110°F)
One ¼-ounce package active dry yeast
1 teaspoon sugar
½ cup olive oil, plus more for the bowl
½ cup semolina flour
3 ½ cups unbleached all-purpose flour, plus more for dusting the work surface and your hands
1 ¼ teaspoons salt

Combine the water with the yeast and sugar in the bowl of a standing electric mixer with the dough hook attached. Let it sit until the mixture begins to foam, about 5 minutes. Add the olive oil, semolina flour, all-purpose flour, and salt and mix on medium speed for 10 minutes, until the dough is smooth, scraping the dough hook midway. Transfer the dough to a lightly floured work surface and knead it with floured hands two to three times, then shape the dough into a ball (see Note). Oil a large mixing bowl, add the dough, and cover with plastic wrap. Set the dough aside in a warm, draft-free place until doubled in size, about 2 hours. Punch down the dough and allow it to rise a second time until nearly doubled in size, about 1 hour. Divide the dough in half; knead each portion into a ball, and use as directed.

Makes enough dough for two 12- to 14-inch pizzas

Note: To make the dough by hand, combine the water, yeast, and sugar in a medium bowl and let it sit until the mixture begins to foam, about 5 minutes. Add the olive oil, semolina, and 2½ cups of the flour and stir with a wooden spoon to combine. Add the remaining 1 cup of flour and the salt and mix well with your hands, working to incorporate it into the dough little by little. Transfer the dough to a lightly floured work surface and knead it with floured hands at least 5 and up to 7 minutes, adding more flour as needed to form a smooth, elastic dough that is not too sticky. Form it into a ball and proceed with the recipe.

MOUSSAKA

This traditional Greek dish needs no introduction ... it's for eggplant lovers only and is Greece's answer to lasagna. It does take a bit of time to assemble, but it's a great make-ahead dish, and, as a bonus, it gets even better as it sits in the fridge for a day or two. Talk about leftovers to die for! Simply reheat leftover portions in a moderate oven and dig in.

3 large eggplants (3 $\frac{1}{2}$ to 4 pounds total), peeled and cut lengthwise into $\frac{1}{4}$-inch-thick slices

$\frac{3}{4}$ cup plus 2 tablespoons olive oil, or more as needed

Salt

3 large baking potatoes (2 pounds total), peeled and cut crosswise into $\frac{1}{4}$-inch-thick slices

1 medium onion, finely chopped

1 pound ground beef

12 ounces ground lamb

2 tablespoons minced garlic

1 teaspoon dried oregano, crumbled between your fingers

2 tablespoons tomato paste

$\frac{1}{2}$ cup dry red wine

$\frac{1}{2}$ cup canned crushed tomatoes

$\frac{3}{4}$ teaspoon freshly ground black pepper

1 cup water

2 tablespoons minced fresh parsley leaves

6 tablespoons ($\frac{3}{4}$ stick) unsalted butter

$\frac{1}{2}$ cup all-purpose flour

5 cups whole milk

1 $\frac{1}{2}$ cups grated kefalotyri or kasseri cheese or a combination of Parmigiano-Reggiano and Romano

2 eggs plus 2 egg yolks, lightly beaten

1.   Preheat the oven to 450°F.

2.   Lay the eggplant slices in a single layer on large baking sheets. Brush both sides of each slice lightly with some of the olive oil (you should use about $\frac{1}{2}$ cup for all the slices) and then season the slices with 1 teaspoon salt. Place the baking sheets in the oven and bake until the eggplant slices are soft and lightly golden, 15 to 20 minutes. Remove and set aside to cool.

3.   Heat 1$\frac{1}{2}$ tablespoons of the remaining oil in a large skillet over medium-high heat. Working in batches, add the potato slices and cook until lightly golden on both sides, 3 to 4 minutes. Transfer to a paper towel–lined plate to drain briefly; repeat with the remaining potato slices, adding 1$\frac{1}{2}$ tablespoons of oil to each batch. (You should be able to cook the potatoes in 4 batches.) Season the potato slices lightly with salt.

4. Add the onion to the skillet and cook until tender, about 4 minutes. Add the ground beef and lamb, garlic, and oregano and cook, stirring to break up any lumps, until the meat is browned, about 6 minutes. Stir in the tomato paste and cook until lightly browned, about 2 minutes. Add the wine and cook until evaporated, then add the crushed tomatoes, pepper, and water and reduce the heat to low. Cook, stirring occasionally, until almost all the liquid is evaporated, 10 to 15 minutes. Stir in the parsley and season with salt to taste; set aside.

5. In a medium saucepan, melt the butter and whisk in the flour. Cook, stirring, for 2 to 3 minutes; do not allow the flour to brown. Gradually whisk in the milk, stirring until smooth and thick. Whisk in 1 cup of the grated cheese and season the sauce with salt to taste. Set aside, partially covered (to keep a skin from forming on the top) until cooled slightly, about 15 minutes. Whisk in the eggs and egg yolks. Cover and set aside while you begin assembling the casserole.

6. Preheat the oven to 350°F.

7. Lightly grease a 9 × 13-inch casserole dish with olive oil and place the browned potatoes in the bottom of the dish in an even layer. Top with half of the eggplant slices and half of the meat sauce. Spoon about a third of the white sauce evenly over the meat sauce. Cover with the remaining eggplant slices, gently pressing down on the layers with your hands to compress. Spoon the remaining meat sauce evenly over the top, followed by the remaining white sauce. Sprinkle with the remaining ½ cup cheese. Bake, uncovered, until the moussaka is golden brown on top and the sauce is set, 50 to 60 minutes. Let stand for at least 40 minutes and up to 60 minutes before cutting into squares and serving.

8 to 10 servings

ROASTED PORK CHOPS WITH JEWELED RICE PILAF

This jeweled rice pilaf was inspired by a dish made for me by a Lebanese friend. The already aromatic basmati rice is spiced with cinnamon, cumin, and allspice and is bespeckled with dried fruits and nuts. The pork chops are glazed with an orange-cardamom reduction that further enhances the flavors of this dish.

Four 12-ounce center-cut bone-in pork chops

1 tablespoon kosher salt

1 ½ teaspoons freshly ground white pepper

2 tablespoons instant flour, such as Wondra flour

2 tablespoons olive oil

3 tablespoons ghee or clarified unsalted butter (see Note)

1 cup small-diced yellow onion

¾ cup small-diced carrot

Two 3-inch cinnamon sticks

½ teaspoon whole allspice berries

¼ teaspoon cumin seeds

1 bay leaf

¼ cup dates, pitted and diced

¼ cup dried apricots, diced small

¼ cup dried currants

2 cups basmati rice

3 ½ cups chicken stock or canned low-sodium chicken broth

⅛ teaspoon saffron threads, crumbled between your fingers

1 tablespoon finely grated orange zest

3 tablespoons Greek-style yogurt

1 cup freshly squeezed orange juice

3 whole cardamom pods, lightly crushed

1 tablespoon apricot jam

¼ cup lightly toasted sliced almonds

¼ cup toasted and coarsely chopped pistachios

1 tablespoon chopped fresh mint leaves

1. Preheat the oven to 350°F.

2. Season the pork chops on both sides with 2 teaspoons of the salt and 1 teaspoon of the pepper. Sprinkle both sides of the pork chops with the flour and set aside. Set a 12-inch flameproof casserole pan over medium-high heat and add the olive oil and 1 tablespoon of the ghee. When the oil is hot, place the pork chops in the pan and sear for 3 minutes per side. Transfer the pork chops to a plate and set aside.

3. Add the remaining 2 tablespoons ghee to the pan and, when hot, add the onion, carrot, cinnamon, allspice, cumin, and bay leaf and cook over medium heat, scraping the bottom of the pan, until the onion

and carrot are lightly caramelized, 3 to 4 minutes. Add the dates, apricots, currants, and basmati rice, stir to coat, and cook until the rice is fragrant, about 1 minute. Stir in the stock, saffron, orange zest, yogurt, and remaining 1 teaspoon salt and ½ teaspoon pepper. Bring the liquid to a boil, reduce the heat to medium-low, cover, and place the pan in the oven for 10 minutes.

4.   Remove the pan from the oven and, working quickly, place the pork chops on top of the rice. Cover and return the pan to the oven. Continue to cook until the pork is cooked through and has reached 140°F, 8 to 10 minutes longer. Remove from the oven and let stand, covered, for 10 minutes.

5.   While the pan is in the oven, combine the orange juice and cardamom pods in a 1-quart saucepan and cook over medium-high heat until the juice has reduced by half, 8 to 10 minutes. Add the apricot jam and stir until melted. Strain the reduction through a fine-mesh sieve. Set aside until ready to serve the pork and rice.

6.   Brush the chops with the orange juice reduction and garnish with the almonds, pistachios, and mint. Serve immediately.

4 servings

Note: Ghee is butter that has been melted slowly until the solids and liquid separate. The solids fall to the bottom, and the butter is cooked until the milk solids are browned and the moisture evaporates, resulting in a nutty, caramel-like flavor. This last step is what distinguishes ghee from regular clarified butter. In both ghee and clarified butter, the milk solids are strained out and discarded before using.

Ghee is used primarily in Indian cooking but is wonderful for any high-heat cooking preparation since it has a higher smoke point than butter. You can find it in many Middle Eastern markets, or you can easily make your own at home.

ROAST LEG OF LAMB WITH LEMON AND OREGANO-SCENTED POTATOES

This meal was inspired by the flavors of Greece...lemony potatoes, peppers, onions, and carrots form a bed upon which an impressive leg of lamb roasts. Take this to your holiday table and make your family and friends happy, happy.

2 green bell peppers, sliced lengthwise into 1-inch strips

2 large yellow onions, peeled and quartered

8 ounces carrots, peeled and cut into 1-inch pieces on the diagonal

¼ cup extra-virgin olive oil

¼ cup (about 12 cloves) minced garlic

5 Idaho Russet potatoes, about 5 pounds, peeled and quartered lengthwise

1 cup chicken stock or canned low-sodium chicken broth

⅓ cup plus ¼ cup freshly squeezed lemon juice

2 ½ tablespoons kosher salt

1 tablespoon coarsely ground black pepper

¼ teaspoon crushed red pepper

3 tablespoons finely chopped fresh oregano leaves

2 tablespoons chopped fresh rosemary leaves

One 5- to 6-pound bone-in leg of lamb

1. Preheat the oven to 500°F.

2. Place the bell peppers, onions, and carrots in a large mixing bowl. Add 2 tablespoons of the olive oil and 1½ teaspoons of the garlic and toss to combine. Place in the center of a 13 × 17-inch roasting pan. To the same bowl, add the potatoes, the remaining 2 tablespoons of oil, and 1½ teaspoons of the remaining garlic and toss to combine. Spread the potatoes along the edges of the pan, circling around the other vegetables. Combine the stock and ⅓ cup lemon juice and pour over the potatoes. Sprinkle all the vegetables with 1 tablespoon of the salt, 1 teaspoon of the black pepper, the crushed red pepper, and 2 tablespoons of the oregano.

3. In a small bowl, combine the remaining 3 tablespoons garlic with the rosemary and remaining 1 tablespoon oregano and stir to mix well. Using your hands, rub the lamb all over with the remaining ¼ cup lemon juice. Pat the garlic and herb mixture evenly over the surface of the meat. Season the meat with the remaining 1½ tablespoons salt and 2 teaspoons black pepper and set the lamb on top of the carrots and onions in the center of the roasting pan. Transfer to the oven and roast for 30 minutes.

4. Reduce the oven temperature to 325°F and roast until a thermometer inserted into the center of the

thickest portion of the lamb (without touching the bone) reaches an internal temperature of 130°F, 30 to 40 more minutes. Remove from the oven and tent with foil. Set aside to rest for 20 minutes before carving.

5. Serve the sliced lamb draped over the roasted vegetables and drizzled with the pan drippings.

8 servings

EGGPLANT INVOLTINI

This is a lighter version of one of my favorite ways to enjoy eggplant—equally delicious as an appetizer or as a vegetarian entree.

3 medium eggplants (about 3 ¾ pounds), cut lengthwise into ½-inch slices

Salt

½ cup olive oil

½ cup fresh whole wheat breadcrumbs or coarse fresh breadcrumbs

1 teaspoon minced garlic

2 tablespoons balsamic vinegar

1 pound fresh mozzarella cheese, cut into ½-inch cubes (2 generous cups)

¼ cup pine nuts, lightly toasted

2 tablespoons chopped fresh basil leaves, plus more for garnish

1 tablespoon chopped fresh oregano leaves, plus more for garnish

1 teaspoon crushed red pepper, or to taste

3 cups drained canned diced tomatoes

1. Lay the eggplant slices in a single layer on a wire rack set on a baking sheet. Sprinkle both sides lightly with salt and let stand for at least 1 hour to allow the juices to drain.

2. Preheat the broiler. Rinse the eggplant under cold water and pat dry. Brush both sides of the eggplant slices with 6 tablespoons of the olive oil and broil until soft and lightly browned on one side, 6 to 8 minutes. Set aside. Change the oven setting to bake and the temperature to 350°F.

3. In a large bowl, combine the breadcrumbs, garlic, vinegar, mozzarella, pine nuts, basil, oregano, crushed red pepper, 1½ cups of the tomatoes, and 1 teaspoon salt. Add the remaining 2 tablespoons olive oil and mix well. Place the remaining 1½ cups tomatoes in the bottom of a 2-inch deep 3 to 3½ quart baking dish and set aside.

4. Place 1 cooked eggplant slice on a clean work surface. Place about 2 tablespoons of the filling at the narrow end of the slice. Roll the eggplant up and around the filling, starting at the stuffing end, and then place the roll in the casserole dish on top of the tomatoes. Repeat the procedure with the remaining slices of eggplant and filling. If you have any filling left, scatter it over the eggplant rolls. Bake until heated through and the cheese is melted, about 20 minutes. Serve warm, garnished with additional basil and oregano.

About 18 pieces, 4 to 6 servings

POTATO AND SALT COD AU GRATIN

This creamy, salty, indulgent dish would be complemented perfectly by crusty bread, a cool salad, and a crisp white wine. You can usually find nice salt cod in specialty stores, particularly Italian markets.

1½ to 2 pounds salt cod, soaked in several changes of water overnight in the refrigerator

4 tablespoons (½ stick) unsalted butter, plus 4 tablespoons (½ stick) softened

1 cup chopped onion

¼ cup minced shallot

¼ teaspoon cayenne

1 tablespoon plus 2 teaspoons minced garlic

4 sprigs fresh thyme

1 sprig fresh tarragon

3 tablespoons all-purpose flour

½ cup dry white wine

3 cups whole milk

3 pounds Idaho potatoes, peeled, sliced into ⅛-inch-thick circles on a mandoline, covered with water, and set aside

1 cup heavy cream

2 cups soft fresh breadcrumbs

¼ cup chopped fresh parsley leaves

½ cup grated Parmigiano-Reggiano cheese

¼ cup extra-virgin olive oil

Lemon wedges, for serving (optional)

1.   Lay the soaked salt cod in a large, shallow skillet and fill with enough water to cover the fish. Bring the water to a gentle simmer and cook until the fish flakes easily with a fork, about 8 minutes. Remove the fillets from the water and set aside until cool enough to handle. Gently pull the tail and bones away from the fillet and discard. Flake the fish into small pieces, taking care to discard any pieces of bone or skin, and set aside in a bowl. You should have 2½ to 3 cups of flaked fish.

2.   Melt 4 tablespoons (½ stick) butter in a medium saucepan set over medium-high heat. Add the onion, shallot, cayenne, and 1 tablespoon of the garlic and cook until soft and translucent, about 3 minutes. Tie the thyme and tarragon together in a bundle and add to the pot. Stir in the flour and cook for 1 minute. Whisk in the wine and milk and continue to simmer until no floury taste remains, about 6 minutes longer. Remove from the heat and allow the sauce to cool for at least 10 minutes. Remove the herb bundle and discard. Stir in the salt cod pieces.

3.   Preheat the oven to 375°F.

4. Grease a 3-quart gratin dish with 1 tablespoon of the softened butter. Using half of the potatoes, line the bottom of the dish by overlapping the slices in two or three rows. Pour ½ cup of the cream over the potatoes and dot with 1½ tablespoons of the remaining softened butter. Add the salt cod mixture and spread evenly over the potatoes. Top with the remaining potatoes, ½ cup cream, and 1½ tablespoons softened butter.

5. In a small bowl, mix the breadcrumbs with the parsley, Parmesan, olive oil, and remaining 2 teaspoons garlic until well combined. Sprinkle the seasoned breadcrumbs over the potatoes. Place the gratin on a baking sheet and bake until the crumbs are golden, the sauce is bubbly, and the potatoes are tender, about 40 minutes. Set aside to cool for at least 20 minutes before serving. Serve with a wedge of lemon if desired.

6 servings

BUTTERNUT SQUASH LASAGNA WITH ITALIAN SAUSAGE AND SAGE

This lasagna is best in the fall, when butternut squash and apples are at their finest. It's a rich dish that incorporates whole-milk ricotta and whole-milk mozzarella. If you must lighten it up, use the skim version of these ingredients and cut back on the sausage. But I happen to think it's worth the splurge!

3 pounds butternut squash, peeled and diced

¼ cup extra-virgin olive oil

½ teaspoon ground cinnamon

4 sprigs fresh thyme

1 bay leaf

1½ teaspoons salt

1 teaspoon freshly ground black pepper

2 tablespoons olive oil

1½ cups small-diced onion

1 cup small-diced fennel

1 cup cored and small-diced Pink Lady or Honeycrisp apple

1½ pounds fresh fennel sausage, removed from casings and crumbled

2 teaspoons chopped fresh marjoram leaves

4 tablespoons (½ stick) unsalted butter

¼ cup plus 1 tablespoon fresh sage leaves, thinly sliced

½ cup chopped lightly toasted hazelnuts

1 pound whole-milk ricotta cheese

8 ounces mascarpone cheese

½ cup heavy cream

2 eggs, lightly beaten

1 pound whole-milk mozzarella cheese, grated (4 cups)

¾ cup finely grated Parmigiano-Reggiano cheese

½ cup chicken stock or canned low-sodium chicken broth

12 sheets no-boil lasagna noodles (about 8 ounces)

1.   Preheat the oven to 350°F.

2.   In a large mixing bowl, combine the butternut squash with the extra-virgin olive oil, cinnamon, thyme, bay leaf, 1 teaspoon of the salt, and ½ teaspoon of the pepper and toss to coat the squash. Transfer the squash to a large baking sheet and cover with aluminum foil. Bake until the squash is tender, about 30 minutes. Set the squash aside, covered, until cool. Remove and discard the thyme sprigs and bay leaf.

3. Heat a medium sauté pan over medium-high heat. When hot, add the olive oil, onion, fennel, apple, sausage, and marjoram and cook for 8 to 10 minutes, stirring occasionally, until the sausage has browned and the vegetables have softened. Remove from the heat, transfer to a large mixing bowl, and set aside to cool. Gently fold the squash into the vegetable-sausage mixture.

4. Heat the butter in a small sauté pan over medium heat. When the butter begins to bubble and brown, add ¼ cup of the sage leaves and cook until they are brown and crisp, 1 to 1½ minutes. Add the chopped hazelnuts and cook for another minute. Remove from the heat and set aside to cool.

5. In a separate large mixing bowl, combine the ricotta, mascarpone, heavy cream, beaten eggs, half of the mozzarella, and

the remaining ½ teaspoon pepper and ½ teaspoon salt. Mix well to combine, then add the cooled brown-butter-sage-hazelnut mixture and mix thoroughly.

6. Increase the oven temperature to 375°F.

7. Assemble the lasagna: Spread half of the butternut squash mixture in the bottom of the pan, sprinkle with ¼ cup of the Parmesan, drizzle ¼ cup of the stock over the top, and cover with 4 pasta sheets, leaving a little space between sheets. Spread 3 cups of the ricotta cheese mixture over the pasta sheets and cover with 4 more pasta sheets. Distribute the remaining half of the butternut squash mixture over the pasta, sprinkle the top with ¼ cup of the remaining Parmesan, and drizzle with the remaining ¼ cup stock. Place the final 4 pasta sheets over the top and spread the remaining ricotta mixture evenly over the pasta. Top with the remaining grated mozzarella and ¼ cup Parmesan.

8. Cover the lasagna tightly with a piece of buttered foil and bake, undisturbed, for 40 minutes. Remove the foil and continue to bake until the top is bubbly and golden brown, about 15 minutes more. Let the lasagna stand for 15 to 20 minutes before serving. Garnish with the remaining tablespoon of sage.

8 to 10 servings

Note: We used a lasagna pan, but you can use any baking dish about 10 × 15 × 3 inches deep.

PICADILLO-STUFFED POBLANOS

This dish was inspired by chiles rellenos, in which poblanos are typically battered and fried. I thought that a simpler, lighter version might be more in line with the way we live and eat today. Poblanos are traditional, but if you can't find them, you can substitute Anaheim peppers—just add a few more. And don't skip the Honduran crema, which is a thicker, richer version of sour cream. It can be found in the refrigerator section of Latin markets, usually near the cheese.

3 tablespoons lard or vegetable oil

3 medium yellow onions, chopped into 1/4-inch pieces

5 cloves garlic, sliced

Two 28-ounce cans whole peeled tomatoes, with juices

2 whole cloves

2 bay leaves

One 3-inch cinnamon stick, preferably Mexican canela, if available

1 teaspoon black peppercorns

1 teaspoon whole coriander seeds

2 teaspoons salt

2 cups chicken stock or canned low-sodium chicken broth

1/4 cup slivered almonds

1/4 cup raw hulled pumpkin seeds (pepitas)

2 pounds coarsely ground pork shoulder or regular ground pork

1/3 cup raisins

1 tablespoon cider vinegar

1 teaspoon chili powder

1/4 teaspoon ground cinnamon

1/4 teaspoon dried Mexican or regular oregano, crumbled between your fingers

1/4 teaspoon ground allspice

6 medium fresh poblano chiles with long stems, preferably not twisted or deeply indented (about 1 pound)

8 ounces queso fresco or queso Chihuahua, grated

1/2 cup Honduran crema or sour cream

Fresh cilantro leaves, for garnish

1.   In a 4-quart saucepan, heat 2 tablespoons of the lard or oil over medium heat. Add two-thirds of the onions and half of the garlic and cook, stirring regularly, until they are very well browned, about 10 minutes.

2.   Meanwhile, puree the tomatoes and their juices in a blender or food processor (in batches if necessary).

3.   When the onions are well browned, increase the heat to medium-high and add the pureed tomatoes. Make a sachet by placing the cloves, bay leaves, cin-

namon stick, black peppercorns, and coriander seeds in a piece of cheesecloth and tying the ends with twine to secure. Add the sachet and ½ teaspoon of the salt to the sauce and cook, stirring frequently, until the sauce reduces to the consistency of a thick tomato sauce, about 35 minutes. Remove 2 cups of the tomato sauce and reserve. Stir the stock into the sauce remaining in the pan. Partially cover and continue to simmer until the sauce thickens, about 45 minutes.

4. While the sauce simmers, prepare the pork picadillo and the chiles. Heat a large sauté pan (preferably nonstick) over medium-high heat. Add the almonds and pumpkin seeds and stir until they are deep golden brown, about 2 minutes. Transfer to a heatproof bowl and set aside. Add the remaining 1 tablespoon lard or oil to the pan along with the remaining onions and garlic. Crumble the pork into the skillet and cook, stirring often, until the pork is completely cooked and the onion is tender, 10 to 15 minutes. If the pork has rendered a lot of fat, drain any excess fat from the pan.

5. Stir the reserved 2 cups tomato sauce, the raisins, vinegar, chili powder, ground cinnamon, oregano, and allspice into the pork mixture. Cook over medium heat, stirring frequently, until the mixture is very thick and most of the excess liquid has evaporated, about 20 minutes. Stir in the almonds and pumpkin seeds, taste, and season with 1 teaspoon of the remaining salt. Set the picadillo aside to cool.

6. While the picadillo is cooking, prepare the chiles by placing them directly onto a fairly high flame or under the broiler. Let the skin blister and burn on all sides of the chiles, turning as necessary and taking care that they do not cook all the way through. Place the chiles in a bowl and cover with plastic wrap.

7. When the chiles are cool enough to handle, rub off the blistered skins and discard the skins. Cut a slit into one side of each chile, starting ½ inch below the stem end and continuing

to within ½ inch of the tip. One by one, work your finger inside the chiles, dislodging all the seeds clustered just below the stem. Quickly rinse under cool water to remove the seeds from inside the chiles, being careful not to rip or tear the opening any wider than is necessary; rinse off any stray bits of charred skin. Drain the chiles on paper towels, cut side down.

8. Preheat the oven to 350°F.

9. Pat each chile dry and then, working carefully, stuff each chile with about 1 cup of the picadillo. Lay the stuffed chiles in a 9 × 13-inch casserole dish.

10. Return the tomato sauce to a boil (if necessary) and check the consistency. It should be similar to a thick tomato soup. If too thick, thin with a little water or broth; if too thin, boil rapidly until thickened slightly. Remove the seasoning sachet and discard. Season the sauce with the remaining ½ teaspoon salt. Ladle about ½ cup of the tomato sauce over each of the stuffed chiles and sprinkle the chiles with the queso fresco. Bake until the chiles are heated through and the cheese has melted, about 30 minutes.

11. Serve the stuffed chiles with a dollop of the crema or sour cream and garnish with fresh cilantro leaves. Serve immediately.

4 to 6 servings

CHICKEN AND BLACK BEANS WITH CHORIZO

Oh, baby, the beans in this dish taste as if they've been slow-cooking with the chorizo all day long, but the truth is that although the chicken does marinate for quite a while, it cooks in just over an hour! The flavors are smoky, reminding me of days spent in Spain, and trust me, this will leave you coming back for more.

½ cup dry sherry

⅓ cup plus 1 ½ tablespoons olive oil

2 teaspoons paprika (hot or sweet)

1 teaspoon sweet pimentón (smoked Spanish paprika)

½ cup thinly sliced yellow onion

1 tablespoon thinly sliced garlic plus ¼ cup minced (about 15 cloves)

5 tablespoons chopped fresh oregano leaves

One 3- to 4-pound whole chicken, halved, with the wishbone, breastbone, backbone, and first 2 digits (tips) of the wings removed

1 teaspoon freshly ground white pepper

1 tablespoon plus 1 teaspoon kosher salt

8 ounces firm Spanish chorizo, cut into ¼-inch-thick half-moons

2 cups finely chopped onion

1 cup finely chopped green bell pepper

1 teaspoon dried Mexican or regular oregano, crumbled between your fingers

¼ teaspoon crushed red pepper

2 cups seeded and small-diced ripe tomatoes

Three 15-ounce cans black beans, drained and rinsed

1 ¼ cups chicken stock or canned low-sodium chicken broth

1. To make the marinade, place the sherry in a small mixing bowl. Slowly whisk in ⅓ cup of the olive oil, then stir in the paprika, pimentón, sliced onion, sliced garlic, and 3 tablespoons of the fresh oregano.

2. Place the chicken in a resealable 1-gallon plastic food storage bag. Pour the sherry marinade over the chicken and squeeze out as much air as possible before sealing the bag. Gently move the chicken around in the marinade to make sure it is well coated. Place the plastic bag with the chicken on a small baking sheet and transfer to the refrigerator to marinate for about 4 hours, turning once midway.

3. Remove the chicken from the marinade and pat dry with paper towels. Discard the marinade. Season

the chicken on both sides with the white pepper and 1 table-spoon of the salt. Preheat the oven to 400°F.

4. Heat the remaining 1½ tablespoons olive oil in a large Dutch oven or a large, heavy skillet over medium-high heat. Sear the chicken, skin side down, until the skin is nicely browned and develops a crust, about 3 minutes. Cook the other side until lightly browned, about 2 minutes. Remove the chicken from the pan and set aside, loosely covered with foil.

5. Reduce the heat to medium and add the chorizo. Cook until crisped and brown, stirring occasionally, 5 to 6 minutes. Remove from the pot and set aside. Add the chopped onion, bell pepper, minced garlic, dried oregano, crushed red pepper, and a pinch of salt and cook until caramelized, stirring fre-quently, about 20 minutes. Add the tomatoes and cook, stir-ring occasionally, until the tomatoes release their juices. Stir in the reserved chorizo, the beans, stock, and the remaining 1 teaspoon salt.

6. Carefully transfer the mixture to a 2- to 3-inch deep 3½- to 4-quart dish. Place the chicken halves skin side up on top of the beans and transfer to the oven. Bake, uncovered, until the chicken reaches an internal temperature of 165°F, 45 to 60 minutes. If necessary, tent the chicken with foil to prevent further browning. Set the dish aside to rest for about 15 min-utes before serving.

7. Cut the chicken into pieces and serve over the black beans. Garnish with the remaining 2 tablespoons chopped fresh oregano.

4 servings

CHEESE ENCHILADAS WITH A SMOKY RED CHILE SAUCE

These enchiladas have an earthy, smoky chile sauce that really makes this dish sing. Feel free to personalize the enchiladas by adding other ingredients. They'd be dynamite with some shredded pulled pork (page 260) or alongside Mexican rice and cooked pinto beans; or add other ingredients to the filling, such as shredded chicken or cooked drained beans. Make 'em your own!

6 cups water

4 large cloves garlic, unpeeled

1 ounce dried guajillo chiles (about 5 chiles), seeded and deveined

1 ounce dried ancho chiles (about 5 chiles), seeded and deveined

7 tablespoons olive oil

1 cup small-diced onion

1 teaspoon salt

1 teaspoon dried thyme, crumbled between your fingers

1 teaspoon dried Mexican or regular oregano, crumbled between your fingers

1 cinnamon stick

One 14.5-ounce can diced tomatoes, drained

2 ½ cups chicken stock or canned low-sodium chicken broth

½ teaspoon freshly ground black pepper

12 corn tortillas

12 ounces Pepper Jack cheese, grated (about 3 cups)

6 ounces queso cotija, Parmigiano-Reggiano, or feta cheese, finely grated (about 1 ½ cups)

2 ounces queso blanco, ricotta salata, or farmer's cheese, finely grated

2 tablespoons roughly chopped cilantro leaves

1. Bring the water to a boil in a medium saucepan. Cover to keep warm and set aside.

2. Heat a 12-inch sauté pan over medium heat. Toast the garlic cloves on one side of the pan and cook, turning frequently, until dark spots appear on the skin and the garlic softens inside its peel, about 15 minutes. Remove from the pan, peel, and set aside. While the garlic is toasting, toast the dried chiles on the other side of the pan until the oils are released, flattening and pressing the chiles down with a spatula, 2 to 3 minutes per side. After toasting, transfer the chiles to the pot of hot water and weight the chiles with a small plate or other heatproof object so that they remain submerged. Cover and soak until the chiles are reconstituted, 2 to 3 hours.

3. Wipe the sauté pan clean with a paper towel. Heat 2 tablespoons of the olive oil over medium-high

heat. When hot, add the onion and ¼ teaspoon of the salt and cook until the onion is lightly caramelized and tender, about 5 minutes. Add the garlic, thyme, oregano, and cinnamon stick and cook until fragrant, about 30 seconds. Add the tomatoes and 2 cups of the stock and bring to a boil. Reduce the heat to a simmer and cook until the flavors have come together, about 4 minutes. Add the black pepper and the remaining ¾ teaspoon salt, stir to combine, and set aside. Remove the cinnamon stick and discard.

4.   Transfer the chiles to a blender and add ½ cup of the soaking water. Blend until pureed, then strain through a fine-mesh sieve, pressing to extract as much of the chile as possible. Discard the solids. Return the pureed chiles to the blender and add the onion-tomato mixture and the remaining ½ cup chicken stock. Place a towel on top of the blender to allow any heat to escape (use caution when blending hot liquids!). Puree until smooth.

5.   Preheat the oven to 375°F. Clean the sauté pan and place it back on the stove. Add 3 tablespoons of the remaining olive oil and heat over medium-high heat. Add a corn tortilla and cook until soft and pliable, about 20 seconds per side. Allow any excess oil to drip from the tortilla back into the pan, then transfer the tortilla to a paper towel–lined baking sheet. Repeat with the remaining tortillas, adding the rest of the oil as needed.

6.   Lightly season the tortillas with salt. Place about ¼ cup of the Pepper Jack and 2 tablespoons of the cotija cheese down the center of each tortilla. Roll the tortillas up, then place them seam side down in a 9×13-inch baking dish. Pour the sauce evenly over the tortillas and sprinkle with the queso blanco. Transfer to the oven and cook until the cheese has melted and the enchiladas have heated through, about 10 minutes. Remove from the oven, sprinkle with the cilantro, and serve immediately.

12 enchiladas, about 6 servings

SPINACH AND PHYLLO TART

Thin, leaf-like sheets of dough are brushed lightly with butter and then sandwiched together to make the crust for this tart. Phyllo can be both magical and infuriating for some—the paper-thin pastry can seem difficult to work with. But here are some good tips: keep the unused phyllo covered by a damp cloth, work quickly, and have all your ingredients ready to go before you get started. Once you learn how to use phyllo, you'll love it for its tender, flaky layers.

¼ cup extra-virgin olive oil

1 cup roughly chopped onion

2 tablespoons minced green onion

1 tablespoon minced garlic

1 ½ pounds baby spinach

1 teaspoon salt

½ teaspoon freshly ground black pepper

8 ounces French goat milk feta or other mild feta, such as Bulgarian, crumbled

½ cup whole-milk ricotta cheese

½ cup toasted chopped walnuts

¼ cup golden raisins

2 tablespoons chopped fresh parsley leaves

1 tablespoon chopped fresh mint leaves

One 16-ounce package frozen phyllo, thawed according to package directions

6 tablespoons (¾ stick) unsalted butter, melted

⅓ cup grated Parmigiano-Reggiano cheese

3 tablespoons toasted sesame seeds

1.   Preheat the oven to 375°F.

2.   In a large sauté pan, heat the olive oil over medium heat. When hot, add the onion, green onion, and garlic and cook until softened, 4 to 5 minutes. Transfer the vegetables to a large mixing bowl and set aside.

3.   Add the spinach to the hot pan, little by little, adding more spinach to the pan as the previous batch wilts. Cook, stirring, until all the spinach has wilted. Season with ½ teaspoon of the salt and ¼ teaspoon of the pepper and place the spinach in a colander set over a bowl to drain.

4.   When the spinach has cooled, squeeze to remove any excess liquid and discard. Add the spinach to the bowl with the onions and garlic. Stir in the feta, ricotta, walnuts, raisins, parsley, mint, and remaining ½ teaspoon salt and ¼ teaspoon pepper until thoroughly combined.

5. Unroll the phyllo. Place 1 sheet of phyllo on a clean, dry work surface and cover the remaining sheets with a piece of plastic wrap and a damp kitchen towel to prevent them from drying out. Using a pastry brush, brush the phyllo lightly with some of the melted butter. Top with a second sheet of phyllo and brush lightly with butter. Repeat until you have a total of 10 layers of phyllo, brushing each layer with butter. Lay the stack of buttered phyllo in an 11-inch round tart pan with a removable bottom. Set the tart pan on a baking sheet. Spread the filling evenly in the phyllo-lined pan.

6. Prepare a second stack of phyllo in the same manner as the first, using the remaining sheets. This should take roughly the whole box of phyllo, considering that several sheets usually tear. Place the second stack of phyllo on top of the spinach filling. Brush lightly with the remaining butter. Sprinkle the Parmesan and sesame seeds evenly over the top of the tart. Roughly trim the edges of any overhanging phyllo so they don't hang too far over the edge of the tart pan. Bake until the phyllo is crispy and deep golden brown, about 45 minutes.

7. Transfer the tart to a cooling rack to cool briefly, then slice and serve warm or at room temperature.

8 servings

TURKEY CLUB CASSEROLE

There is some speculation that club sandwiches may have gotten their name because they were served at private men's social clubs—or perhaps the sandwich was originally called a "two-decker" and served in the double-decker club cars on the railroad. Either way, club sandwiches today usually consist of three pieces of toast layered with sliced tomato, lettuce, turkey, bacon, and sometimes cheese. In this recipe, we have layered club sandwiches in a baking dish, soaked them in an egg royale, and baked them in the oven. Oh, yeah, babe, this dish is great for any occasion—a cross between French toast and a club sandwich. You don't get any better than that.

8 large eggs

1 cup heavy cream

1 cup whole milk

1/2 teaspoon salt

1/2 teaspoon spicy brown mustard

1/4 teaspoon cayenne

1/8 teaspoon freshly grated nutmeg

5 tablespoons unsalted butter

Two 1-pound loaves very thinly sliced sandwich bread, preferably Pepperidge Farm

1 recipe Béchamel Sauce (recipe follows)

1 pound thinly sliced oven-roasted turkey breast

2 medium tomatoes, cored and thinly sliced

1 pound bacon, cooked until crisp and drained

8 ounces thinly sliced honey-glazed ham

8 ounces thinly sliced sharp cheddar cheese

1. In a large mixing bowl, whisk together the eggs, cream, milk, salt, mustard, cayenne, and nutmeg. Set the egg-cream mixture aside while you prepare the sandwiches.

2. Grease the bottom and sides of a 9 × 13-inch glass baking dish with 1 tablespoon of the butter.

3. Using a serrated knife, cut the crusts off the bread. Assemble 16 sandwiches by combining the ingredients for each sandwich in this order, from the bottom up: 1 slice of bread spread with 1 teaspoon of the béchamel, topped with 1 ounce of turkey, 1 slice of tomato, and 1 piece of the bacon (broken to fit on the sandwich); another slice of bread spread with 1 teaspoon béchamel, 1/2 ounce of the ham, and 1/2 ounce cheese; and one more piece of bread spread with 1 teaspoon béchamel (béchamel side down). As the

sandwiches are assembled, place 8 of them in the prepared casserole dish. Repeat with the remaining sandwiches, placing them directly on top of the first layer.

4. When all the sandwiches are positioned in the casserole, pour the egg-cream mixture evenly over the top. Place a piece of parchment or wax paper on top of the casserole and place a second casserole dish on top of the paper to weight the casserole. Refrigerate for at least 1 hour and up to 2 hours. The bread should absorb most of the egg mixture.

5. Preheat the oven to 350°F and remove the casserole from the refrigerator, slice the remaining 4 tablespoons (½ stick) of butter into 8 pieces, and place one piece on top of each sandwich stack. Bake the casserole, uncovered, until puffed and golden, usually about 40 minutes.

6. Set the casserole aside to cool briefly before serving. Serve the casserole warm.

8 to 10 servings

BÉCHAMEL SAUCE

---

2 tablespoons unsalted butter
2 tablespoons all-purpose flour
2 cups whole milk
¼ teaspoon salt
⅛ teaspoon freshly ground white pepper
Pinch of freshly grated nutmeg

1. In a medium saucepan, melt the butter over medium heat. Add the flour and cook, stirring constantly with a wooden spoon, for about 2 minutes; do not allow to brown.

2. While whisking constantly, add the milk, salt, pepper, and nutmeg. Cook the mixture, stirring constantly, until it comes to a boil. Reduce the heat to medium-low and continue to

cook until the sauce has thickened and any floury taste is gone, about 8 minutes.

3. Remove the sauce from the heat and transfer to a small heat-resistant bowl. Place a piece of plastic wrap on the surface of the béchamel and then set aside to cool. The béchamel can be stored in a resealable container in the refrigerator for up to 5 days.

1 1/2 cups

LEEK AND BACON QUICHE IN A POTATO CRUST

Here is a unique quiche for you. The filling is baked in a grated potato crust and is flavored with bacon, cheese, sour cream, and green onions—all the fixin's we love on a baked potato. The quiche makes a perfect lunch or brunch entree since it is just as good (if not better) the day after you make it. Once it cools in the fridge, the texture becomes even creamier. Just slice, reheat, and enjoy.

Nonstick cooking spray

2 tablespoons butter, plus 1 tablespoon softened and 2 tablespoons melted

7 eggs

2 ½ teaspoons salt

1 ¼ teaspoons freshly ground white pepper

¼ teaspoon plus a pinch of cayenne

2 pounds Idaho potatoes, peeled and set in a bowl of water to prevent browning

1 egg white, lightly beaten

8 ounces bacon, diced

1 large leek (about 1 pound), root end and dark green leaves discarded, thinly sliced and cleaned

1 cup sour cream

1 ½ cups whole milk

1 ½ cups heavy cream

1 tablespoon fresh thyme leaves

¼ cup thinly sliced green onion

4 ounces sharp cheddar cheese, grated (about 1 cup)

1. Preheat the oven to 450°F.

2. Using the cooking spray, grease the bottom and sides of a 9-inch springform pan. Grease a large sheet of parchment paper with the softened butter and cut it into pieces to fit the bottom and sides of the pan (one circle and one long rectangle). Line the pan with the parchment paper, buttered side up.

3. Whisk 1 egg in a medium bowl. Add 1 teaspoon of the salt, ½ teaspoon of the white pepper, and the pinch of cayenne.

4. Set a box grater on a clean kitchen towel. Grate the potatoes on the large holes of the grater onto the towel. Gather the ends of the towel up around the grated potatoes, hold it over the sink, and squeeze to release the excess moisture from the potatoes. Transfer the potatoes to another clean towel and squeeze again. You may need to do this in batches.

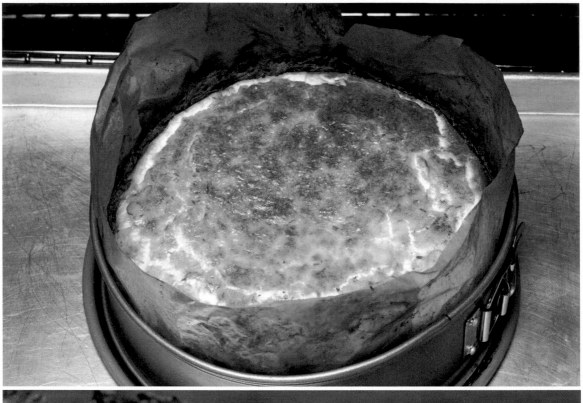

5. When the potatoes are dry, add them and the melted butter to the egg mixture and toss to combine. Pat the potato mixture evenly on the bottom and up the sides of the prepared pan. Place the pan on a baking sheet and bake until golden around the edges, about 30 minutes. Brush some of the beaten egg white all over the potato crust to seal any cracks. Set the crust aside to cool for at least 5 minutes (leave it on the baking sheet for easier transporting). Reduce the oven temperature to 375°F.

6. Add the bacon to a small skillet and set over medium heat. Cook until the fat is rendered and the bacon is crispy, about 10 minutes. Using a slotted spoon, transfer the bacon to a paper towel–lined plate and reserve. Discard all but 2 tablespoons of the bacon fat from the pan.

7. Add the remaining 2 tablespoons butter to the pan. When the butter has melted, add the leek, ½ teaspoon of the remaining salt, and ¼ teaspoon of the remaining white pepper. Cook, stirring as needed, until the leek is soft, 6 to 7 minutes. Remove from the heat.

8. In a large bowl, whisk the remaining 6 eggs with the sour cream, milk, cream, thyme, green onion, grated cheddar, and remaining 1 teaspoon salt, ½ teaspoon white pepper, and ¼ teaspoon cayenne until smooth. Add the bacon and leek and stir to combine. Carefully ladle the filling into the potato crust. The filling may come up past the edges of the crust, depending on how high you pressed the potato crust—if so, don't worry.

9. Bake for 30 minutes. Reduce the oven temperature to 350°F and cook for 25 minutes. Rotate the pan from front to back and continue to cook until the quiche is nearly set in the center, about 25 minutes longer. It will continue to set as it cools. Remove the quiche from the oven and set aside at least 20 minutes before slicing and serving.

8 servings

EGGS FLORENTINE

This is a favorite for brunch at my house. It is so simple to put together that you could almost do it in your sleep. The creamed spinach can be made the day before and spooned into the casserole dish, leaving you with the simple task of cracking a few eggs, sprinkling with breadcrumbs, and popping it in the oven. Voilà—brunch!

4 tablespoons (½ stick) unsalted butter

3 pounds baby spinach

1 teaspoon salt

½ teaspoon freshly ground white pepper

1 onion, roughly chopped

2 cloves garlic, minced

2 tablespoons all-purpose flour

½ cup whole milk

¼ cup heavy cream

4 ounces Neufchâtel cheese, cubed

Pinch of freshly grated nutmeg

6 large eggs, at room temperature

¼ cup fresh breadcrumbs

¼ cup grated Parmigiano-Reggiano cheese

1. Preheat the oven to 350°F.

2. Melt 1 tablespoon of the butter in a large sauté pan over medium heat. Add the spinach, little by little, stirring and adding more spinach as the previous addition has wilted, until all the spinach has wilted. Season with ½ teaspoon of the salt and ¼ teaspoon of the white pepper and place the spinach in a colander over a bowl to drain.

3. Add 1 tablespoon of the remaining butter to the pan. When it begins to bubble, add the onion and garlic and cook over medium-low heat until the onion is translucent and tender, about 4 minutes. Transfer the onion and garlic to a medium mixing bowl.

4. In a small, heavy saucepan, heat the remaining 2 tablespoons butter over medium-high heat. When the butter begins to bubble, add the flour and cook, stirring, for 1 minute. Gradually whisk in the milk and cream and, while whisking constantly, bring to a boil, about 3 minutes. Add the Neufchâtel cheese, nutmeg, ¼ teaspoon of the remaining salt, and the remaining ¼ teaspoon white pepper. Once the sauce has thickened, remove it from the heat and continue to whisk for 1 minute more.

5. When the spinach has cooled, squeeze out any excess liquid, coarsely chop, and add back to the mixing bowl with the onion and garlic. Add the warm sauce and stir well to combine.

6. Spread the spinach mixture in an even layer in the bottom of a 9 × 13-inch glass baking dish. Using a spoon, make 6 wells in the spinach for the eggs. Crack an egg into each well. Combine the breadcrumbs, Parmesan, and remaining ¼ teaspoon salt in a small mixing bowl. Sprinkle the breadcrumb mixture evenly over the eggs and spinach. Bake until the spinach is warmed through and the eggs are set and cooked to the desired degree of doneness, 12 to 15 minutes. Serve with warm crusty bread.

6 servings

MAKE-AHEAD SAVORY BREAKFAST CASSEROLE

This dish is easily prepared ahead of time and then baked just before serving for a super kicked-up breakfast, brunch, or dinner with no effort whatsoever.

6 ounces thick-cut smoked bacon (about 4 strips), diced

1 1/4 cups chopped yellow onion

3/4 cup chopped mixed red and green bell peppers

2 3/4 teaspoons Emeril's Original Essence or Creole Seasoning (page 3)

4 large croissants (about 12 ounces total), cut into 1-inch pieces

1/4 cup minced green onion

6 ounces medium yellow cheddar cheese, grated (about 1 1/2 cups)

7 large eggs

1 1/4 cups milk

3/4 cup heavy cream

1/4 teaspoon salt

1. In a medium skillet over medium-high heat, cook the bacon until crisp and the fat has rendered, 4 to 6 minutes. Remove the bacon using a slotted spoon and transfer to a paper towel–lined plate to drain. Remove all but 1½ tablespoons of the bacon drippings from the pan and reserve the drippings on the side. Add the onion, bell peppers, and ¾ teaspoon of the Essence to the pan and cook, stirring often, until the vegetables are soft and lightly caramelized, 4 to 6 minutes. Return the bacon to the pan and stir to combine.

2. Using a bit of the reserved bacon drippings, lightly grease a 1½-quart oval gratin dish or other shallow baking dish of similar size. Add half the croissant pieces to the dish, then spoon half the vegetable-bacon mixture over the bread. Sprinkle with half of the green onion and then top with half of the cheese. Repeat to form a second layer with the remaining bread, vegetables, green onion, and cheese.

3. In a medium mixing bowl, combine the eggs, milk, cream, salt, and remaining 2 teaspoons Essence and whisk to combine. Pour the egg-milk mixture slowly over the casserole so that it is evenly distributed. Cover with plastic wrap and refrigerate for at least 4 hours or up to overnight.

4. Preheat the oven to 325°F and remove the breakfast casserole from the refrigerator while the oven is preheating.

5. Discard the plastic wrap and cover the casserole with a piece of buttered aluminum foil (buttered side down). Bake for 30 minutes, then uncover and bake until the casserole is puffed, set in the middle, and golden brown on top, 30 to 35 minutes more. Allow the casserole to sit for 10 to 15 minutes before serving.

6 servings

DUTCH
Ovens

COLA-BRAISED POT ROAST
WITH VEGETABLES

Here's a comfort-food classic with a sauce that gets a hint of sweetness when you add your favorite cola. Choose a chuck roast that is nicely marbled—the meat will remain moist and flavorful after the slow braising.

4 pounds boneless beef chuck roast

2 teaspoons freshly ground black pepper

1 tablespoon plus 1 teaspoon kosher salt

2 tablespoons minced garlic

2 teaspoons minced fresh rosemary leaves

2 tablespoons vegetable oil

2 cups beef stock or canned low-sodium beef broth, plus more as needed

One 12-ounce can cola soda

1 tablespoon tomato paste

2 medium onions, peeled and cut into 2-inch chunks

2 large Idaho potatoes, peeled and cut into 2-inch chunks

2 medium parsnips, peeled and cut into 2-inch chunks

2 medium carrots, peeled and cut on the bias into 2-inch chunks

3 celery ribs, cut on the bias into 2-inch chunks

2 ½ tablespoons all-purpose flour

1. Preheat the oven to 325°F.

2. Season the roast well on all sides with the pepper and 2 teaspoons of the salt. Combine the garlic, rosemary, and remaining 2 teaspoons salt on a cutting board and use the side of a knife to mash them into a paste. Using a small paring knife, make thin slits on all sides of the roast, about 2 inches apart, and fill the holes with the garlic-rosemary paste. Repeat until you have used all the paste.

3. Heat a Dutch oven over high heat and add the oil. When the oil is hot, add the roast and cook until very well browned on all sides, 10 to 12 minutes total. Add the stock and cola and bring to a boil, scraping the bottom of the pan with a wooden spoon to release any browned bits. Add the tomato paste and stir to blend. The liquid should reach about halfway up the sides of the roast; add a little more stock or water if needed. Cover the Dutch oven, place in the oven, and roast for 2 hours, turning the meat after 1 hour and adding extra water if necessary to keep the liquid level at about one-third of the way up the sides of the roast. Add the vegetables, making sure they are completely submerged in the liquid, and continue to cook, covered, until the roast is fork-tender and the vegetables are tender, about 1½ hours longer.

4. Remove the roast from the oven and carefully transfer the meat to a serving platter. Cover loosely to keep warm. Remove the vegetables with a slotted spoon, set aside in a bowl, and cover to keep warm.

5. Skim off as much of the fat from the surface of the cooking liquid as possible and discard all but 2 tablespoons of the fat. Transfer the reserved skimmed fat to a small heatproof bowl and stir in the flour to make a smooth paste. Add ½ cup of the hot braising liquid to the bowl and whisk to combine. Slowly whisk this mixture into the liquid remaining in the Dutch oven, then place the pan over high heat on the stovetop. Cook, whisking frequently, until the mixture comes to a boil and thickens. Continue to cook for about 5 minutes, or until the sauce is thick enough to coat the back of a spoon and any floury taste is gone. Taste and adjust the seasoning if necessary.

6. Slice the roast and serve with the hot gravy and vegetables.

4 to 6 servings

RED WINE AND PORT BRAISED SHORT RIBS

This hearty dish is not necessarily something for every day, but it's perfect for a dinner party or a special occasion because it can be made ahead of time. The short ribs are particularly rich, so I like to serve them on a bed of braised veggies. If you're looking for something a little more filling, try serving the ribs with creamy polenta or over stone-ground grits.

2 tablespoons olive oil

8 beef short ribs (about 6 pounds)

1 tablespoon salt

1 ½ teaspoons freshly ground black pepper

4 cipollini onions, peeled and quartered

4 baby white turnips, peeled and quartered

2 parsnips, peeled and cut into 1-inch chunks

8 cloves garlic, peeled and smashed

3 tablespoons all-purpose flour

2 cups full-bodied red wine, such as Pinot Noir, Burgundy, or Zinfandel

2 cups tawny port

3 cups beef stock or canned low-sodium beef broth

4 sprigs fresh flat-leaf parsley

4 sprigs fresh thyme

2 bay leaves

5 whole black peppercorns

1. Preheat the oven to 325°F.

2. Heat the olive oil in a 6-quart Dutch oven over medium-high heat. Season the short ribs with 2 teaspoons of the salt and 1 teaspoon of the ground black pepper. When the oil is hot, brown half of the short ribs until well caramelized on all sides, about 10 minutes. Transfer the ribs to a platter and repeat with the remaining short ribs.

3. Remove and discard all but 2 tablespoons of the fat from the pan and reduce the heat to medium. Add the onions, turnips, and parsnips and cook until the vegetables begin to caramelize, 6 to 8 minutes. Add the garlic and cook for 1 to 2 minutes longer. Stir in the flour and continue to cook, stirring, for 3 minutes. Add the wine to the pan and bring to a simmer, scraping to release any browned bits that have stuck to the bottom. Stir in the port, stock, parsley, thyme, bay leaves, and black peppercorns, adjust the heat to medium-high, and bring to a boil.

4. Return the short ribs to the pan, along with any accumulated juices, then cover the pan and place it in the oven. Cook until the meat is fork-tender and beginning to pull away from the bones, basting the ribs occasionally with the braising liquid, 2½ to 3 hours.

5. Transfer the ribs to a large platter, discard any loose bones, and cover the ribs to keep them warm. Skim the fat from the top of the braising liquid and discard. Gently strain the braising liquid through a fine-mesh sieve, carefully transferring the vegetables from the pot to a platter (discard the parsley and thyme sprigs and bay leaves). Return the braising liquid to a clean Dutch oven and bring to a boil over medium-high heat. Simmer until the liquid has reduced to a sauce consistency and is thick enough to coat the back of a spoon, about 10 minutes. Season the sauce with the remaining 1 teaspoon salt and ½ teaspoon ground black pepper. Return the meat and the vegetables to the Dutch oven and simmer briefly until heated through. Serve hot.

4 servings

Note: These short ribs may be made up to 2 days in advance and refrigerated (covered and in the sauce) until ready to serve. Reheat gently and return to a simmer before serving.

CAJUN SHRIMP STEW

This comforting, simple stew is a Cajun dish that many home cooks in Louisiana enjoy, especially during the Lenten season. It is easy to make and feeds a bunch. The trick is getting the roux to the right color... about a notch darker than peanut butter should do the trick. A homemade shrimp stock makes all the difference in the world. Make sure to add the shrimp just before serving so that they stay nice and tender. Some families boil eggs in their shrimp stew (as it simmers) to make the dish even heartier.

1 cup vegetable oil

1 ½ cups all-purpose flour

2 ½ cups finely chopped onion

¼ cup minced garlic (about 12 cloves)

10 cups Rich Shrimp Stock (page 173)

2 bay leaves

1 ¼ teaspoons freshly ground black pepper

¾ teaspoon cayenne

2 teaspoons chopped fresh thyme leaves

1 ½ tablespoons kosher salt

3 large baking potatoes (2 ½ to 3 pounds), peeled and cut into 2-inch pieces

2 pounds small or medium shrimp, peeled and deveined

¼ cup chopped green onion, green part only

2 tablespoons chopped fresh parsley leaves

Steamed long-grain white rice, for serving

1. Heat the oil in a heavy-bottomed Dutch oven over medium-high heat and, when hot, add the flour. Whisk to combine and continue to cook, stirring constantly, until a medium roux is formed (it should look a bit darker than peanut butter), about 10 minutes. (If the roux begins to brown too quickly, reduce the heat to medium or medium-low and take your time—it is important that the roux not be burned at all or the stew will have a bitter taste.) As soon as the roux is the right color, add the chopped onion and cook until soft, stirring occasionally, 4 to 6 minutes. Add the garlic and cook for 2 minutes. Stir in the stock, little by little, and bring the sauce to a gentle boil. Add the bay leaves, black pepper, cayenne, thyme, and 4 teaspoons of the salt and reduce the heat so that the sauce just simmers. Cook, stirring occasionally, until the floury taste is gone, 30 to 45 minutes.

2. Add the potatoes and continue to cook, uncovered and stirring occasionally, until the potatoes are very tender and the sauce is thick and flavorful, 30 to 40 minutes longer. (Add a bit of water or chicken broth to thin the gravy should the stew get too thick during the cook time. The sauce is meant to be thick and rich but not pasty.)

3. Toss the shrimp with the remaining ½ teaspoon salt. Stir the shrimp, green onion, and parsley into the stew and continue to cook until the shrimp are just cooked through, 3 to 4 minutes. Taste and adjust the seasoning if necessary. Remove the bay leaves. Serve the stew in shallow bowls over hot white rice.

6 to 8 servings

CHICKEN CACCIATORE

Use San Marzano tomatoes in this classic Italian dish for the best flavor. They are prized for their less acidic taste and almost bittersweet complexity, which is said to come from the unique, protected Italian soil on which they are grown. Another secret to the success of this dish: a piece of Parmesan rind thrown into the pot for an added layer of flavor. Now that's what I'm talkin' about!

One 3 ½- to 4-pound whole chicken, cut into 8 pieces

1 teaspoon freshly ground black pepper

2 teaspoons salt

3 tablespoons olive oil

3 cups chopped onion

1 ½ tablespoons minced garlic

8 ounces mushrooms, such as shiitake, baby bella, or button, stems trimmed, sliced

½ teaspoon crushed red pepper

2 tablespoons fresh rosemary leaves

1 bay leaf

1 cup dry white wine

One 28-ounce can San Marzano whole peeled tomatoes, with juice

1 or 2 chunks Parmigiano-Reggiano cheese rind, about 6 inches total

½ teaspoon sugar

¼ cup chopped fresh parsley leaves

2 tablespoons extra-virgin olive oil

Steamed rice or cooked egg noodles, for serving

1. Season the chicken with the black pepper and 1 teaspoon of the salt and set aside. Heat the olive oil in a large, preferably shallow, Dutch oven over medium-high heat. Add the chicken, skin side down (in batches if necessary), and cook until browned on all sides, 6 to 8 minutes. Remove the chicken and set it aside. Repeat with any remaining chicken.

2. Add the onion and garlic to the pan and cook until the onion is translucent, about 3 minutes. Add the mushrooms and cook for 3 minutes longer. Stir in the crushed red pepper, rosemary, bay leaf, wine, and tomatoes, breaking them up with a wooden spoon, and simmer for 5 minutes. Add the Parmesan rind, sugar, and remaining 1 teaspoon salt and return the chicken to the pan. Bring the sauce to a boil, reduce the heat to simmer, cover, and cook until the chicken is tender and the sauce is flavorful, about 45 minutes.

3. Remove the chicken from the pan with a slotted spoon and set it aside on a serving platter. Continue to simmer the sauce until reduced to the desired consistency, about 5 minutes longer. Remove and discard the Parmesan rind and bay leaf, stir in the parsley and extra-virgin olive oil, and spoon the sauce over the chicken. Serve immediately with rice or noodles.

4 to 6 servings

MOJO-MARINATED PORK AND BLACK BEAN STEW

Who can resist the quintessential Cuban flavors of citrus, oregano, and garlic with pork and black beans? We put all these things together for one big pot packed full of flavor. The meat is marinated overnight and ends up perfectly seasoned and falling-apart tender. All you need to round things out is a steaming bowl of yellow rice and perhaps some sliced avocado and fresh cilantro.

½ cup freshly squeezed orange juice

¼ cup freshly squeezed lime juice

¼ cup freshly squeezed lemon juice

8 large cloves garlic, peeled and smashed, plus 2 tablespoons minced garlic

1 tablespoon plus 1 ½ teaspoons salt

1 teaspoon whole black peppercorns

2 tablespoons chopped fresh oregano leaves

3 ½ to 4 pounds boneless Boston butt pork roast, cut into 1 ½- to 2-inch cubes

½ teaspoon freshly ground black pepper

2 tablespoons vegetable oil

3 cups small-diced onion

1 cup small-diced green bell pepper

1 cup small-diced poblano chile

2 tablespoons ground cumin

1 tablespoon dried oregano, crumbled between your fingers

1 teaspoon dried thyme leaves, crumbled between your fingers

1 ½ tablespoons red wine

8 cups chicken stock or canned low-sodium chicken broth

1 bay leaf

1 pound dried black beans, rinsed, picked over, and soaked overnight

1 cup finely chopped tomato

2 tablespoons chopped fresh cilantro leaves

1 tablespoon Crystal or other red Louisiana hot sauce

Cooked yellow rice, for serving (optional)

1. Combine the orange juice, lime juice, lemon juice, smashed garlic, 1½ teaspoons of the salt, the peppercorns, and the fresh oregano in a small mixing bowl and set aside at room temperature for about 15 minutes to let the flavors come together. Add the pork and toss to coat well. Transfer the pork and marinade to a resealable 1-gallon plastic food storage bag. Remove as much air as possible, seal the bag, and

place it in a shallow baking dish. Refrigerate overnight, turning the bag at least once to ensure even marinating.

2.   Remove the pork and discard the marinade. Lightly pat the pork pieces dry with paper towels. Season the pork with 1 teaspoon of the remaining salt and the ground black pepper.

3.   Heat the vegetable oil in a 6-quart Dutch oven over medium-high heat. Cook the pork in batches until it is nicely browned on all sides, 3 to 4 minutes on each side. Remove the pork and transfer to a paper towel–lined plate to drain briefly. Discard all but 2 tablespoons of the fat in the pan.

4.   Add the onion, bell pepper, poblano, minced garlic, 1 tablespoon of the cumin, $1\frac{1}{2}$ teaspoons of the dried oregano, and $\frac{1}{2}$ teaspoon of the thyme and sauté over medium-high heat until the onion is soft and lightly caramelized, 6 to 7 minutes. Add the wine and cook, stirring to release any browned bits on the bottom of the pan. Stir in the stock, add the bay leaf, and bring to a boil. Add the pork, cover, and cook at a simmer for 30 minutes.

5.   Drain the beans and add to the pot, along with the remaining 2 teaspoons salt, 1 tablespoon cumin, $1\frac{1}{2}$ teaspoons dried oregano, and $\frac{1}{2}$ teaspoon thyme and stir to combine. Partially cover the pot and continue cooking, stirring occasionally, until the pork and beans are tender, $1\frac{1}{2}$ to 2 hours longer. Remove the bay leaf and stir in the tomato, cilantro, and hot sauce and serve immediately, spooned over yellow rice if desired.

6 to 8 servings

CHICKEN AND ANDOUILLE JAMBALAYA

The trick to any jambalaya recipe is to make sure the rice is perfectly cooked. Since there are many ingredients, it isn't as simple as just getting the rice-to-liquid ratio right. Make sure you use the correct rice: long-grain white. And, after stirring in the parsley, be sure to cover again and allow the rice to finish steaming. The flavor of this jambalaya is truly out of this world!

3 pounds chicken thighs (about 6), trimmed of excess fat

2 1/2 teaspoons salt

1 1/2 teaspoons freshly ground black pepper

3 tablespoons canola oil

1 1/2 pounds smoked andouille sausage, diced

2 large yellow onions, chopped

4 medium celery stalks, chopped

1 green bell pepper, chopped

1 bunch green onions, finely chopped, green and white parts reserved separately

6 cloves garlic, minced

2 tablespoons tomato paste

One 4-ounce can chopped green chiles, with juice

1 teaspoon dried thyme leaves, crumbled between your fingers

1 bay leaf

1/2 teaspoon crushed red pepper

1/2 teaspoon Tabasco or other hot pepper sauce

1 1/2 teaspoons Emeril's Original Essence or Creole Seasoning (page 3)

4 cups chicken stock or canned low-sodium chicken broth

One 14.5-ounce can diced tomatoes, with juice

3 cups long-grain white rice

1/2 cup chopped fresh parsley leaves

1. Season the chicken on both sides with 1 teaspoon of the salt and 1 teaspoon of the black pepper. Heat the oil in a large Dutch oven over high heat. Add the chicken and cook until browned on both sides, 3 to 4 minutes per side, working in batches as necessary. Transfer the browned chicken to a platter and set aside.

2. Add the sausage to the Dutch oven, reduce the heat to medium-high, and cook, stirring, until the sausage is browned, 4 to 5 minutes. Transfer the sausage to the same platter as the chicken. Add the onions, celery, bell pepper, white part of the green onions, garlic, and tomato paste to the Dutch oven, reduce the heat to medium, and sauté until the vegetables are tender, about 5 minutes. Stir in the green

chiles, thyme, bay leaf, crushed red pepper, hot sauce, and Essence.

3. Return the chicken and sausage to the pan. Add the stock and tomatoes and bring to a brisk simmer. Cover, reduce the heat to low, and cook for 30 minutes, or until the chicken is nearly tender and the broth has absorbed the flavor of the sausage and the seasonings.

4. Increase the heat to high and add the rice, chopped green parts of the green onions, and remaining 1½ teaspoons salt and ½ teaspoon pepper. Stir well and return to a boil. Immediately reduce the heat to low, cover, and simmer until the rice is cooked and has absorbed all the liquid, about 20 minutes. Remove from the heat, remove the bay leaf, gently stir in the parsley, cover, and let stand for 15 minutes before serving.

6 to 8 servings

CREAMY WHITE BEANS WITH SMOKED TURKEY

I love using smoked turkey to flavor all sorts of soups and stews; it's a nice alternative to the more commonplace ham hock (though it's no secret that I love those too!). We used spinach here, but substitute whatever type of green you prefer or whichever happens to be in season.

2 pounds smoked turkey legs

8 cups chicken stock or canned low-sodium chicken broth

2 cups water

3 bay leaves

¼ teaspoon cayenne

2 tablespoons vegetable oil

1 ½ cups small-diced onion

¾ cup small-diced celery

2 ½ teaspoons salt

2 teaspoons minced garlic

2 teaspoons chopped fresh thyme

½ teaspoon crushed red pepper

1 pound dried white beans (great Northern or navy is fine), rinsed, picked over, and soaked overnight

8 ounces butternut squash, diced (2 generous cups)

6 ounces fresh spinach, cleaned and any tough ribs removed (see Note)

1. Place the turkey legs, 4 cups of the stock, the water, 2 of the bay leaves, and the cayenne in a 6-quart Dutch oven and bring to a boil over high heat. Reduce the heat so that the liquid just simmers, cover, and cook until the meat is falling from the bones, 2½ to 3 hours. Remove the turkey legs from the broth and, when cool enough to handle, shred the meat into bite-sized pieces. Discard the bones and skin. Strain the broth through a fine-mesh sieve and discard any solids. Set the broth and turkey meat aside.

2. Clean the Dutch oven and dry well. Add the oil and heat over medium-high heat. Add the onion, celery, and ½ teaspoon of the salt and cook, stirring, until the vegetables have softened, about 4 minutes. Add the garlic, thyme, and crushed red pepper and cook until fragrant, about 30 seconds. Drain the beans and add them to the pot, along with the reserved turkey broth and the remaining 4 cups chicken stock and 1 bay leaf, and bring to a boil. Reduce the heat to simmer and stir in the remaining 2 teaspoons salt. Cover and cook, stirring occasionally, for 1 hour. Partially uncover the pot and continue to cook until the beans are nearly tender, about 30 minutes longer. Add the squash and continue to cook until the beans and squash are tender, about 30 minutes longer.

3. Remove the lid and smash some of the beans against the side of the pot with the back of a spoon. Bring the sauce to a boil and cook until reduced and slightly thickened, 3 to 4 minutes. Remove the bay leaves. Stir in the reserved turkey and the spinach and heat through. Serve hot, in shallow bowls.

4 to 6 servings

Note: You can substitute kale or chard, but these tougher greens should be coarsely chopped and added a bit earlier than the spinach so that they're tender by the time the stew is done.

CARIBBEAN-STYLE OXTAILS

Oxtails' great flavor and texture make them perfect for slow braising in a Dutch oven. We spiced these up with Caribbean influences...and after a long, slow cooking they just melt in your mouth, leaving your taste buds dancing with the flavors of ginger, garlic, and allspice.

2 tablespoons olive oil, plus more as needed

1 teaspoon freshly ground black pepper

1 teaspoon ground allspice

1 1/2 tablespoons salt

4 pounds beef oxtails (the meatiest ones you can find)

2 cups small-diced onion

1 cup small-diced carrot

1 cup small-diced celery

1/4 cup minced garlic (about 12 cloves)

1/4 cup minced green onion, white part only

1/4 cup peeled and minced fresh ginger

2 1/2 tablespoons all-purpose flour

One 14.5-ounce can diced tomatoes, drained

2 cups veal stock or canned low-sodium beef broth

1 tablespoon whole allspice

5 whole cloves

Two 3-inch cinnamon sticks

4 bay leaves

1 habanero chile, pierced with the tip of a paring knife

1 1/2 pounds sweet potatoes, peeled and cut into 1 1/2- to 2-inch pieces

1 tablespoon chopped fresh parsley

1. Preheat the oven to 325°F.

2. Heat the olive oil in a 6-quart Dutch oven over medium-high heat. In a small bowl, combine the pepper, ground allspice, and 4 teaspoons of the salt. Season the oxtails all over with the salt mixture. Working in batches, add the oxtails to the Dutch oven and cook until well browned on all sides, adding a bit more oil if necessary, about 3 to 4 minutes per side. Transfer the seared oxtails to a platter and repeat with the remaining oxtails.

3. Add the onion, carrot, celery, and the remaining 1/2 teaspoon salt to the Dutch oven and cook, scraping the bottom of the pot to release any browned bits, until the vegetables are soft, 3 to 4 minutes. Add the garlic, green onion, and ginger and cook for 1 minute, stirring often. Sprinkle the flour over the vegetables and cook, stirring, for about 3 minutes. Add the tomatoes and stock and bring to a boil. Place the whole allspice, cloves, and cinnamon sticks in a small piece of cheesecloth and secure with twine. Add the spice

bag to the Dutch oven along with the bay leaves and habanero. Return the oxtails to the Dutch oven, bring the liquid to a boil, cover, and transfer to the oven. Cook until the oxtails are nearly tender, 2 to 2½ hours, turning them after 1 hour.

4.   Add the sweet potatoes and cook until the meat and potatoes are fork-tender, about 1 hour longer. Remove the lid and discard the spice bag, bay leaves, and habanero chile (if desired). Garnish with the parsley and serve immediately.

4 to 6 servings

BUTTERNUT SQUASH AND CHICKPEA TAGINE

A tagine is a slow-cooked North African stew, and it's also the name of the traditional cooking vessel in which it is prepared. Typically made of earthenware, a tagine has a distinctive conical lid that ensures the simmering juices remain inside. Most often the dish is made of meat and vegetables, but here we have a slight twist: chickpeas and vegetables braise with raisins, apricots, and aromatic saffron. Don't worry if you don't have the traditional pot; it is easily made in your Dutch oven.

3 tablespoons olive oil

1 ½ cups small-diced onion

1 cup small-diced carrot

1 teaspoon ground turmeric

1 teaspoon ground cinnamon

1 teaspoon ground coriander

½ teaspoon crushed red pepper

3 cups peeled and diced butternut squash

1 ½ cups peeled and diced sweet potato

1 tablespoon minced garlic

½ cup golden raisins

½ cup small-diced dried apricots (about 4 ounces)

4 saffron threads, crumbled between your fingers

4 cilantro sprigs, tied together with twine

1 tablespoon kosher salt

4 cups chicken stock or canned low-sodium chicken broth, plus more if needed

Two 14.5-ounce cans chickpeas, drained and rinsed

1 tablespoon chopped Simple Preserved Lemons (page 146)

¼ cup chopped fresh parsley leaves

½ cup small-diced red bell pepper

½ teaspoon freshly ground black pepper

Grated zest of 1 lemon

10 ounces couscous

2 tablespoons freshly squeezed lemon juice

1 tablespoon extra-virgin olive oil

1. Heat 2 tablespoons of the olive oil in a tagine or Dutch oven over medium-high heat. Add the onion, carrot, turmeric, cinnamon, coriander, and crushed red pepper and cook until the onion is translucent, about 3 minutes. Add the butternut squash and sweet potato and cook for 7 minutes longer, stirring occasionally. Add the garlic, raisins, dried apricots, saffron, cilantro sprigs, 2 teaspoons of the kosher salt, and 2 cups of the stock and bring the mixture to a boil. Reduce the heat to medium-low and cook, covered, for 15 minutes. Add the chickpeas and preserved

lemon and cook for 30 minutes longer. Remove from the heat and sprinkle half of the parsley over the top. Set aside while you prepare the couscous.

2.   In a 2-quart or larger saucepan, heat the remaining 1 table-spoon olive oil over medium-high heat. Add the bell pepper, black pepper, and remaining 1 teaspoon kosher salt and cook until soft, about 2 minutes. Stir in the lemon zest and remain-ing 2 cups stock and bring to a boil. Add the couscous, cover, and remove from the heat. Allow the couscous to steam for 5 minutes, then add the lemon juice, extra-virgin olive oil, and remaining half of the parsley and stir to combine. Serve the couscous in shallow bowls, with some of the stew ladled over the top.

6 servings

CHICKEN VINDALOO

If you like spicy Indian food—and I don't mean just a blend of different spices, I mean spicy *hot*—then this is the dish for you. In this dish, chicken is marinated overnight in an aromatic mixture of spices and seasonings, resulting in intense Indian flavors that'll knock your socks off! When cooking the chicken, take care to stir it often: the sauce is very thick and tends to stick and will easily burn on the pan's bottom if left unattended. A heavy-bottomed Dutch oven is key here—don't even think of making this in a thin pot. When the chicken is done, you can either leave it in whole pieces or remove it from the pot, shred the meat, and return it to the sauce for easier eating.

2 teaspoons cumin seeds

2 teaspoons black mustard seeds

Seeds from 8 cardamom pods

18 whole cloves

1 large onion, roughly chopped, plus 3 cups thinly sliced

3 tablespoons finely chopped garlic

2 tablespoons peeled and finely chopped fresh ginger

3 tablespoons cider vinegar

1/4 cup plus 1 tablespoon vegetable oil

One 4-pound whole chicken, cut into 8 pieces

1 tablespoon plus 1 teaspoon tamarind pulp

1 1/4 cups boiling water

1 tablespoon plus 1/2 teaspoon kosher salt

1/4 cup chicken stock or canned low-sodium chicken broth

1 cup seeded and chopped tomato

1 tablespoon ground turmeric

1 tablespoon cayenne

1 tablespoon hot paprika

3 bay leaves

1 cinnamon stick

Steamed basmati rice, for serving

1.   Toast the cumin seeds, mustard seeds, cardamom, and cloves in a small sauté pan over medium heat, stirring, until they are fragrant and change color, about 3 minutes. Transfer to a spice blender or a clean coffee mill and blend to a powder. Using a spatula, scrape out as much of the spice mixture as possible and set aside.

2.   Place the chopped onion, garlic, ginger, vinegar, and ground spice mixture in a food processor and puree. While the machine is still running, drizzle in 2 tablespoons of the oil, scraping the sides of the bowl as necessary.

3. In a large mixing bowl, combine the chicken and onion puree and toss to coat. Transfer to a resealable 1-gallon plastic food storage bag and refrigerate overnight.

4. Place the tamarind pulp in a small bowl and add the boiling water. Cover with plastic wrap and set aside until softened, about 10 minutes. Uncover the bowl and, using the back of a spoon, smash the pulp in the water to dissolve the tamarind. Strain through a fine-mesh sieve, pressing the pulp through the strainer. Discard the seeds and fibrous parts and reserve the tamarind juice.

5. Remove the chicken from the marinade, scraping any excess marinade from the chicken into the marinade remaining in the bag. Pat the chicken dry with a paper towel and season with 1 teaspoon of the salt. Reserve the marinade.

6. In a 6-quart Dutch oven, heat the remaining 3 tablespoons oil over medium-high heat. In batches, cook the chicken pieces until browned on both sides, about 10 minutes total. If the bottom of the pan begins to darken, add a bit of the chicken stock as needed to help dissolve any browned bits. Remove the chicken from the pot and set aside.

7. Reduce the heat to medium, add the sliced onions and ½ teaspoon of the remaining salt and cook, stirring, until browned, about 10 minutes. Add the tomato and cook until just tender, about 2 minutes. Add the turmeric, cayenne, paprika, bay leaves, and cinnamon stick and sauté until fragrant, about 30 seconds. Stir in the tamarind juice, reserved marinade, any remaining chicken stock, and the remaining 2 teaspoons salt and bring to a boil. Add the chicken, reduce the heat to a gentle simmer, partially cover with a lid, and cook until fork-tender, 50 to 60 minutes. Discard the bay leaves and cinnamon stick. Remove the chicken from the bones if desired and serve immediately over basmati rice.

4 servings

SPICY VEGETABLE COCONUT CURRY

Thai curry paste comes in many varieties, with red, green, and yellow being the most popular. It is used in many ways—in soups, stir-fries, and marinades to name a few. Though it is easily made from scratch, I prefer to use the packaged ones because the flavor is consistent and it is easy to use; try the Mae Ploy brand. It can be found in Asian markets as well as online, as can fried tofu (and in many health food stores, too).

2 tablespoons vegetable oil

1 tablespoon minced garlic

1 tablespoon peeled and minced fresh ginger

1 tablespoon minced green onion

1 tablespoon minced shallot

1 tablespoon seeded and minced fresh red Thai bird chile

¼ cup minced lemongrass, white part only

2 tablespoons Thai red curry paste

1 yellow onion, peeled and cut into wedges

1 pound sweet potatoes, peeled and cut into large chunks

2 cups cauliflower florets

1½ cups broccoli florets

1 cup ½-inch sliced carrot rounds

¾ cup diced red bell pepper

¾ cup diced yellow bell pepper

¾ cup diced orange bell pepper

6 ounces fried tofu, cut into ½-inch cubes

4 cups vegetable stock or canned low-sodium vegetable broth

2 cups unsweetened coconut milk

2 teaspoons kosher salt

2 cups steamed jasmine rice, for serving

¼ cup fresh cilantro leaves, for garnish

¼ cup chopped unsalted roasted peanuts, for garnish

1. Heat the vegetable oil in a 6-quart Dutch oven over medium heat. Add the garlic, ginger, green onion, shallot, red chile, and lemongrass and cook until the vegetables have wilted, about 3 minutes. Stir in the curry paste and cook for 1 minute. Add the yellow onion, sweet potato, cauliflower, broccoli, carrot, bell peppers, tofu, stock, coconut milk, and salt. Bring to a boil, then reduce the heat to simmer, cover, and cook until all the vegetables are tender, 35 to 40 minutes. Taste and adjust the seasoning if necessary.

2. Serve the curry in bowls over jasmine rice, garnished with the cilantro and peanuts.

4 servings

GRILLADES AND STONE-GROUND GRITS

Now here's a Creole classic that'll definitely make you feel as if you're in New Orleans (if you're not here already)! Thin slices of beef are quickly sautéed and then braised in a rich sauce until fork-tender—who needs a knife? Grillades are usually served over grits, and we didn't change a thing.

½ teaspoon freshly ground black pepper

½ teaspoon cayenne

1 tablespoon salt

1 ½ pounds sliced beef top round, cut into roughly 3-inch pieces and then pounded to ⅛-inch thickness

½ cup all-purpose flour

¼ cup plus 2 tablespoons vegetable oil

1 tablespoon unsalted butter

2 cups small-diced onion

1 cup small-diced red bell pepper

1 cup small-diced celery

2 tablespoons minced shallot

1 tablespoon minced garlic

5 bay leaves

¼ teaspoon dried thyme leaves, crumbled between your fingers

¼ teaspoon dried oregano leaves, crumbled between your fingers

¼ teaspoon dried basil leaves, crumbled between your fingers

1 ½ cups peeled, seeded, and chopped tomato

½ cup dry red wine

2 cups beef stock or canned low-sodium beef broth

Stone-Ground Grits (recipe follows), for serving

¼ cup chopped green onion, for garnish

2 tablespoons chopped fresh parsley leaves, for garnish

1.   Preheat the oven to 325°F.

2.   Combine the black pepper, cayenne, and 2 teaspoons of the salt in a small bowl and stir to blend. Season the pieces of beef evenly on both sides with the salt mixture. Place the flour in a shallow bowl or plastic bag and lightly dredge the beef in the flour, shaking to remove any excess.

3.   In a large Dutch oven, heat ¼ cup of the oil over medium-high heat. When the oil is smoking hot, add the meat in batches and cook until browned on both sides, 2 to 3 minutes per side. Transfer to a baking sheet and repeat with the remaining meat.

4.   Add the remaining 2 tablespoons of oil and the butter to the pan. When the butter has melted, add the onion, bell pepper, and celery to the pan and

cook, scraping the bottom and sides to loosen any browned bits, until the vegetables are softened, about 4 minutes. Add the shallot and garlic and cook until fragrant, 30 seconds. Add the bay leaves, dried herbs, and tomato and cook until the tomato begins to give up its liquid, about 4 minutes. Stir in the wine, stock, and remaining 1 teaspoon salt and bring to a boil. Return the beef to the pan, cover, and transfer to the oven. Cook until the grillades are fork-tender, stirring occasionally, about 2 hours. Remove the bay leaves.

5. Serve over the grits, garnished with the green onions and parsley.

4 to 6 servings

STONE-GROUND GRITS

1 cup milk
3 cups water
1 cup stone-ground grits
1 $\frac{1}{2}$ teaspoons salt
$\frac{1}{4}$ teaspoon freshly ground black pepper
1 cup finely grated cheddar cheese
2 tablespoons butter

Place the milk and water in a medium saucepan and bring to a boil over medium-high heat. Add the grits and lower the heat to produce a gentle simmer. Cook, partially covered and stirring often, until the grits are tender, adding more water if the grits get too thick before they are tender, 45 to 60 minutes. Add the salt, pepper, cheese, and butter and stir to combine. Serve immediately.

4 to 6 servings

COQ AU VIN BLANC

In the Burgundy region of France, coq au vin is typically made with red wine, bacon, and mushrooms. When this dish is made with white wine, it is referred to as coq au vin blanc. My version of this dish has been slightly modernized by the addition of fennel, leeks, and parsnips.

6 ounces thick-cut bacon, cut into thin strips

Two 3-pound whole chickens, cut into 8 pieces each

1 tablespoon plus 1 teaspoon salt

2 1/2 teaspoons freshly ground white pepper

1/2 cup plus 3 tablespoons all-purpose flour

3 tablespoons unsalted butter

2 medium fennel bulbs, cored and cut into 1/2-inch wedges

2 cups 1/2-inch sliced leek, white part only

1 1/2 cups 1/2-inch sliced parsnip rounds

1 cup 1/4-inch sliced celery

3 cloves garlic, peeled and smashed

One 750-ml bottle good-quality dry white wine, such as Chardonnay or Meursault

1 cup seedless green grapes

2 cups chicken stock or canned low-sodium chicken broth

4 sprigs fresh thyme

1 bay leaf

Cooked egg noodles, steamed rice, or French bread, for serving

1. Preheat the oven to 325°F.

2. In a large Dutch oven, cook the bacon over medium-high heat until crisp and golden brown, about 8 minutes. Using a slotted spoon, transfer the bacon to a paper towel–lined plate and set aside.

3. Season the chicken with 1 tablespoon of the salt and 2 teaspoons of the white pepper. Add 1/2 cup of the flour to a resealable 1-gallon plastic food storage bag. Place the chicken in the bag a few pieces at a time and shake until well coated with flour. Remove the chicken from the bag and, working in batches, brown the chicken pieces in the rendered bacon fat over medium-high heat until golden on all sides, 3 to 4 minutes per side. Once browned, transfer the chicken to a platter and set aside. Repeat with the remaining chicken.

4. Pour off and discard any remaining fat and any dark bits left in the pan and return the pan to the stove. Add the butter and heat over medium heat. When it begins to bubble, add the fennel, leek, pars-

nip, celery, and garlic and cook until the vegetables are tender, 6 to 8 minutes. Stir in the remaining 3 tablespoons flour until combined and cook for 2 minutes. Add 1 cup of the wine and cook, stirring and scraping up any browned bits from the bottom of the pan, until the liquid is almost evaporated.

5. Add the grapes, stock, thyme, bay leaf, and remaining wine, 1 teaspoon salt, and ½ teaspoon white pepper and bring to a brisk simmer. Add the bacon and the browned chicken back to the pan, cover, and place the pan in the oven. Cook until the chicken is tender and the sauce has thickened, 2 to 2½ hours.

6. Remove the thyme sprigs and bay leaf and discard, then serve the dish directly from the Dutch oven over cooked egg noodles or rice or with warm French bread.

6 to 8 servings

LAMB AND POTATO STEW WITH ARTICHOKES AND OLIVES

This rich and aromatic dish combines the bold flavors of the Middle East with the subtle flavors of the Mediterranean. The blend of spices stands up surprisingly well to the assertive flavor of the lamb, while mint, feta, and lemon zest really complement the artichokes to make this dish truly original.

1/2 teaspoon freshly ground black pepper

1 teaspoon hot paprika

1 teaspoon ground coriander

1 teaspoon ground cumin

2 1/2 teaspoons salt

1/2 cup all-purpose flour

4 pounds boneless lamb shoulder, trimmed and cut into 1 1/2- to 2-inch pieces

1/4 cup olive oil

2 cups 1/4-inch sliced onion

1/2 teaspoon dried rosemary leaves, crumbled between your fingers

1/2 teaspoon dried thyme leaves, crumbled between your fingers

1/2 teaspoon dried oregano leaves, crumbled between your fingers

2 tablespoons minced garlic

1 cup dry white wine

2 tablespoons Dijon mustard

4 cups chicken stock or canned low-sodium chicken broth

One 14-ounce can artichoke hearts (in water), drained, rinsed, and halved

1 pound Yukon Gold potatoes, quartered

1 packed tablespoon finely grated lemon zest (from about 3 or 4 lemons)

1/2 cup sliced pitted Kalamata olives

2 tablespoons chopped fresh oregano leaves

1/4 cup chopped fresh mint leaves

12 ounces feta cheese, crumbled, for garnish (optional)

1.   Combine the black pepper, 1/2 teaspoon of the paprika, 1/2 teaspoon of the coriander, 1/2 teaspoon of the cumin, and 1 teaspoon of the salt in a large mixing bowl and put the flour in a second large mixing bowl. Toss the lamb in the seasoning to coat well, then transfer the lamb to the second bowl and coat lightly with the flour, shaking to remove any excess flour.

2.   Heat 2 tablespoons of the olive oil in a 6-quart Dutch oven over medium-high heat. Working in three batches, cook the lamb until nicely browned and caramelized, 3 to 4 minutes per side, adding 1 tablespoon of the remaining oil before the last batch. Set the lamb aside.

3. Add the remaining 1 tablespoon olive oil to the pan along with the onion, dried herbs, ½ teaspoon of the remaining salt, and the remaining ½ teaspoon each of paprika, coriander, and cumin. Cook, stirring, over medium-high heat until the onion is soft and lightly caramelized, about 3 minutes. Add the garlic and cook until fragrant, about 30 seconds. Stir in the wine, mustard, stock, lamb, and artichoke hearts, mix well, and bring to a boil. Cover, reduce the heat to a simmer, and cook, undisturbed, until the lamb is nearly tender, about 1½ hours.

4. Add the potatoes and the remaining 1 teaspoon salt and continue to cook, partially covered, until the lamb and potatoes are fork-tender, about 1 hour longer. Remove the lid and stir in the lemon zest, olives, and fresh herbs. Serve the stew in shallow bowls, garnished with crumbled feta cheese if desired.

6 servings

CASSOULET WITH CONFIT AND GARLIC SAUSAGE

A most fancy baked bean dish with an incredible *wow* factor! It's got confit duck, for goodness' sake. This recipe is for the person who likes to cook for company. And though it is cooked slowly in stages over two days, it's a snap to assemble and serve. A key traditional ingredient in this French dish is garlic sausage, a country-style sausage that may be difficult to find. If you can't find any, don't let that stop you. Simply substitute a flavorful fresh Polish, Italian, or other garlic sausage. If you choose to buy confit duck legs (instead of cooking them yourself as described here), be sure to read the directions carefully, omitting any unnecessary cooking steps (see Note 2).

2 pounds great Northern beans, rinsed and picked over

4 quarts chicken broth, plus more as needed

6 sprigs fresh parsley

1 celery stalk, with leaves if possible, halved crosswise

2 bunches fresh thyme

1 1/2 teaspoons whole black peppercorns

16 garlic cloves plus 2 tablespoons minced garlic

10 small bay leaves

2 small onions, peeled and root ends left intact to keep the onions whole

4 whole cloves

2 whole ducks, about 5 pounds each, cut into quarters, trimmed of excess fat, fat reserved, or 8 purchased confit duck legs and 1 cup store-bought duck fat

1/4 cup tomato paste

12 ounces pancetta (or salt pork blanched for 5 minutes), chopped

1 1/2 pounds garlic sausage or fresh kielbasa, pricked with the tip of a knife in several places

2 tablespoons plus 2 teaspoons kosher salt

1 teaspoon freshly ground white pepper

2 1/2 pounds boneless Boston butt pork roast, rinsed and patted dry

1 cup vegetable oil, purchased duck fat, or goose fat, as needed

3 cups fresh breadcrumbs (made from French bread)

1/2 cup chopped fresh parsley

1. Add the beans and broth to a large pot. Tie the parsley sprigs, celery pieces, and 6 sprigs of the thyme together with twine and add the bundle to the pot. Make a cheesecloth pouch and fill with ¼ teaspoon of the peppercorns, 8 cloves of the garlic, and 2 of the bay leaves. Tie it closed with twine and add it to the pot. Stud the onions with 2 cloves each and add them to the pot. Bring the beans to a boil and turn off the heat. Allow the beans to soak for 1 hour.

2. Meanwhile, put the reserved duck fat (skin) in a separate small pot over very low heat and cook, scraping the bottom of the pot to prevent sticking, as necessary, until all the fat is rendered and the skin is crispy. This can take up to 3 hours (see Note 1). Strain the fat and set aside, covered, in the refrigerator. You should have about 1 cup. If desired, sprinkle the duck cracklings with salt and enjoy as a snack or reserve for garnish.

3. Stir the tomato paste, pancetta, and sausage into the pot with the beans and return the beans to a boil. Reduce the heat to simmer and cook for 45 minutes, or until the beans are just tender. You want the beans to remain intact for the finished cassoulet, so do not overcook.

4. Turn off the heat and stir in 1½ teaspoons of the salt and the white pepper. Use tongs to remove the onions, herb bundle, and cheesecloth pouch and discard. Remove the sausage and set it aside to cool, then cover and refrigerate. Strain the beans, reserving the broth and the beans separately, cover, and refrigerate until ready to assemble the cassoulet.

5. Cut the pork into 3-inch chunks, about 18 pieces, and add to a medium bowl. Smash 4 cloves of the remaining garlic and add them to the bowl as well. Add 1 teaspoon of the remaining peppercorns, 8 sprigs of the remaining thyme, 4 of the remain-

ing bay leaves, and 1½ tablespoons of the remaining salt. Mix well to combine. Cover and refrigerate overnight.

6.   Lay 4 pieces of the duck skin side down in a shallow container. Smash the remaining 4 garlic cloves and place one on top of each piece. Sprinkle the flesh with the remaining 2 teaspoons of the salt and the remaining ¼ teaspoon peppercorns. Lay a bay leaf and a sprig of thyme on top of each. Top with a matching piece of duck, flesh to flesh (leg to leg; breast to breast). Cover and refrigerate overnight.

DAY TWO

---

1.   Preheat the oven to 300°F.

2.   Rinse the pork, pat it dry, and place it in a 3½- to 4-quart shallow baking dish. Rinse the duck, pat it dry, and place it in the dish with the pork. Add the rendered duck fat and enough vegetable oil to cover the meat (the fat will melt once you put it in the oven). Cover the dish with heavy-duty aluminum foil, set it on a rimmed baking sheet, and bake for 3 hours, or until the meat is very tender.

Note 1: Rendering duck fat can also be done in the oven at 300°F. Set the pot, covered, in the oven, and check intermittently.

3.   Remove the confit pork and duck from the oven and set it aside to cool in its fat at least 1 hour before proceeding. Reserve ½ cup of the confit fat. Alternatively, the duck and pork can remain stored in their fat, covered, and refrigerated for up to 1 week.

4.   Combine the breadcrumbs, chopped parsley, minced garlic, and ¼ cup of the reserved confit fat in a small bowl and mix well.

5.   Preheat the oven to 450°F.

6.   Assemble the cassoulet: Add one-third of the beans to the bottom of a 6-quart or larger Dutch oven. Slice the sausage

into 2-inch-thick pieces and nestle a third of the pieces into the beans. Nestle in one-third of the confit pork. Repeat twice more with the beans, sausage, and pork. If there is any congealed fat on the bean liquid, remove and discard. Add 7 cups of the reserved bean liquid to the Dutch oven, or enough to just cover the beans. Nestle the confit duck pieces on top and cover with the breadcrumb mixture. Drizzle the remaining ¼ cup reserved confit fat over the top.

7.   Bake the cassoulet, uncovered, for 30 minutes. Reduce the oven temperature to 350°F and cook for 1 hour longer, or until the liquid is thick and bubbly and the cassoulet is browned and crispy on top. Remove from the oven and pour in 1 more cup of the reserved bean liquid or chicken broth, avoiding the crispy top, as room allows. Serve the cassoulet directly from the pot, making sure that the meat is divided equally among the guests.

8 to 10 servings

Note 2: If using purchased confit duck legs, omit the duck in Day Two, steps 2 and 3, and cook the pork as written, in a smaller dish, using the store-bought duck fat to cover. Use the purchased confit duck legs when it is time to assemble the cassoulet (Day Two, step 6).

BRAISED BREAST OF VEAL WITH FENNEL AND GREEN OLIVES

Breast of veal is an often underrated cut of meat. It is naturally self-basting and, after long, slow cooking, will provide you with the most unbelievable pan juices to drizzle over everything. It is an extremely rich and flavorful dish—serve over creamy polenta, mashed potatoes, or pasta, and you're there.

4 ounces pancetta, diced

1 cup small-diced onion

1/2 cup small-diced carrot

1/2 cup small-diced celery

1 tablespoon salt

2 cups dried breadcrumbs

One 14-ounce can artichoke hearts (in water), drained and chopped

3 tablespoons minced garlic

2 teaspoons dried Italian herbs, crumbled between your fingers

Grated zest of 1 lemon

1/2 cup finely grated Parmigiano-Reggiano cheese

1/2 cup olive oil

4 pounds boneless breast of veal

1 1/4 teaspoons freshly ground black pepper

1 cup white wine

1 cup chicken stock or canned low-sodium chicken broth

1 1/2 tablespoons freshly squeezed lemon juice

1/2 teaspoon fennel seeds

2 medium fennel bulbs, cored and thinly sliced

1 1/4 cups sliced pitted green olives

1/4 cup chopped fresh parsley leaves, for garnish

1. Heat a 6-quart Dutch oven over medium heat. Add the pancetta and cook until the fat is rendered and the pancetta is just crisp, about 10 minutes. Transfer the pancetta to a paper towel–lined plate and set aside. Remove 1 tablespoon of the rendered fat and reserve separately, leaving the rest of the fat in the Dutch oven.

2. Increase the heat to medium-high. Add the onion, carrot, celery, and 1/4 teaspoon of the salt. Cook, stirring, until just soft, about 4 minutes. Remove the vegetables using a slotted spoon and set aside on a plate to cool.

3. In a medium mixing bowl, combine the breadcrumbs, cooled vegetable mixture, pancetta, artichoke hearts, garlic, dried herbs, lemon zest, Parmesan, olive oil, and 1/2 teaspoon of the remaining salt. Stir the mixture until it resembles wet sand.

4. Preheat the oven to 350°F.

5. Lightly pound or butterfly the breast of veal to 1- to 1½-inch thickness, forming a roughly rectangular piece of meat of even thickness. Season on both sides with 2 teaspoons of the remaining salt and 1 teaspoon of the black pepper. Lay the veal so that it is fatty (skin) side down on the cutting board and spread the breadcrumb mixture evenly over the veal to come within 1 inch of all edges. Carefully roll the meat lengthwise and then tie along the length of the roulade every 1½ inches with kitchen twine. Tie the roulade in the opposite direction, end to end, with one long piece of twine to secure the ends. Reserve any stuffing that falls out while rolling the veal.

6. Return the Dutch oven to the stovetop over medium-high heat. Add the reserved 1 tablespoon rendered pancetta fat. When hot, add the veal and cook until well browned on all sides, 10 to 12 minutes. Stir in the wine, stock, lemon juice, fennel seeds, and remaining ¼ teaspoon salt and ¼ teaspoon black pepper and bring to a boil. Add any stuffing that has fallen out while rolling the veal, cover with a tight-fitting lid, and transfer to the oven. Cook until the veal is very tender, about 3½ hours, turning every hour and adding the fennel and olives for the last hour of cooking.

7. Remove from the oven and set aside, still covered, for 10 minutes. Transfer the roulade from the Dutch oven to a cutting board, cover loosely with aluminum foil, and let it rest for 15 to 30 minutes. Remove the twine, cut the roulade crosswise into ½-inch-thick slices, and spoon the braising liquid over all. Garnish with the parsley and serve.

6 to 8 servings

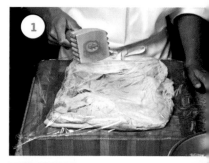

BEEF BOURGUIGNON

This dish is a timeless classic, but the key to making this humble beef stew outstanding is using both good-quality beef and good red wine. Use a drinkable wine rather than anything labeled "cooking" wine. Serve this dish with buttered noodles, rice, or a loaf of warm, crusty bread. Whatever you do, don't skip the balsamic-glazed pearl onions—they are this dish's crowning glory.

6 ounces thick-cut bacon, cut crosswise into thin strips

3 pounds boneless beef chuck, cut into 1-inch cubes

1 tablespoon plus 1 teaspoon salt

1 tablespoon freshly ground black pepper

8 ounces button mushrooms, stems trimmed, sliced

1 tablespoon tomato paste

1½ cups large-diced shallot

1½ cups ¼-inch sliced carrot rounds or half-moons

3 garlic cloves, smashed

¼ cup all-purpose flour

½ cup cognac

One 750-ml bottle red wine, such as Pinot Noir

4 cups beef stock or canned low-sodium beef broth

2 bay leaves

2 sprigs fresh thyme

4 sprigs fresh parsley

12 ounces small fingerling potatoes, such as Russian banana, cut in half lengthwise

10 ounces red pearl onions

3 tablespoons balsamic vinegar

2 teaspoons sugar

Cooked buttered egg noodles, rice, or crusty bread, for serving

¼ cup roughly chopped fresh parsley, for garnish

1. Preheat the oven to 325°F.

2. In a large Dutch oven, render the bacon over medium-high heat until crisp and golden brown, about 8 minutes. Using a slotted spoon, transfer the bacon from the pan to a paper towel–lined plate and set aside.

3. Season the beef with 2 teaspoons of the salt and 1½ teaspoons of the pepper and brown the beef in the bacon fat, working in batches so as not to overcrowd the pan. Transfer the browned beef to a platter and repeat with the remaining beef.

4. Add the mushrooms to the pan and cook over medium-high heat until caramelized, 4 to 5 minutes. Transfer the mushrooms to the platter with the meat. Add the tomato paste to the pan and cook for 1 to 2 minutes. Add the shallot, carrot, and garlic and cook

until the shallot begins to wilt, 3 to 4 minutes. Return the beef and mushrooms to the pan, along with any juices that have accumulated. Sprinkle the flour and the remaining 2 teaspoons salt and 1½ teaspoons pepper over the contents of the pan and stir well to coat evenly. Cook for 2 minutes, then deglaze the pan with the cognac, scraping up any browned bits from the bottom of the pan. Stir in the wine, stock, bay leaves, thyme, and parsley sprigs and bring to a simmer.

5.   Cover and place in the oven. Cook for 1½ hours, remove the pan from the oven, and add the potatoes. Make sure the potatoes are completely submerged in the liquid. Cover, return the pan to the oven, and cook until the meat and potatoes are fork-tender, 1 to 1½ hours longer.

6.   While the meat is cooking, prepare the pearl onions: Bring a small pot of water to a boil. Add the onions and cook for 3 minutes. Using a slotted spoon, transfer the onions to a bowl of ice water. Once cooled, use a paring knife to cut off the root end of each onion. Squeeze the onion from the opposite end; it should pop out of its skin. Discard the skin.

7.   Heat the balsamic vinegar and sugar in a medium sauté pan over medium heat. When the sugar is dissolved and the vinegar begins to bubble, add the pearl onions. Increase the heat to medium-high and toss the onions in the syrup. Cook, tossing or stirring frequently, just until the onions are glazed; remove from the heat and set aside.

8.   When you're ready to serve, remove the bay leaves and stir in the glazed onions. Serve with cooked noodles, rice, or a loaf of crusty French bread. Garnish with the chopped parsley.

6 to 8 servings

RABBIT RAGOUT OVER PAPPARDELLE

Though this is traditional hunter's fare, here's a great recipe for domesticated rabbit. It's stewed with vegetables and garlic in red wine until mouth-wateringly tender and served with pasta. But, hey, enjoy it with rice if you like. This also makes a wonderful do-ahead meal for guests since the sauce gets even better after sitting a day or two in the fridge.

½ cup olive oil

2 whole rabbits, cut into pieces (about 3 pounds)

1½ teaspoons salt, plus more for cooking the pasta

2 teaspoons freshly ground black pepper, plus more for garnish

1 cup instant flour such as Wondra

2 cups minced onion

1 cup minced carrot

1 cup minced celery

2 tablespoons minced garlic

3 cups fruity red wine

½ cup chopped canned whole tomatoes with juice

2 bay leaves

1 sprig fresh thyme

1 sprig fresh rosemary

1 teaspoon crushed red pepper

1 teaspoon dried oregano leaves, crumbled between your fingers

1 cup chicken stock or canned low-sodium chicken broth

1 pound dried pappardelle or other wide pasta, such as tagliatelle, fettuccine, or linguine

Extra-virgin olive oil

1½ tablespoons all-purpose flour

1½ tablespoons unsalted butter, softened

¼ cup chopped fresh parsley leaves

¼ cup finely grated Parmigiano-Reggiano, for garnish

1.   In a large Dutch oven, heat the olive oil over medium-high heat. Season the rabbits with 1 teaspoon of the salt and the pepper. Dredge the rabbit pieces in the instant flour and shake off any excess. Add the rabbit pieces to the pan and cook until golden brown, about 3 minutes per side. Transfer the rabbit to a paper towel–lined plate and set aside.

2.   Reduce the heat to medium-low, then add the onion, carrot, and celery and cook until the vegetables are caramelized, stirring occasionally, about 30 minutes. It's important to caramelize the vegetables slowly, as this forms the basis of the sauce. Next add the remaining salt, the garlic, wine, tomatoes, bay leaves, thyme, rosemary, crushed red pepper, and oregano and cook for 10 minutes longer. Return the rabbit to the pan along with the stock and bring to a

boil. Reduce the heat to simmer, cover, and cook until the rabbit is very tender, 1¼ to 1½ hours. Transfer the rabbit pieces to a plate and set aside until cool enough to handle. Remove the bay leaves. When cool, remove the meat from the bones and shred the meat into bite-sized pieces. Discard the bones and return the meat to the sauce.

3. Bring a large pot of salted water to a boil. Add the pappardelle and cook according to the package directions until al dente, about 12 minutes. Drain the pasta, toss with enough extra-virgin olive oil to coat, and set aside, covered, until ready to serve.

4. Combine the all-purpose flour and butter in a small bowl and mix with a spoon to form a smooth paste.

5. Whisk half the butter-flour mixture into the rabbit ragout to thicken the sauce. Add more of the butter-flour mixture as necessary to achieve the desired consistency. Simmer the sauce for 1 minute (do not boil). Remove the pot from the heat and stir in the parsley.

6. In a large mixing bowl, toss the pasta with the sauce. Mound onto serving plates and garnish with the Parmesan, additional extra-virgin olive oil, and fresh pepper to taste.

4 to 6 servings

TAGINE OF CHICKEN WITH PRESERVED LEMONS AND CERIGNOLA OLIVES

Preserved lemons are a key ingredient in Moroccan cuisine, and this well-known Moroccan dish really highlights their tangy and intensely lemony flavor. You can make your own preserved lemons at home or purchase them in jars at specialty markets. We have included a simple recipe here for those of you who wish to make them. Once you've become accustomed to their bright, briny flavor, you'll find them indispensable in soups, stews, vinaigrettes, and salads.

One 3 1/2- to 4-pound whole chicken, cut into 8 pieces

1/2 lemon

1 teaspoon salt

1 teaspoon freshly ground black pepper

1/4 cup olive oil

2 medium yellow onions, thinly sliced

3 garlic cloves, smashed

1/2 teaspoon ground ginger

1/4 teaspoon saffron threads, crumbled between your fingers

1/4 cup chopped fresh cilantro leaves

1/4 cup chopped fresh flat-leaf parsley leaves

1 1/2 cups chicken stock or canned low-sodium chicken broth

2 tablespoons chopped peel from Simple Preserved Lemons (recipe follows)

1 cup pitted and sliced Cerignola or other unstuffed mild green olives

Steamed white rice or couscous, for serving

1.   Rub the chicken with the juice from the lemon and season with the salt and pepper. Place the chicken in a large Dutch oven or tagine with the olive oil, onions, garlic, ginger, saffron, cilantro, parsley, and stock. Take care that the chicken is covered with the herbs and onions. Cover the pan and cook over medium-low heat for 1 1/4 hours. Add the preserved lemon and olives and cook for 15 to 20 minutes longer, until the chicken literally begins to fall from the bone.

2.   Transfer the chicken to a serving platter. Spoon the sauce over the chicken and serve immediately with rice or couscous.

4 servings

SIMPLE PRESERVED LEMONS

If you can get homegrown lemons, this is the perfect way to preserve their fresh flavor in a unique way. Any variety can work—thick skinned, thin skinned, Meyer, you name it—as long as the lemons aren't waxed or treated with chemicals. They need to sit for at least 4 weeks before using, but will keep for up to 1 year after maturing, and their flavor improves with age.

4 unwaxed lemons, preferably organic, well washed and dried
$\frac{1}{4}$ cup sea or kosher salt
$\frac{1}{2}$ cup freshly squeezed lemon juice, or as needed

1. Using a sharp knife, cut each lemon lengthwise almost through to the stem end, and then rotate the lemon 45 degrees and cut so that the lemon is almost quartered; the lemon should still be connected at one end, but you should be able to open it up, much like a flower. Spoon 1 tablespoon of the salt into the center of each lemon and press to close. Squeeze the lemons into a sterilized jar with a tight-fitting lid (it's okay if you need to squeeze firmly to compact the lemons; they will soften over time) and add any salt that has fallen from the lemons to the jar. Cover the jar and set aside in a cool, dark place for several days.

2. Uncover the jar and press down on the lemons with your fingers or the back of a spoon. Add enough lemon juice to cover them completely—the amount of lemon juice will vary depending on their ripeness (I have had batches where no additional lemon juice was necessary because the lemons themselves exuded so much juice). Close the jar and once again set aside in a cool, dark place for 1 month, shaking the jar occasionally to distribute the salt and brine.

3. When the lemons are ready, the peel and flesh will be very soft and you will see that the flesh easily peels away. Discard the flesh, rinse the peel briefly under cool water, and use as needed.

4 preserved lemons

TRUE
BOLOGNESE

Be forewarned: this is not your typical tomato-laden American-style meat sauce for pasta. It is based heavily on the simple meat ragùs of northern Italy, where meat sauces are cooked low and slow for a rich, meaty flavor and a thick, deceptively creamy sauce. If you've never tried a traditional ragù such as this, I suggest you give it a go. It's a favorite at my house; my entire family looks forward to the days when I prepare this simple, comforting dish.

1 tablespoon olive oil

8 ounces pancetta, finely chopped

1 1/2 cups small-diced onion

3/4 cup small-diced carrot

3/4 cup small-diced celery

3/4 teaspoon freshly ground black pepper

1 1/2 teaspoons salt

1 pound ground sirloin

1/2 pound ground veal

3 tablespoons tomato paste

3/4 cup dry white wine

1 1/2 tablespoons minced garlic

1 1/2 cups beef stock or canned low-sodium beef broth

1 cup half-and-half

2 tablespoons finely chopped fresh parsley leaves

1 pound dried pasta, such as tagliatelle or pappardelle, cooked until al dente, for serving

Grated Parmigiano-Reggiano cheese, for garnish

1.   In a medium Dutch oven, heat the oil over medium-high heat and cook the pancetta until it is crisp and the fat is rendered, 6 to 8 minutes. Add the onion, carrot, celery, pepper, and 1 teaspoon of the salt and cook until the vegetables are lightly caramelized, stirring occasionally, 4 to 6 minutes. Increase the heat and stir in the sirloin and veal. Cook, stirring and breaking the meat into small pieces, until the meat is well browned, about 5 minutes. Add the tomato paste and cook, stirring, for 2 minutes. Stir in the wine and garlic and cook until the wine is nearly evaporated, about 2 minutes. Add the stock and reduce the heat to low. Cook, partially covered, until the liquid is almost completely evaporated, about 10 minutes.

2. Add ½ cup of the half-and-half and continue cooking for 30 to 40 minutes, adding the remaining half-and-half little by little as the sauce reduces. The sauce should be very thick and rich. Season with the remaining ½ teaspoon salt and additional black pepper to taste; you may not need any more seasoning, depending on the stock that you used. Stir in the parsley.

3. Serve the sauce tossed with cooked pasta and garnish with grated cheese.

5 cups meat sauce, 4 servings

BIG
Pots

The BIG POT isn't just for stocks. This bad boy is generously sized for other one-pot wonders.

CHEDDAR CHEESE SOUP WITH CHICKEN AND PEPPERS

Here's a different spin on cheese soup. It's a bit lighter than other versions you may have tried but still wonderfully spiced and definitely satisfying. Cheese soup doesn't reheat easily—it tends to separate—so make it when the gang comes over to watch the game and it can be gobbled up in one evening.

2 to 2 ½ pounds chicken leg quarters (about 4)

1 tablespoon salt

1 tablespoon sweet or hot pimentón (smoked Spanish paprika)

5 tablespoons olive oil

2 poblano chiles, seeded and minced

1 red bell pepper, minced

1 jalapeño chile, seeded and minced

1 cup minced red onion

¼ cup minced celery

¼ cup chopped cilantro stems

1 teaspoon chili powder

¼ teaspoon ground cumin

¼ teaspoon dried ground oregano

¼ teaspoon cayenne

1 tablespoon minced garlic

¼ cup plus 2 tablespoons all-purpose flour

1 cup dry white wine

8 cups chicken stock or canned low-sodium chicken broth

2 pounds Idaho Russet potatoes, peeled and cut into ½-inch dice (about 4 cups)

1 cup whole milk

1 pound sharp cheddar cheese, coarsely grated (about 4 cups)

4 ounces queso cotija, finely grated (about 1 cup), for garnish

4 ounces queso fresco or ricotta salata, crumbled (about 1 cup), for garnish

¼ cup chopped fresh cilantro leaves, for garnish

Mexican hot sauce, such as Cholula, for serving (optional)

1.   Preheat the oven to 400°F.

2.   Season the chicken with 1 teaspoon of the salt and the pimentón. Heat the olive oil in a 6-quart or larger soup pot over medium-high heat. Add the chicken, in batches if necessary, and cook until browned on both sides, 3 to 4 minutes per side. Transfer the browned chicken to a baking dish or baking sheet and roast in the oven until cooked through, about 25 minutes. Remove the chicken from the oven

and set aside until cool enough to handle. When cool, remove the meat from the bones and shred into bite-sized pieces. Discard the skin and bones.

3.   While the chicken is roasting, add the poblanos, bell pepper, jalapeño, red onion, celery, cilantro stems, chili powder, cumin, oregano, cayenne, and 1 teaspoon of the remaining salt to the drippings remaining in the pot and cook until the vegetables are soft, about 6 minutes. Stir in the garlic and flour and cook for 2 minutes more. Stir in the wine, cook for 1 minute, and add the stock. Bring the soup to a boil, reduce the heat to simmer, and cook for 15 minutes. Stir in the potatoes, reserved chicken, and the remaining 1 teaspoon salt. Return the soup to a gentle simmer and cook until the potatoes are just tender, about 15 minutes longer. Stir in the milk.

4.   Remove the soup from the heat and set aside to cool for 5 minutes. Add the cheddar and whisk until melted.

5.   Serve the soup hot, garnished with the queso cotija, queso fresco, cilantro leaves, and hot sauce to taste if desired.

4 quarts, 10 servings

SOUTHERN-STYLE CHICKEN AND DUMPLINGS

This is the real-deal down-South chicken and dumplings. The dumplings feel like little pillows in your mouth, the chicken is meltingly tender, and the broth, well, it's simply delicious. It's easy to prepare—you just enrich broth with chicken and vegetables, make your dumplings, and simmer gently.

5 pounds chicken leg quarters (8 to 10)

4 carrots, cut into thirds, plus 1 cup diced

3 onions, cut into large pieces, plus 1 cup chopped

2 celery stalks, cut into thirds, plus ½ cup chopped

6 cloves garlic, peeled and smashed

6 sprigs fresh thyme

Leaves from 1 large sprig fresh rosemary

2 bay leaves

8 cups chicken stock or canned low-sodium chicken broth

4 cups water

1 tablespoon plus ½ teaspoon salt

¼ teaspoon freshly ground black pepper

¼ teaspoon crushed red pepper

3 cups all-purpose flour, plus more for dusting

1 teaspoon baking powder

⅓ cup chopped mixed fresh herbs such as parsley, thyme, oregano, and chives

½ cup plus 3 tablespoons vegetable shortening

1 cup whole milk

1 tablespoon unsalted butter

2 cups frozen green peas

1. In an 8-quart or larger heavy-bottomed pot, combine the chicken, carrot pieces, onion pieces, celery pieces, garlic, thyme, rosemary, bay leaves, stock, water, 2 teaspoons of the salt, the black pepper, and the crushed red pepper. Bring to a simmer and cook until the chicken is very tender, about 1 hour.

2. While the chicken is cooking, make the dumplings. In a medium mixing bowl, mix the flour, remaining 1½ teaspoons salt, the baking powder, and the chopped herbs well with a fork. Add the shortening and work it into the flour with your fingers, a pastry blender, or a fork until the mixture resembles coarse crumbs. (It's okay for a few large flat pieces of shortening coated with flour to remain.) Add the milk and stir with a fork until incorporated.

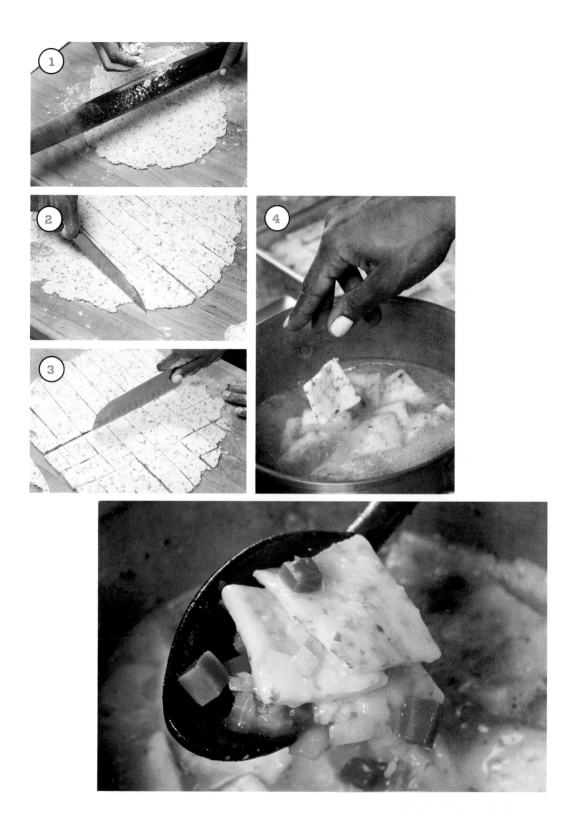

3. Gather the dough together and press gently into a rough ball. Turn the dough out onto a lightly floured surface and pat together (with lightly floured hands if necessary). Knead the dough gently 6 or 7 times, then divide it into 3 pieces. Working with 1 piece at a time, roll the dough out with a lightly floured rolling pin to a ¹⁄₁₆-inch thickness. Cut the dough into 1½-inch-wide strips, then cut the strips crosswise into roughly 1½-inch squares. Transfer the dumplings to a parchment-lined baking sheet and repeat with the remaining dough, putting a piece of parchment paper between the layers. Refrigerate the dumplings until ready to use, up to 1 day in advance.

4. Remove the chicken from the pot and set aside until cool enough to handle. Discard the skin, remove the meat from the bones, and reserve the meat. Discard the bones.

5. Strain the broth into another large pot or container and reserve. Discard the solids. Return the original pot to the stove over medium heat. Add the butter and, when melted, add the chopped carrot, onion, and celery. Cook for 2 minutes, then add the strained broth and increase the heat to high. When the broth comes to a boil, add the dumplings in batches, stirring between additions. When the liquid returns to a boil, reduce the heat to low, cover the pot, and simmer for 15 minutes. Stir the dumplings once, very gently, to prevent them from sticking to the bottom of the pot, and continue to cook, covered and undisturbed, until the dumplings are very tender, about 15 minutes longer.

6. Stir in the reserved chicken and the peas. Return the sauce to a gentle boil, cover, and remove from the heat. Let the chicken and dumplings sit, covered, for 20 minutes before serving.

4 quarts, 6 to 8 servings

MEATBALLS WITH SWISS CHARD AND FARFALLE IN BROTH

This recipe was inspired by a dish I featured on an Italian-themed episode of *Emeril Live* that's just stuck with me. It's a great alternative to traditional spaghetti and meatballs . . . a comforting soup for a chilly evening.

2 slices white bread

½ cup whole milk

3 cloves garlic, peeled

1 tablespoon kosher salt

½ pound ground beef chuck (85% lean)

½ pound ground veal

¼ pound ground pork

¼ cup minced yellow onion plus ½ cup chopped

¼ cup finely chopped green onion

1 teaspoon dried oregano leaves, crumbled between your fingers

1 teaspoon freshly ground black pepper

3 tablespoons vegetable oil

3 medium carrots, cut into ¼-inch-thick rounds (about 1½ cups)

8 cups beef stock or canned low-sodium beef broth

4 cups chicken stock or canned low-sodium chicken broth

1 pound Swiss chard, stemmed and roughly chopped

½ pound dried farfalle pasta

4 ounces Parmigiano-Reggiano cheese, grated (about 1½ cups)

1. Place the bread in a large mixing bowl and add the milk. Allow it to sit for 10 minutes. Use your hands to squeeze the bread together, then tear the bread into small pieces.

2. Smash the garlic on a cutting board with the blade of a knife. Add the salt. Chop the garlic and salt together, periodically mashing the garlic with the knife blade, until you have a paste.

3. To the bowl with the soaked bread, add the ground beef, veal, and pork, the minced onion, green onion, oregano, black pepper, and half of the garlic paste. Mix gently but thoroughly enough to combine. This is best done with your hands, but you can use a rubber spatula if you prefer. Portion the meatball mixture with a 1-tablespoon scoop onto a parchment-lined baking sheet or platter. Rub the meat between the palms of your hands to form smooth, round balls.

4. In an 8-quart or larger stockpot, heat 1 tablespoon of the vegetable oil over medium-high heat.

Add the chopped onion and the carrots and cook until the onion is translucent, about 2 minutes. Add the beef stock, chicken stock, and the remaining garlic paste and bring to a simmer.

5.   Meanwhile, heat the remaining 2 tablespoons vegetable oil in a large skillet over medium heat. Add enough meatballs to fill the pan without crowding and cook until nicely browned on all sides, about 4 minutes. Add the browned meatballs to the pot of broth and repeat with any remaining meatballs.

6.   Add the Swiss chard (see Note) to the broth and bring to a boil. Add the pasta and cook until the pasta is al dente, about 8 minutes. Remove the soup from the heat. To serve, ladle the soup into individual bowls and garnish with the cheese.

4 quarts, 6 to 8 servings

Note: If you prefer your Swiss chard to have a soft texture, sauté it in the stockpot with the onion and carrot before adding the stock.

TUSCAN WHITE BEAN SOUP
WITH BROCCOLI RABE

This is a comforting, hearty soup with flavors reminiscent of northern Italy. We used baby lima beans because we just love their tender, creamy consistency, although in Italy it would likely be made with cannellini beans or great Northern beans. Use whichever beans you love or have on hand; just take note that the cooking time will vary slightly.

2 tablespoons olive oil

2 cups small-diced onion

1 cup small-diced celery

1 cup small-diced red bell pepper

1 tablespoon plus 1 teaspoon salt

1/2 teaspoon freshly ground black pepper

2 tablespoons minced garlic

1 teaspoon dried Italian herbs

1/4 teaspoon crushed red pepper

8 cups chicken stock or canned low-sodium chicken broth

2 pounds dried white beans (cannellini, baby lima, or great Northern), rinsed, picked over, soaked overnight, and drained

1 piece Parmigiano-Reggiano cheese rind, about 1 × 3 inches

1 bay leaf

4 cups water

1 1/2 pounds broccoli rabe, tough stem ends trimmed, chopped into bite-sized pieces

1 sprig fresh rosemary

Grated zest of 1 lemon

2 teaspoons freshly squeezed lemon juice

6 ounces Parmigiano-Reggiano cheese, finely grated (about 1 1/2 cups)

Extra-virgin olive oil, for drizzling

1. Heat the olive oil in an 8-quart soup pot or stockpot over medium-high heat. Add the onion, celery, bell pepper, 1 teaspoon of the salt, and 1/4 teaspoon of the black pepper and cook, stirring, until the vegetables are tender, about 6 minutes. Add the garlic, dried Italian herbs, and crushed red pepper and cook, stirring, until fragrant, about 1 minute. Add the stock, beans, Parmesan rind, bay leaf, and water and bring to a low boil. Reduce the heat to simmer gently and cook, partially covered and stirring occasionally, until the beans are tender, 45 to 60 minutes.

2. Using a slotted spoon, transfer about 1 cup of the beans from the pot to a small bowl and mash them with the back of a spoon. Return the mashed beans to the soup and add the remaining 1 tablespoon salt.

Bring to a simmer over medium-high heat and continue to cook, uncovered, until the broth thickens slightly, about 15 minutes. Add the remaining black pepper, the broccoli rabe, and rosemary sprig and continue to cook until the broccoli rabe is just tender, about 5 minutes. Stir in the lemon zest and lemon juice. Remove the Parmesan rind, bay leaf, and rosemary sprig and discard them. Serve the soup in wide, shallow bowls, garnished with grated Parmesan and a drizzle of extra-virgin olive oil.

13 cups, about 6 servings

SHRIMP AND ASPARAGUS RISOTTO

Asparagus is available all year long in some supermarkets, flown in from all corners of the world, but it's really best when eaten in spring, its season here in the United States. Its delicate flavor can make any dish feel like an indulgence. The simple yet luxurious pairing of shrimp and asparagus in a creamy risotto makes for a dazzling springtime dinner.

1 bunch medium asparagus, ends trimmed, cut on the diagonal into $\frac{1}{2}$-inch pieces

1 $\frac{1}{4}$ teaspoons salt, plus more for cooking the asparagus

1 $\frac{1}{2}$ pounds medium shrimp, peeled and deveined, shells reserved separately

2 teaspoons olive oil

1 onion, halved

1 carrot, coarsely chopped

1 celery stalk, coarsely chopped

1 clove garlic, smashed, plus 1 tablespoon minced garlic

1 bay leaf

$\frac{1}{4}$ teaspoon whole black peppercorns

8 cups water

$\frac{1}{4}$ cup extra-virgin olive oil

1 $\frac{1}{2}$ teaspoons Emeril's Original Essence or Creole Seasoning (page 3)

4 tablespoons ($\frac{1}{2}$ stick) unsalted butter

$\frac{1}{4}$ cup minced shallot

2 cups Arborio or Carnaroli rice

$\frac{1}{2}$ cup dry white wine

$\frac{1}{2}$ teaspoon freshly ground black pepper

2 tablespoons chopped mixed fresh herbs, such as chives, chervil, lemon thyme, parsley, and/or basil

2 teaspoons finely grated lemon zest

1 cup finely grated Parmigiano-Reggiano cheese

1. Prepare a medium bowl of ice water and set aside.

2. Blanch the asparagus in a large pot of boiling salted water for $1\frac{1}{2}$ minutes. Immediately remove the asparagus from the boiling water and immerse in the ice water. Once completely cool, drain the asparagus and set it aside.

3. In a medium saucepan, combine the shrimp shells and olive oil over medium-high heat and cook, stirring frequently, until the shells are toasted and fragrant, 3 to 4 minutes. Add the onion, carrot, celery, smashed garlic, bay leaf, peppercorns, and water and bring to a boil. Reduce the heat to a simmer and cook, skimming the top of any foam, for 30 minutes. Strain through a fine-mesh sieve and discard the solids. You should have about 6 cups of shrimp stock. Pour the stock into a clean saucepan and season to taste with salt. Keep hot.

4. Heat 2 tablespoons of the extra-virgin olive oil in a heavy-bottomed 4- or 6-quart pot until very hot. In a small bowl, combine the shrimp with the Essence and ¼ teaspoon of the salt and toss to distribute the seasoning thoroughly. Add 2 tablespoons of the butter to the pot and, when the butter begins to foam, add the shrimp and cook until lightly golden on both sides, 1 to 2 minutes. Transfer the shrimp and any accumulated juices to a heatproof bowl and set aside.

5. Add the remaining 2 tablespoons butter and 2 tablespoons extra-virgin olive oil to the same pot. Once the butter is bubbling, add the shallot and minced garlic and cook, stirring, until fragrant, about 1 minute. Add the rice and cook, stirring frequently, until fragrant and opaque, about 2 minutes. Stir in the wine and cook until it evaporates, then reduce the heat to medium.

6. Add 2 cups of the hot shrimp stock and season with the remaining 1 teaspoon salt and ¼ teaspoon of the pepper. Cook, stirring constantly, until the broth has been completely absorbed. Continue to cook, adding more broth 1 cup at a time as each previous addition is absorbed, until the rice is al dente, 18 to 20 minutes total cooking time. If you use all the stock before the rice is al dente, add a bit of hot water as needed. (You should have just the right amount of stock.) Add the herbs, lemon zest, and remaining ¼ teaspoon pepper. Taste and adjust the seasoning if necessary.

7. Add the shrimp, asparagus, and half of the Parmesan to the pot and stir to combine. Cook until the shrimp and asparagus are heated through, the cheese is melted, and the risotto has a creamy texture, 1 to 2 minutes. Serve immediately, in shallow bowls, garnished with the remaining Parmesan.

4 to 6 servings

ARTICHOKE SOUP
WITH POACHED OYSTERS

Artichoke and oyster soup is a New Orleans favorite, and just about everyone and his or her mother has a favorite recipe for it. I've made this version slightly more elegant by adding an herbed mascarpone. Pureeing the soup also gives it a silky texture, and since the oysters are added at the very last minute, they are gently poached to perfection. Serve this soup with a nice salad and a loaf of warm, crusty bread for a light evening meal.

½ cup mascarpone cheese

1 tablespoon chopped fresh parsley leaves

1 tablespoon thinly sliced fresh chives

1 tablespoon chopped fresh tarragon leaves

1 teaspoon grated lemon zest

1 teaspoon freshly squeezed lemon juice

50 small raw oysters (about 1 pint), picked over carefully for shell pieces, oyster liquor reserved

2 cups clam juice, or as needed

8 tablespoons (1 stick) unsalted butter

2 shallots, minced

2 leeks, white part only, minced

2 celery stalks, minced

2 cloves garlic, minced

2 tablespoons all-purpose flour

1 cup dry white wine

Four 14.5-ounce cans quartered artichoke hearts, drained and rinsed

4 cups chicken stock or canned low-sodium chicken broth

4 cups heavy cream

2 teaspoons salt

½ teaspoon cayenne

1 tablespoon fresh chervil leaves

1 tablespoon chive blossoms, if available, or snipped chives, for garnish

1. In a small bowl, combine the mascarpone, parsley, sliced chives, tarragon, lemon zest, and lemon juice. Mix well and set aside in the refrigerator.

2. Strain the oysters over a fine-mesh sieve and reserve the oysters and strained liquor separately. Add enough of the clam juice to bring the oyster liquor up to 2 cups.

3. Heat the butter in a large, heavy pot over medium heat. Add the shallots, leeks, celery, and garlic and cook, stirring frequently, until translucent, about

8 minutes. Sprinkle the flour over the vegetables and cook, stirring constantly, for about 1 minute. Stir in the wine and simmer until thickened and bubbly, about 30 seconds. Add the artichoke hearts, stock, cream, oyster liquor/clam juice mixture, salt, and cayenne and bring to a brisk simmer. Cook for 10 minutes, then remove the soup from the heat and puree in batches in a blender. (Note: use caution when pureeing hot liquids.) Strain the soup through a fine-mesh sieve, pressing to extract as much liquid as possible. Discard the solids and return the soup to a clean pot. Warm the soup gently over low heat until it returns to a simmer.

4.   Add the oysters to the soup and return the soup to a simmer, cooking until the edges of the oysters curl and they are just cooked through, 2 to 3 minutes. Remove the soup from the heat and stir in 1/4 cup of the mascarpone mixture. Adjust the seasoning if necessary. Serve the soup immediately, each bowl garnished with a dollop of the remaining mascarpone mixture, chervil leaves, and chive blossoms.

About 3 quarts, 6 to 8 servings

POT-AU-FEU

This boiled dinner is based on the classic French dish. The name, when translated, roughly means "a pot always left on the fire." Though making it is a continuous affair in which meats, vegetables, and herbs are added to the pot in stages (to build layers of flavor), this is a lazy-day endeavor, and the only major effort is in the gathering of ingredients. In the end, you have a platter of delicious abundance that should be served with a green salad, crusty bread, and your favorite wine.

1 pound oxtails, tied together to hold their shape

2 pounds beef rump roast, tied to hold its shape

8 cups beef stock or canned low-sodium beef broth

12 cups chicken stock or canned low-sodium chicken broth

8 small to medium carrots, root ends trimmed (about 2 pounds)

4 small onions, peeled, root ends trimmed but left intact

8 whole cloves

3 celery stalks, halved crosswise

8 sprigs fresh parsley

8 sprigs fresh thyme

4 bay leaves

20 peppercorns

1 head of garlic, split crosswise

One 2-pound boneless Boston butt pork roast, rinsed, patted dry, and tied to hold its shape

One 3-pound chicken, rinsed, patted dry, and tied to hold its shape

1 pound fresh kielbasa or garlic sausage, casings pierced with the tip of a knife

1 tablespoon kosher salt

2 pounds leeks, dark green parts removed, halved lengthwise, rinsed, and tied to hold their shape

1 pound turnips, peeled, roots trimmed, cut into large wedges or halved depending on the size

Caper Parsley Aïoli (recipe follows), for serving

Freshly ground black pepper, for serving

Coarse sea salt, for serving

1. Place the oxtails, rump roast, beef stock, and 8 cups of the chicken stock in a 12-quart or larger stockpot. Set the pot over medium heat.

2. While the beef is coming to a simmer, divide the carrots into 2 bunches and tie each bunch in two places with kitchen twine. Add 1 bunch of carrots to the pot and set the other bunch aside on a tray. Stud each of the onions with 2 cloves. Add half of the onions to the pot and the other half to the tray with the

carrots. Add 1 of the celery stalks to the pot. Make a bouquet garni by tying 1 of the remaining celery stalks with half of the parsley sprigs and half of the thyme sprigs. Repeat with the remaining celery stalk, parsley, and thyme sprigs. Add 1 bouquet garni to the pot and the other to the tray. Add half of the bay leaves to the pot and the other to the tray. Make 2 cheesecloth pouches, each holding half of the peppercorns and ½ head of garlic. Add 1 bundle to the pot and the other to the tray.

3.   Once the broth comes to a simmer, reduce the heat to low so that it continues to cook at a gentle simmer. The heat should be low enough that the bubbles burst in one spot (see Note). As the pot simmers, foam will rise to the top. Have a large ladle and container near the stove. Remove the foam by skimming the surface of the broth and discarding it into the container as needed. The longer the broth simmers, the lighter in color the foam will become. Allow the beef to cook gently for 1 hour, checking the heat, never allowing the broth to come to a rolling boil, and skimming as necessary. At the end of cooking you will have a clear and flavorful broth.

4.   Add the pork butt to the pot and raise the heat to medium. Once the broth returns to a simmer, reduce the heat to low and continue to cook for 1 hour longer, skimming the broth as necessary.

5.   Using long tongs, carefully remove the vegetables, the herb bundle, and the cheesecloth bundle from the pot and discard. Add the chicken, the sausages, the remaining 4 cups chicken stock, and the ingredients reserved on the tray. Raise the heat to medium and add the salt. Once the broth returns to a simmer, reduce the heat to low and simmer gently for 20 minutes, skimming as necessary. Add the leeks and turnips and continue to simmer for 40 minutes longer. Turn off the heat.

Note: If you are not cooking on a gas burner, you may need to move the pot slightly off the heating element for more control so that the broth simmers gently in one spot. Extremely gentle simmering is important in producing a clear broth.

6.   Set a large carving board and a large serving platter next to the pot. Using long tongs, very carefully remove the chicken, pork butt, rump roast, and oxtails and set aside on the carving board. Remove the strings. Remove the onions from the pot and discard. Carefully remove the remaining vegetables and sausages and arrange them in neat piles on the serving platter. Remove the strings. If desired, halve the carrots.

7.   Set a chinois or other fine-mesh sieve over a large bowl or pot and strain the broth. You will have a clear, flavorful broth. If you would like to refine your broth further, you may strain the broth again through several layers of cheesecloth. Ladle some of the broth over the vegetables. Slice the rump roast into 6 to 8 slices and arrange on the platter. Slice the pork butt into 6 to 8 slices and arrange on the platter. Carve the chicken and place on the platter as well. Remove the oxtail meat from the bones and arrange on the platter. Moisten the meats with some of the broth.

8.   Serve the guests individual small bowls of hot broth and Caper Parsley Aïoli to accompany their choice of meats. Serve the pot-au-feu family style, passing the peppermill and coarse sea salt.

Serves 8

CAPER PARSLEY AÏOLI

This simple condiment really makes this dish. Should you happen to have any left over, it would be right at home next to roasted or grilled meats, fish, or veggies. Or try it with your favorite fried seafood in place of tartar sauce.

2 eggs
4 to 5 cloves garlic, peeled and smashed

2 teaspoons Dijon mustard

1 1/2 teaspoons kosher salt

1 teaspoon freshly ground black pepper

1 anchovy fillet

1 tablespoon plus 1 teaspoon freshly squeezed lemon juice

1 1/2 cups vegetable oil

1/2 cup olive oil

1/4 cup roughly chopped fresh parsley leaves

1 1/2 tablespoons drained nonpareil or regular capers

Add the eggs, garlic, mustard, salt, pepper, and anchovy fillet to a food processor and puree. Add the lemon juice and puree to combine. With the machine still running, add the oils in a slow, steady stream and process until the mixture has formed a thick emulsion. Add the parsley and pulse to combine. Transfer the aïoli to a small nonreactive bowl and stir in the capers. Refrigerate until ready to use, up to 1 week.

Generous 2 cups

STEAMED MUSSELS WITH TOASTED ISRAELI COUSCOUS

The addition of Israeli couscous elevates this simple mussel dish to something unique. Israeli couscous is made from wheat pasta and is quite a bit larger than the traditional variety of couscous. This dish could also be made with fregola, a pasta from Sardinia that is made in a similar fashion but is toasted and has more of an irregular shape. Should you decide to use fregola, the cooking time will vary and you will likely need more cooking liquid to achieve an al dente texture.

3 tablespoons extra-virgin olive oil, plus more for drizzling

1 tablespoon minced garlic

1/4 cup minced shallot

1 teaspoon salt

1/2 teaspoon crushed red pepper

1 1/3 cups Israeli couscous

1 3/4 cups water

1 1/4 cups white wine

2 tablespoons Pernod

1 cup peeled, seeded, and diced tomato

3 tablespoons unsalted butter, cubed

1 teaspoon finely grated lemon zest

4 pounds mussels, scrubbed well and debearded

1 tablespoon chopped fresh parsley leaves

2 teaspoons thinly sliced fresh basil

1 teaspoon chopped fresh tarragon leaves

1. Heat the oil in a 6-quart saucepan over medium-high heat. When hot, add the garlic, shallot, salt, and crushed red pepper and cook for 1 minute. Add the couscous and cook, stirring, until toasted, about 2 minutes. Pour in the water and bring to a boil over high heat. Cover, reduce the heat to medium-low, and continue to cook at a simmer until the couscous is al dente, about 8 minutes.

2. Uncover the pot and add the wine, Pernod, tomato, butter, lemon zest, and mussels. Cover, increase the heat to medium-high, and cook until all the mussels have opened, 6 to 8 minutes. (Discard any unopened mussels.) Remove the pan from the heat, then stir in the parsley, basil, and tarragon.

3. Serve in large, shallow bowls, drizzled with extra-virgin olive oil.

4 servings

BOUILLABAISSE

Bouillabaisse is a Provençal fish soup that, according to local lore, was once made in big cauldrons on the beaches of Provence by local fishermen and fishmongers. They used the fish that was least likely to sell at market to make this soup, and they flavored it with dried herbs and served it with chunks of fresh peasant bread. This dish has come a long way since then and today is enjoyed as a delicacy by city dwellers. In my version, a simple shrimp stock provides the backbone for this delicious soup, which is then infused with aromatic Pernod and further enriched with clams and mussels. It's a real crowd pleaser!

½ cup olive oil

1 cup thinly sliced onion

½ cup thinly sliced leek, white and light green parts only, in half-moons

½ cup thinly sliced fennel bulb

2 tablespoons thinly sliced garlic

One 14.5-ounce can petite diced tomatoes, with juice

½ cup Pernod or Herbsaint

½ cup dry white wine

¼ teaspoon crushed saffron threads, crumbled between your fingers

1 pound small Yukon Gold potatoes, peeled and diced

1 teaspoon salt

½ teaspoon freshly ground black pepper

2 ½ quarts Rich Shrimp Stock (recipe follows)

1 bay leaf

2 sprigs fresh thyme

2 sprigs fresh parsley

5 black peppercorns

16 littleneck clams, scrubbed and purged, (see page 32)

16 mussels, scrubbed and debearded

2 pounds mixed firm-fleshed skinless white fish fillets, such as rockfish, cod, or halibut, cut into 2-inch pieces

1 recipe Roasted Red Pepper Aïoli (recipe follows), for serving

Chopped fresh parsley leaves, for garnish

Warm baguettes, for serving

1. In an 8-quart or larger pot, heat the olive oil over medium heat. Add the onion, leek, fennel, and garlic and cook, stirring, until soft, about 6 minutes. Add the tomatoes and cook, stirring, for 1 minute. Stir in the Pernod, wine, and saffron, increase the heat to medium-high, and cook for 1 minute more. Add the potatoes, salt, and pepper and stir well, then add the

stock and bring to a boil. Add the bay leaf, thyme, parsley, and peppercorns, lower the heat, and simmer until the potatoes are just tender but still firm, 20 minutes. Add the clams, mussels, and fish, cover the pot, and cook for another 10 minutes, or until the clams and mussels have opened and the fish is just cooked through. Remove from the heat and discard any unopened clams or mussels.

2.   Ladle about 1 cup of the hot broth into a heatproof bowl and briskly whisk in 3 tablespoons of the aïoli to form an emulsion. Pour the emulsified broth-aïoli mixture back into the bouillabaisse and stir to combine.

3.   To serve, ladle the soup into large soup bowls and garnish with chopped parsley. Serve with warm baguettes and the remaining aïoli.

4 to 6 servings

RICH SHRIMP STOCK

This stock is so easy to make, yet so flavorful—make a batch every time you have shells and heads from fresh shrimp and you'll never have to worry about where to get shrimp stock again. You'll find that toasting the shells in oil before adding the water gives added depth to this stock, which can be used in countless ways.

1 to 1 ½ pounds shrimp shells and heads
1 tablespoon vegetable or olive oil
14 cups water
1 large onion, unpeeled, roughly chopped (the onion peel
    deepens the color of the stock)
½ cup roughly chopped celery
2 small carrots, roughly chopped
2 cloves garlic, peeled and smashed

2 bay leaves
1 teaspoon salt
2 teaspoons black peppercorns
3 sprigs fresh thyme
2 large sprigs fresh parsley

1. Rinse the shrimp shells and heads in a large colander under cold running water and allow to drain.

2. In a large stockpot, heat the oil over medium-high heat. When hot, add the shrimp shells and cook, stirring occasionally, until the shells are pink and toasty-fragrant, 4 to 6 minutes. Add the water and all the remaining ingredients and bring to a boil over high heat, skimming any foam that comes to the surface. Reduce the heat to medium-low and continue to cook at a slow simmer until the stock is flavorful, 45 to 60 minutes.

3. Strain the stock through a fine-mesh sieve into a large heatproof bowl and allow it to cool completely. Cover and refrigerate for up to 3 days before using. (The stock may also be placed in airtight containers and frozen for up to several months.)

About 12 cups

Note: You can easily double the ingredient amounts to make a larger batch of stock. To save spacc in the freezer, you can reduce the stock further after straining and discarding the solids. Just add water to the defrosted stock to reconstitute as needed.

ROASTED RED PEPPER AÏOLI

Aïoli is a Provençal garlic mayonnaise served as a condiment for fish, meat, and poultry. It makes a nice accompaniment to steamed and raw vegetables and can be stirred into brothy soups. I have substituted this version, with roasted red peppers, in place of the more traditional rouille typically served with bouillabaisse in France.

6 large cloves garlic, peeled
3/4 teaspoon kosher salt
2 egg yolks
1 teaspoon freshly squeezed lemon juice

½ cup roasted red peppers (jarred or homemade),
roughly chopped
¾ cup Spanish or other mild-flavored olive oil

Place the garlic in a blender or food processor and pulse until finely chopped, stopping to scrape down the sides as needed. Add the salt, egg yolks, lemon juice, and roasted red peppers and process until well combined. While the machine is still running, add the oil in a thin, steady stream until it is completely incorporated and the mixture is thickened. Taste and adjust the seasoning if necessary.

1 1/4 cups

BRACIOLE

This is traditional Italian Sunday fare. It can be made with one big roulade of beef (with one large piece of bottom round) or as individual roulades using sliced bottom round, as we do here. We like the look of the small rolls of stuffed meat—and this way, when it's time to serve, there's no slicing to contend with. It does take a bit of time to put together—but once it's all in the pot simmering, there's nothing to do but enjoy its outrageous aroma and anticipate its arrival at the table.

Twelve $\frac{1}{4}$-inch-thick slices beef bottom round (2 to 2 $\frac{1}{2}$ pounds)

$\frac{1}{2}$ cup plus 1 tablespoon olive oil

1 tablespoon kosher salt

1 teaspoon freshly ground black pepper

$\frac{3}{4}$ cup Italian-style dry bread-crumbs

4 hard-boiled eggs, chopped

$\frac{1}{2}$ cup chopped fresh parsley leaves

$\frac{1}{4}$ cup plus 2 tablespoons finely grated Parmigiano-Reggiano cheese, plus more for serving

2 tablespoons drained capers

1 tablespoon finely chopped anchovies

$\frac{1}{4}$ cup plus 2 tablespoons chopped fresh basil leaves

$\frac{1}{4}$ cup plus 1 tablespoon minced garlic (about 15 cloves)

1 teaspoon crushed red pepper

1 large onion, minced

1 cup dry red wine

One 28-ounce can Italian-style whole plum tomatoes, broken up with your hands, with juice

One 28-ounce can Italian-style crushed tomatoes

One 1 × 3-inch Parmigiano-Reggiano rind

2 bay leaves

1 teaspoon finely chopped fresh oregano leaves or $\frac{1}{4}$ teaspoon dried

2 cups water

1 pound pasta, such as spaghetti, linguine, or fettuccine, cooked until al dente, for serving

1.   Place the beef slices between sheets of plastic wrap, working with 1 or 2 at a time, and pound to a thickness of $\frac{1}{8}$ inch. Remove the plastic wrap and repeat with the remaining meat slices. Brush the meat on both sides with $\frac{1}{4}$ cup of the olive oil and season with 1 teaspoon of the salt and the black pepper.

2.   In a mixing bowl, combine 3 tablespoons of the remaining olive oil with the breadcrumbs, eggs, parsley, Parmesan, capers, anchovies, $\frac{1}{4}$ cup of the basil,

3 tablespoons of the garlic, ½ teaspoon of the crushed red pepper, and 1 teaspoon of the remaining salt and stir to blend thoroughly. Divide the breadcrumb mixture evenly among the slices of meat (about ¼ cup stuffing for each), spreading it to within 1 inch of the edges. Carefully roll each piece of meat into a tight cylinder so that it resembles a fat cigar. Use toothpicks to secure the meat or tie on both ends using kitchen twine.

3. In a large nonstick skillet, heat the remaining 2 tablespoons olive oil over medium-high heat and brown the meat rolls well on all sides, 8 to 10 minutes. Transfer the browned meat to a large pot and set aside. Add the onion and the remaining 2 tablespoons garlic to the drippings still left in the skillet and cook until lightly caramelized, 4 to 6 minutes. Pour in the wine and cook until nearly evaporated, 3 to 4 minutes. Add the plum tomatoes and crushed tomatoes and bring to a simmer.

4. To the pot with the browned meat, add the tomato-onion sauce, Parmesan rind, bay leaves, oregano, water, and the remaining 1 teaspoon salt and ½ teaspoon crushed red pepper. Place the pot over medium heat and bring the sauce to a gentle simmer. Reduce the heat to medium-low and cook, stirring occasionally, until the meat is very tender and the sauce is thick and flavorful, 2 to 2½ hours.

5. Stir in the remaining 2 tablespoons of basil, taste the sauce, and adjust the seasoning if necessary. Remove the rind and the bay leaves. Remove the meat rolls from the sauce and remove the toothpicks or twine. Serve the meat over cooked pasta, with the sauce spooned over all. Garnish with additional Parmesan.

6 servings

BIG BOY MEATBALLS AND SPAGHETTI

These meatballs are for the big boys out there—you know who you are! These big babies are so tender and flavorful, I doubt you'll have any meatball leftovers, but if you happen to, warm them up and make sandwiches on lightly toasted French bread. Serve these and you'll have friends for life!

4 slices white bread, crusts removed, torn into pieces

3/4 cup buttermilk

1 1/2 pounds ground beef chuck (85% lean)

3/4 pound sweet Italian sausage, removed from casings

2 ounces Parmigiano-Reggiano cheese, finely grated (about 1/2 cup), plus more for garnish if desired

2 tablespoons minced fresh parsley leaves

1/4 cup minced garlic (about 12 cloves)

3/4 teaspoon salt

3/4 teaspoon freshly ground black pepper

3 tablespoons olive oil

2 cups chopped yellow onion

1 teaspoon crushed red pepper

3/4 cup dry red wine

One 28-ounce can tomato puree

One 28-ounce can crushed tomatoes

2 bay leaves

1 1/2 cups water

1/3 cup chopped fresh basil leaves

1 tablespoon chopped fresh oregano leaves

2 tablespoons evaporated milk (optional)

1 pound dried spaghetti, cooked until al dente, for serving

1.   Place the bread and buttermilk in a small bowl and set aside for 10 minutes. Mash the bread with a fork to form a paste. Place the ground chuck, sausage, Parmesan, parsley, 2 tablespoons of the garlic, salt, and pepper in a large bowl. Add the bread-buttermilk mixture and mix gently but thoroughly to combine. Shape into about 10 large meatballs (about 1/2 cup each) and refrigerate briefly to firm up, about 15 minutes.

2.   In a large nonstick skillet, heat the olive oil over medium-high heat. Add the meatballs, in batches if necessary, and cook until very well browned on all sides, 8 to 10 minutes. Transfer the browned meatballs to a large pot.

3.   Add the onion and crushed red pepper to the oil remaining in the skillet and cook, stirring occasion-

ally, until the onion is soft and lightly browned, 6 to 8 minutes. Add the remaining 2 tablespoons garlic and cook, stirring, for 2 minutes. Pour in the wine and cook, scraping any browned bits from the pan, until reduced by half, 1 or 2 minutes. Add the tomato puree, crushed tomatoes, bay leaves, and water and bring the sauce to a simmer.

4. Carefully transfer the hot tomato sauce to the pot with the meatballs. Place the pot over medium-high heat and bring the sauce to a gentle boil so as not to disturb the meatballs. Reduce the heat so that the sauce just simmers and cook until the sauce is thick and the meatballs are tender, 45 to 60 minutes, stirring occasionally once the meatballs have firmed up and have begun floating in the sauce. Stir in the basil and oregano and season the sauce with salt to taste. If the sauce seems too acidic, add the evaporated milk and cook for a few minutes longer. Remove the bay leaves. Serve the meatballs and sauce ladled over the cooked spaghetti, garnished with additional Parmesan if desired.

About 10 large meatballs, 4 to 6 servings

CONGEE

This soothing Asian rice soup will warm you through and through. It's all about cooking the rice in a rich broth and then garnishing it with tasty tidbits. Take care not to overseason the soup, since you will be drizzling it with soy sauce and fish sauce before serving. Also, if you don't want to make your own crispy garlic and shallots to garnish, you can purchase them already cooked in Asian markets, where they're sold in airtight containers, ready to go. But nothing beats fresh!

1 pound chicken wings or necks

1 pound boneless Boston butt pork roast, cut into 2-inch chunks

1 large onion, peeled and quartered

One 4-inch piece fresh ginger, peeled and cut crosswise into ¼-inch-thick slices

6 green onions, 4 smashed with a knife and 2 thinly sliced, reserved separately

4 cloves garlic, peeled and smashed

30 sprigs fresh cilantro, stems and leaves reserved separately

1 tablespoon kosher salt

1 teaspoon soy sauce, plus more for serving

6 quarts water

1 pound boneless, skinless chicken breasts

3 ½ cups steamed jasmine rice

⅓ cup Crispy Garlic (recipe follows), for serving

½ cup Crispy Shallots (recipe follows), for serving

Fish sauce (see page 213), for serving

Toasted sesame oil, for serving

Hot sesame oil, for serving (optional)

1. In an 8-quart or larger stockpot or soup pot, add the chicken wings, pork butt, onion, ginger, smashed green onions, garlic, cilantro stems, salt, soy sauce, and water. Bring to a boil, reduce the heat to a gentle simmer, and cook, skimming any foam that rises to the surface, until the broth is flavorful and the pork is tender, about 2½ hours. Add the chicken breasts and cook at a bare simmer until they are just cooked through, 15 to 20 minutes. Strain the broth through a sieve into a large bowl. Remove the pork pieces and chicken breasts and set aside until cool enough to handle. Shred both meats and reserve separately until ready to serve. Discard the remaining solids.

2. Return the broth to the large stockpot and bring to a simmer. Stir in the steamed rice. Cover the pot and return to a boil. Reduce the heat to a simmer and cook, stirring occasionally, for 1 hour. Remove the cover and whisk the rice well to encourage it to break into very small pieces. Increase the heat slightly to

produce a brisk simmer and continue cooking until the rice is broken into very tiny pieces and has thickened the broth to the consistency of a thick porridge, 45 to 60 minutes longer. Note: it is important to stir or whisk the soup frequently near the end of cooking as it has a tendency to stick to the bottom of the pot as it thickens.

3. Serve the soup ladled into shallow bowls, garnished with the shredded chicken and pork. Allow guests to garnish their bowls to taste with cilantro leaves, soy sauce, sliced green onions, crispy garlic and shallots, fish sauce, and toasted or hot sesame oil.

10 cups, 4 to 6 servings

CRISPY GARLIC

Cloves from 1 head of garlic, peeled
Vegetable oil or peanut oil, for frying
Salt

1. Slice each garlic clove (on a mandoline if available) to ⅛-inch thickness or even thinner if possible.

2. Heat about 1 inch of oil in a small skillet until very hot. Working in small batches, add some of the garlic and cook, stirring with a slotted spoon or skimmer, until golden brown, 10 to 20 seconds. Immediately remove the browned garlic slices and transfer to a paper towel–lined plate or small baking sheet. Sprinkle with salt and set aside to cool. Repeat with the remaining garlic.

About 1/3 cup

CRISPY SHALLOTS

3 large shallots, peeled and cut crosswise into $1/8$-inch slices
Vegetable oil or peanut oil, for frying
Salt

1. Separate the shallot slices into individual rings.

2. Heat about 1 inch of oil in a small skillet until very hot. Working in small batches, add some of the shallot rings and cook, stirring with a slotted spoon or skimmer, until golden brown, 30 to 60 seconds. Immediately remove the browned rings and transfer to a paper towel–lined plate or small baking sheet to drain. Sprinkle with salt and set aside to cool. Repeat with the remaining shallots.

About 1/2 cup

GIGANTE BEAN SOUP WITH ARUGULA PESTO

Gigante beans are very large white beans with a creamy, almost buttery texture. They are also known as hija or gigande beans and are a staple in Spanish and Greek cuisine. These large beans make great soups and stews. If you cannot find gigante beans in your area, feel free to substitute large lima beans.

2 sprigs fresh thyme

2 sprigs fresh parsley

1 bay leaf

5 white peppercorns

4 ounces pancetta, diced small

2 tablespoons olive oil

2 medium carrots, diced small

2 celery stalks, diced small

1 onion, diced small

1 small fennel bulb, diced small

1 pound dried gigante beans, picked over, rinsed, soaked overnight, and drained

3 cups chicken stock or canned low-sodium chicken broth

2 ½ teaspoons salt

1 yellow bell pepper, seeded and diced small

1 orange bell pepper, seeded and diced small

1 red bell pepper, seeded and diced small

½ teaspoon freshly ground black pepper

¼ cup Arugula Pesto (recipe follows), for garnish

1.   In the center of a piece of cheesecloth, combine the thyme, parsley, bay leaf, and peppercorns. Gather the ends together and tie securely with a piece of kitchen twine to form a sachet. Set aside.

2.   In a large soup pot over medium heat, cook the pancetta in the olive oil until it is brown and crispy and has rendered most of its fat, 3 to 5 minutes. Remove the pancetta from the pot using a slotted spoon and transfer to a paper towel–lined plate to drain.

3.   Add the carrots, celery, onion, and fennel to the pot and sauté until the vegetables begin to wilt and caramelize lightly, about 10 minutes. Add the beans, the herb sachet, chicken stock, and enough water to cover the beans by 1 inch (about 5 cups). Season the beans with 1½ teaspoons of the salt. Bring the beans to a boil, reduce the heat so that the broth just simmers, and cook, uncovered, until the beans are almost tender, about 1 hour. Add the bell peppers and pancetta and cook until the beans are tender, about 30 minutes longer. Remove the sachet from the pot and discard.

4. Season the soup with the pepper and the remaining 1 teaspoon salt.

5. Serve the soup in large bowls, garnished with a generous spoonful of the pesto, to taste. Serve with a loaf of warm, crusty bread.

4 to 6 servings

ARUGULA PESTO

---

4 ounces baby arugula, washed and spun dry
1 ounce fresh mint leaves (about 1 packed cup)
$\frac{1}{2}$ cup grated Parmigiano-Reggiano cheese
$\frac{1}{2}$ cup toasted pine nuts
1 teaspoon grated lemon zest
2 teaspoons freshly squeezed lemon juice
$\frac{1}{2}$ cup extra-virgin olive oil
$\frac{1}{2}$ teaspoon salt

1. Combine the arugula, mint, Parmesan, pine nuts, lemon zest, and lemon juice in a food processor. Puree until smooth, then add the olive oil in a slow, steady stream. Process just until the olive oil is incorporated. Add the salt and pulse just to blend.

2. Transfer the pesto to an airtight container until ready to use. The pesto can be stored in the refrigerator for up to 2 weeks and in the freezer for up to 6 months.

1 cup

EMERIL'S MULLIGATAWNY SOUP

Though the ingredient list here may look daunting, this soup is a breeze to put together. Have your junior sous-chef help with assembling, chopping, and measuring the ingredients and you will be rewarded with a hearty, aromatic soup that will delight family and friends.

¼ cup ghee (page 69) or clarified butter

1 ½ pounds boneless, skinless chicken thighs, cut into ½-inch pieces

2 tablespoons garam masala

1 ¾ teaspoons salt

2 cups small-diced onion

½ cup small-diced carrot

½ cup small-diced celery

2 tablespoons minced garlic

2 tablespoons peeled and minced fresh ginger

2 cups peeled, cored, and diced Granny Smith apple

1 cup peeled and diced Yukon Gold potato

1 cup peeled and diced sweet potato

1 cup dried red lentils

6 cups chicken stock or canned low-sodium chicken broth

¾ cup diced zucchini

¾ cup diced yellow squash

1 cup tightly packed baby spinach

One 14-ounce can unsweetened coconut milk

¾ teaspoon freshly ground black pepper

1 cup peeled, seeded, and chopped tomato

1 tablespoon apple cider vinegar

3 cups steamed white basmati rice, for serving

½ cup toasted finely ground cashews, for garnish

¼ cup chopped fresh cilantro leaves, for garnish

1. Set a 4- or 5-quart stockpot or soup pot over medium heat and add the ghee. While the ghee is heating, season the chicken with the garam masala and ¼ teaspoon of the salt. Once the ghee is hot, add the chicken and cook, turning often, until golden brown and fragrant, 6 to 8 minutes. Transfer the chicken to a plate and set aside to cool.

2. Add the onion, carrot, and celery to the hot pan and sauté until lightly caramelized, 4 to 5 minutes. Add the garlic, ginger, and apples and sauté until the apples are caramelized, 7 to 8 minutes. Add the potatoes, sweet potatoes, lentils, and 4 cups of the chicken stock, increase the heat to high, and bring to a boil. Reduce to a simmer and cook the soup until the potatoes are tender, about 10 minutes. Add the zucchini, squash, spinach, coconut milk, pepper, tomato,

the reserved chicken, and the remaining 1½ teaspoons salt and 2 cups chicken stock. Simmer the soup until the lentils and chicken are tender, 10 to 15 minutes longer. Remove from the heat and stir in the cider vinegar. Taste and adjust the seasoning if necessary.

3.   To serve the soup, place ½ cup of the rice in a warmed large bowl and pour 2 cups of the soup over the rice. Garnish with the ground cashews and cilantro.

12 cups, 6 servings

MATZOH BALL SOUP

Also known as "Jewish penicillin," matzoh ball soup is a quintessential comfort food and is considered by many to be a surefire cure for the common cold. The trick to a good matzoh ball soup is starting with a rich chicken broth and adding light, fluffy matzoh balls. Though this soup can be enjoyed year-round, for members of the Jewish faith it is an essential dish during Passover and is often eaten on Shabbat.

One 5-pound chicken, cut into quarters

8 quarts cold water

2 large celery stalks with leaves, chopped, plus 1 cup thinly sliced celery

2 large carrots, peeled and cut into big chunks, plus 1 cup thinly sliced carrot rounds

1 onion, quartered, plus 1 cup thinly sliced onion

3 sprigs fresh parsley, plus $1/4$ cup chopped fresh parsley leaves

1 bay leaf

$1/2$ cup chicken fat, either store-bought or reserved from making the stock, plus grapeseed oil if necessary

4 eggs, separated

1 tablespoon plus 1 teaspoon and a pinch of salt

1 cup matzoh meal

$1/4$ cup seltzer water

1 teaspoon freshly ground white pepper

1 teaspoon snipped fresh chives

1 cup thinly sliced leek, white and light green parts

1. Rinse the chicken under cold running water and place in a 12-quart soup pot or stockpot. Cover with the cold water and bring to a boil over high heat, skimming off any foam that comes to the surface. Add the chopped celery stalks, carrot chunks, quartered onion, parsley sprigs, and bay leaf and simmer over medium-low heat, partially covered, for 3 hours, skimming as needed, until the chicken is very tender and pulls away from the bone and the broth is very flavorful.

2. Strain the broth through a fine-mesh sieve lined with cheesecloth and set aside to cool. Discard the vegetables. When the chicken is cool enough to handle, remove the meat from the bones and discard the skin and bones. Shred the meat with a fork and set aside.

3. When the broth has cooled completely, skim any fat from the surface and reserve for making the mat-

zoh balls. You should have about ½ cup of rendered fat; if not, add grapeseed oil to bring the volume up to ½ cup.

4. In a medium mixing bowl, whisk the egg whites with a pinch of salt to soft peaks. Soft peaks are formed when the whites appear thick and fluffy but will droop slightly when the beaters are removed.

5. In a medium mixing bowl, combine the 4 egg yolks and ¼ cup of the reserved chicken fat. Stir in the matzoh meal, seltzer, white pepper, chives, 1 teaspoon of the salt, and 2 teaspoons of the chopped parsley and mix well. Gently fold in the beaten egg whites until they are fully incorporated. Cover and refrigerate for at least 1 hour. Using a small ice cream scoop or a small spoon, form the matzoh dough into balls the size of walnuts, about 1 tablespoon each (about 36 matzoh balls). In a large pot, bring 4 cups of the chicken broth to a brisk simmer, season with 1 teaspoon of the remaining salt, add the matzoh balls, cover, and cook until the balls float to the top and are cooked through, about 10 minutes.

6. In a separate large stockpot, heat the remaining ¼ cup reserved chicken fat over medium-high heat. When hot, add the sliced celery, carrot, onion, and leek. Season with the remaining 2 teaspoons salt and cook until the vegetables are very tender, stirring occasionally, about 8 minutes. Add the shredded chicken and the remaining chicken broth to the pot and bring to a brisk simmer. Add the matzoh balls and their cooking broth to the soup pot along with the remaining chopped parsley. Taste and adjust the seasoning if necessary. Serve immediately.

5 quarts, 8 to 10 servings

THAI CHICKEN AND
COCONUT SOUP

Here's an easy one for you. Steep chicken broth with aromatics, strain, add the rest of the ingredients, and simmer briefly. This soup is spicy—if you need to make a milder version, either remove the seeds from the chiles or don't include them at all.

1 tablespoon vegetable oil

½ cup thinly sliced shallot

3 cloves garlic, smashed

2 red Thai chiles, chopped, plus 1 fresh red Thai bird chile, seeded and thinly sliced

2 ounces fresh ginger (about a 6-inch piece), peeled and sliced

1 lemongrass stalk, root end and tough outer leaves removed, trimmed to 12 inches and cut into 1-inch pieces

Strips of zest from 1 lime

¼ cup chopped fresh cilantro stems plus ¼ cup chopped fresh leaves

4 cups chicken stock or canned low-sodium chicken broth

Two 14-ounce cans unsweetened coconut milk

2 tablespoons Thai red curry paste (preferably Mae Ploy brand)

¼ cup freshly squeezed lime juice

2 tablespoons palm sugar or light brown sugar

2 tablespoons fish sauce (see page 213)

1½ teaspoons salt

1 pound boneless, skinless chicken breasts, cut into strips

4 ounces shiitake mushrooms, stemmed and thinly sliced (about 2 cups)

4 ounces snow peas, diced small

¼ cup thinly sliced green onion, green parts only

Steamed jasmine rice, for serving (optional)

1.   Heat the oil in a 6-quart or larger stockpot or soup pot over medium-high heat. Add the shallot, garlic, chopped chiles, ginger, and lemongrass and cook, stirring as needed, for 2 minutes. Add the lime zest, cilantro stems, and chicken broth. Bring to a boil, reduce the heat to low, and simmer for 30 minutes.

2.   Strain the broth through a fine-mesh sieve into another pot or bowl, discard the solids, and return the broth to the pot set over medium heat. Stir in the coconut milk, curry paste, lime juice, palm sugar, fish sauce, salt, and sliced chile. Bring the broth to a sim-

mer and cook for 2 minutes. Add the chicken, mushrooms, and snow peas to the pot and cook for 2 minutes longer, or until the chicken is just cooked through. Stir in the green onion and cilantro leaves and remove from the heat. Serve the soup hot, over steamed rice if desired.

12 cups, 4 to 6 servings

HUNTER'S GUMBO

This is a project for a long, lazy day . . . you really can't rush a good gumbo. That said, if you don't have all day to spend tending the stock and then simmering the gumbo, the work is easily divided into two distinct segments: make the stock and shred the meat on the first day and then make the roux and simmer the gumbo the next. Just keep in mind the golden rule of combining roux and stock—you should always add a cool roux to hot stock or vice versa. If they are both hot, they will have a tendency to separate once combined.

4 quarts chicken stock or canned low-sodium chicken broth, plus more for thinning if desired

8 cups water

1 onion, peeled and quartered, plus 3 cups small-diced onion

2 celery stalks, halved, plus 1 1/2 cups small-diced celery

4 large cloves garlic, peeled and smashed, plus 3 tablespoons minced garlic

3 sprigs fresh parsley, plus 1/4 cup chopped leaves

1 dried hot red pepper or 1/4 teaspoon crushed red pepper

5 sprigs fresh thyme

4 bay leaves

1 1/4 cups vegetable oil

3 pounds dressed whole wild ducks (see Note)

3 pounds rabbit pieces

1 1/2 tablespoons kosher salt

1 teaspoon freshly ground black pepper

2 cups all-purpose flour

1 cup small-diced green bell pepper

3/4 teaspoon cayenne

2 teaspoons Crystal or other Louisiana hot sauce

1 teaspoon Worcestershire sauce

1 1/2 pounds venison sausage or andouille sausage, halved lengthwise and cut crosswise into half-moons

1 bunch green onions, thinly sliced, green and white parts reserved separately

Steamed long-grain white rice, for serving

1.   In an 8-quart or larger stockpot, combine the stock and water. Add the quartered onion, celery stalks, smashed garlic, parsley sprigs, dried pepper, 3 of the thyme sprigs, and 2 of the bay leaves.

2.   Heat 2 tablespoons of the oil in a large heavy skillet or Dutch oven over medium-high heat. Pat the ducks and rabbit pieces dry with paper towels. Season the ducks with 2 teaspoons of the kosher salt and

½ teaspoon of the black pepper (seasoning inside the cavity as well). Season the rabbit pieces with 2 teaspoons of the remaining kosher salt and the remaining ½ teaspoon black pepper. When the oil is hot, add the ducks and cook until golden brown on all sides, turning as necessary, about 20 minutes total. Transfer the ducks to the stockpot. Add the rabbit pieces to the pan and cook, in batches if necessary, until golden brown, about 5 minutes per side. Transfer the rabbit to the stockpot. (Discard any remaining oil in the skillet, wipe the pan clean, and set aside until you are ready to make the roux.) Bring the liquid to a boil, reduce the heat to a simmer, and cook until the rabbit is tender, 1 to 1½ hours. Remove the rabbit pieces from the stock and, when cool enough to handle, remove and shred the meat. Reserve the rabbit meat in the refrigerator until ready to use.

3. Return the rabbit bones to the stockpot and continue to cook until the ducks are tender, about 1 hour longer. When the ducks are tender and the meat easily pulls away from the bones, remove the ducks and, when cool enough to handle, discard the skin and bones. Shred the meat into bite-sized pieces. Reserve the duck meat in the refrigerator until ready to use. Strain the stock through a fine-mesh sieve and discard the solids. Return the stock to the stockpot.

4. While the stock is simmering, heat 1 cup of the remaining vegetable oil in the large heavy skillet or Dutch oven over medium-high heat. When hot, add 1½ cups of the flour and whisk to blend. Cook, stirring constantly and reaching every corner of the pot so as not to allow the roux to burn, until it has reached a dark copper penny color, 45 to 50 minutes. (If the roux begins browning too quickly, reduce the heat to medium-low.) During the last 10 minutes of cooking the roux, add the remaining ½ cup flour and continue stirring. As soon as the roux reaches the desired color, immediately add the diced onion, celery, and bell pepper and cook, stirring fre-

Note: Any wild ducks that are available in your area may be used to make this gumbo, although some folks think that diving ducks have a "fishy" flavor. Hunters here in Louisiana prefer the flavor of teal, Mallard, and gray ducks (Gadwall), but by all means use ducks that you like and can procure. Also, it is not necessary for the duck to have its skin (since any hunter knows that it is easier to clean a duck by skinning than by painstakingly plucking the birds), but the skin does provide an awesome duck flavor to the stock.

quently, until the vegetables have softened, 6 to 8 minutes. Add the minced garlic and cook for 2 minutes. Set the roux-vegetable mixture aside to cool until the stock is strained.

5.   When the hot stock has been strained and returned to the stockpot, bring it to a simmer over medium-high heat. Carefully whisk in the cooled roux-vegetable mixture. Add the cayenne, hot sauce, Worcestershire, and the remaining 2 thyme sprigs and 2 bay leaves. Return the stock to a simmer over medium-high heat, reduce the heat so that the sauce just simmers, and cook the gumbo, stirring occasionally, until any floury taste is gone, about 1 hour.

6.   Meanwhile, heat the remaining 2 tablespoons of vegetable oil in a nonstick sauté pan over medium-high heat. In batches, cook the sausage until browned on all sides, 4 to 6 minutes. Transfer to a paper towel–lined plate and reserve until ready to use.

7.   After the gumbo has cooked for about an hour, add the browned sausage and the green onion bottoms (white parts) and cook for 1 hour longer. Add the reserved rabbit and duck meat and the remaining ½ teaspoon kosher salt. Continue to cook for 1 more hour, so that the gumbo has cooked for 3 hours in all. Adjust the consistency to your liking by thinning with additional stock or water if the broth seems too thick, or cook for a bit longer if it is still on the soupy side; tastes vary, and you're the boss of your gumbo. Once you obtain the desired thickness, stir in the green onion tops (green parts) and chopped parsley, taste and adjust the seasoning if necessary, and serve the gumbo in wide, shallow bowls ladled over hot white rice.

About 4 quarts plus 2 cups, 8 to 12 servings

WONTON SOUP

You'll love this. No fighting over the wontons. There's plenty . . . nine for each person if you're serving four, but who's counting?

8 ounces shrimp, peeled, deveined, and finely chopped

4 ounces lean ground pork

1 cup finely sliced green onion, white and green parts, plus 1 tablespoon minced green parts

½ teaspoon honey

1 tablespoon plus ½ teaspoon peeled and minced fresh ginger

1 tablespoon plus ½ teaspoon minced garlic

3 ½ tablespoons soy sauce

1 tablespoon plus 1 teaspoon toasted sesame oil

1 tablespoon plus 1 teaspoon rice vinegar

½ teaspoon salt

36 wonton wrappers

14 cups chicken stock or canned low-sodium chicken broth

8 ounces shiitake mushrooms, stemmed and thinly sliced

4 cups shredded Napa cabbage

2 cups snow peas or sugar snap peas, tips and string removed, halved on the diagonal

2 cups grated carrot

¼ teaspoon crushed red pepper

1. In a medium bowl, combine the shrimp, pork, 1 tablespoon minced green onion, honey, ½ teaspoon of the ginger, ½ teaspoon of the garlic, 1½ teaspoons of the soy sauce, 1 teaspoon of the sesame oil, 1 teaspoon of the rice vinegar, and ¼ teaspoon of the salt. Mix thoroughly to combine.

2. Pour some water into a small bowl. Working on a flat surface, lay out about 6 wonton wrappers. Place a heaping teaspoon of the filling in the center of each wrapper. Using your fingers or a brush, lightly wet the edges of the wrapper with the water. Bring two opposite corners of the wonton together to form a triangle and enclose the filling, pressing the edges firmly around the mound of filling to eliminate any air pockets, and press to seal. Moisten the opposite ends of the long side and then bring the ends together, overlapping, and press to form a seal. Set the wontons aside on a plate. Repeat with the remaining filling and wrappers. When all the wontons are assembled, refrigerate them, uncovered, until ready to cook—up to overnight (see Note).

3. Add the stock, the remaining 1 tablespoon ginger and 1 tablespoon garlic, and ½ cup of the finely sliced green onion to a 6-quart or larger pot. Bring to a boil,

reduce the heat to low, and simmer for 30 minutes. Strain the broth through a fine-mesh sieve into another pot or bowl, discard the solids, and return the broth to the pot. Return the soup to a simmer. Stir in the mushrooms, cabbage, snow peas, carrot, crushed red pepper, wontons, and remaining 3 tablespoons soy sauce, 1 tablespoon sesame oil, 1 tablespoon vinegar, and ¼ teaspoon salt. Bring the soup to a boil, reduce the heat to a simmer, and cook until the wontons are just cooked through, about 5 minutes.

4. Add the remaining ½ cup sliced green onions, remove from the heat, and gently ladle the soup into soup bowls. Note: the wontons are tender; take care not to break them when serving.

About 12 cups, 4 servings

Note: Prepared wontons may also be frozen (uncovered) on a plate or baking sheet. Once frozen, transfer the wontons to a resealable plastic food storage bag and keep frozen until ready to use, up to 1 month. There is no need to defrost before adding to the soup; just add 3 to 4 more minutes to the simmering time.

BEEF AND BARLEY SOUP WITH GARLIC-BASIL OIL

You will love this hearty Madeira-flavored soup with tender beef chunks and fresh basil-garlic oil. The barley will really soak up the broth as the soup cools, so have extra broth on hand to add if you plan to hold the soup for any length of time.

1 pound cubed beef stew meat (1 ½ to 2 inches)

1 tablespoon kosher salt

1 ¼ teaspoons freshly ground black pepper

1 tablespoon olive oil

14 cups beef stock or canned low-sodium beef broth

3 small cloves garlic, smashed, plus 1 tablespoon minced

1 cup roughly chopped fresh basil leaves

¾ cup extra-virgin olive oil

1 ½ cups Madeira

½ cup chopped canned San Marzano tomatoes, with juice

2 cups small-diced onion

1 ½ cups small-diced carrot

1 cup small-diced celery

1 cup small-diced red bell pepper

1 bay leaf

½ teaspoon crushed red pepper (optional)

12 ounces shiitake mushrooms, stemmed and thinly sliced (about 2 generous cups)

¾ cup barley

¼ cup chopped fresh parsley leaves

1. Season the beef with 1½ teaspoons of the salt and ¼ teaspoon of the black pepper. Heat the olive oil in a 6-quart or larger stockpot over high heat. Brown the beef on all sides, about 7 minutes, and add 4 cups of the beef stock. Bring to a boil, reduce the heat to low, cover, and simmer the beef for 2 hours.

2. Lay the garlic cloves on a cutting board and sprinkle with 1 teaspoon of the remaining salt. Chop the garlic with the salt, occasionally mashing the garlic with the side of the blade of your knife, until it forms a paste. Add the basil on top of the garlic and continue to chop, mixing with the side of your knife as needed, until the basil and garlic come together and form a roughly textured paste. Transfer the basil-garlic mixture to a small bowl, stir in the extra-virgin olive oil and ¼ teaspoon of the black pepper, and set aside until ready to serve the soup. (This basil-garlic oil may be made ahead and kept covered in the refrigerator for up to 1 week.)

3. Remove the lid from the stockpot and skim any foam that has risen to the surface of the broth. Add the Madeira to the pot and simmer for 5 minutes. Add the tomatoes, onion, carrot, celery, bell pepper, minced garlic, bay leaf, crushed red pepper (if using), and remaining 10 cups beef broth. Return the liquid to a simmer and cook for 20 minutes. Add the mushrooms and barley and simmer until the barley is tender, about 40 minutes longer. Remove the bay leaf and discard. Stir in the chopped parsley, ¼ teaspoon of the black pepper, and the remaining ½ teaspoon salt.

4. Serve the soup in bowls, drizzled with the basil-garlic oil.

14 cups, 6 to 8 servings

WOKS

Built for speed and incredible versatility, the WOK does far more than stir fry. It can also be used for steaming, deep-frying or braising.

SWEET AND SOUR PORK

No need to call for take-out...this Chinese favorite can be prepared easily at home and is well worth the effort. Use fresh pineapple if it's in season. The pork is married with the sauce just at the end to keep it nice and crispy. Now that's sweet and sour pork!

½ cup plus 3 tablespoons soy sauce

½ cup plus 2 tablespoons sugar

1 pound pork tenderloin, trimmed and cut into 1-inch pieces

½ cup cider vinegar or rice vinegar

1 ½ cups plus 2 tablespoons cornstarch

½ cup chicken stock or canned low-sodium chicken broth

1 teaspoon crushed red pepper

1 ½ cups all-purpose flour

2 eggs

2 tablespoons water

2 cups peanut oil

1 bunch green onions, cut into 2-inch pieces on the diagonal (about 1 cup)

1 tablespoon peeled and minced fresh ginger

1 tablespoon minced garlic

½ cup chopped onion

¾ cup 1-inch diced green bell pepper

¾ cup thinly sliced carrot

2 cups fresh pineapple chunks or one 14-ounce can pineapple chunks in juice, drained

Steamed rice, for serving

1. Whisk together ½ cup of the soy sauce with 2 tablespoons of the sugar until dissolved; transfer to a small bowl or resealable plastic food storage bag. Add the pork and cover or seal; set aside to marinate for 15 minutes.

2. In a 2-cup liquid measure or other small container, whisk together the remaining 3 tablespoons soy sauce, the remaining ½ cup sugar, the vinegar, 2 tablespoons of the cornstarch, the stock, and the crushed red pepper. Set the sauce aside.

3. Set up a breading station using three small containers. Add the flour to one, combine the eggs and water in another, and place the remaining 1½ cups cornstarch in the third.

4. Remove the pork from the marinade and add half of the pieces to the flour and coat evenly, then dip in the egg wash, then finally dredge in the cornstarch. Set the breaded pork aside on a plate and repeat with the remaining pork.

5. Heat a large wok over high heat. Add the peanut oil and heat to 350°F. Add a third of the pork to the oil and fry on all sides until browned, about 4 minutes. Using a slotted spoon, transfer the pork to a paper towel–lined bowl or plate and set aside. Repeat with the remaining pork. Strain the peanut oil through a fine-mesh sieve into a heatproof bowl. (Discard the solids.) Return 2 tablespoons of the strained hot oil to the wok. (Allow the remaining oil to cool, then discard.)

6. Add the green onions, ginger, garlic, and onion to the wok and cook, stirring continuously, for 1 minute. Add the bell pepper and cook for 1 minute. Add the carrot and cook for 1 minute longer. Add the pineapple and stir briefly. Whisk the sauce, then add it to the wok. Just before serving, bring the sauce to a rolling boil and add the pork—you don't want to add the pork too soon and lose its crispiness. Stir to combine and cook until the pork is warmed through, about 1 minute. Remove the wok from the heat. Transfer the stir-fry to a platter or serve immediately from the wok over steamed rice.

4 servings

SCALLOPS AND SNOW PEAS IN BLACK BEAN GARLIC SAUCE

Whenever you're sautéing scallops, sear them on one side until a deep, browned crust develops—about 5 minutes. I know it's hard to resist turning them, but when you add the scallops back to the pan with the vegetables and sauce, they will retain their color for striking visual appeal.

¼ cup fermented black beans (black bean paste)

¼ cup distilled white vinegar

½ cup light brown sugar

½ teaspoon crushed red pepper

1 pound large diver scallops (about 10)

¼ teaspoon freshly ground black pepper

3 tablespoons peanut oil

1 tablespoon minced garlic

1 tablespoon peeled and minced fresh ginger

1 bunch green onions, cut into 2-inch pieces on the diagonal (about 1 cup)

1 cup red bell pepper strips

4 ounces fresh baby corn, halved crosswise, or drained canned baby corn

4 ounces fresh snow peas, ends trimmed

Steamed rice, for serving

1. In a 2-cup measure or other small container, combine the black beans, vinegar, sugar, and crushed red pepper. Set this sauce aside.

2. Pat the scallops dry with a paper towel. Season them with the black pepper.

3. Heat 1 tablespoon of the oil in a large wok over high heat. Add the scallops and cook on one side until well browned and caramelized, 4 to 5 minutes. Turn the scallops over and cook for 1 more minute. Transfer the scallops to a plate and set aside.

4. Add the remaining 2 tablespoons peanut oil to the wok. Add the garlic, ginger, and green onions and cook, stirring continuously, for 1 minute. Add the bell pepper and baby corn and cook, stirring, for 1 minute. Add the snow peas and cook for 30 seconds. Whisk the sauce and add it to the wok. Return the scallops to the pan and toss with the vegetables and sauce until warmed through, about 1 minute longer. Remove the wok from the heat and immediately transfer the scallops and vegetables to a serving platter or serve directly from the wok over steamed rice.

4 servings

10-VEGETABLE STIR-FRY

The keys to a successful stir-fry are using the highest heat and stirring constantly. So crank up that stove! Adding just a few veggies at a time and constantly stirring keeps the temperature of your wok from dropping dramatically and allows the veggies to cook—yes, even the broccoli. In just 10 minutes you'll have a beautiful mixture of perfectly cooked veggies that make a power-packed vegetarian entree when served over steamed jasmine rice. Eat up, kids!

$\frac{1}{4}$ cup low-sodium soy sauce

$\frac{1}{4}$ cup dry sherry

3 tablespoons canned low-sodium vegetable, chicken, or beef broth

2 tablespoon fermented black beans (black bean paste)

1 teaspoon toasted sesame oil

1 teaspoon cornstarch

1 teaspoon sugar

3 tablespoons peanut or grapeseed oil

$1\frac{1}{2}$ tablespoons peeled and minced fresh ginger

$1\frac{1}{2}$ tablespoons minced garlic

1 bunch green onions, cut into 2-inch pieces on the diagonal (about 1 cup)

2 to 3 small dried hot red chiles

$\frac{1}{2}$ green bell pepper, cut into 1-inch dice (about $\frac{3}{4}$ cup)

$\frac{1}{2}$ red bell pepper, cut into 1-inch dice (about $\frac{3}{4}$ cup)

3 small carrots, halved lengthwise and cut into $\frac{1}{8}$-inch-thick half-moons on the diagonal (about $1\frac{1}{2}$ cups)

1 celery stalk, thinly sliced on the diagonal (about $\frac{1}{2}$ cup)

2 cups halved broccoli florets

2 cups sliced shiitake mushrooms (about 4 ounces)

2 cups $\frac{1}{4}$-inch sliced red cabbage

1 cup snow peas, ends trimmed (about 4 ounces)

1 cup bean sprouts

1 teaspoon hot sesame oil (optional)

Steamed jasmine or other rice, for serving

1.   In a medium bowl, whisk together the soy sauce, sherry, broth, fermented black beans, toasted sesame oil, cornstarch, and sugar. Set the sauce aside.

2.   Heat a large wok over high heat until smoking. Add 2 tablespoons of the peanut oil, then add the ginger, garlic, green onions, and chiles and cook for 1 minute, stirring frequently (keep stirring as you make each addition). Add the bell peppers and cook for 1 minute, then add the carrots and celery and cook

for 1 minute. Add the broccoli and cook for 1 minute. Last, add the mushrooms and cook for 1 minute.

3. Make a hole in the center of the vegetables, moving them as far to the sides of the wok as possible. Add the remaining 1 tablespoon oil to the center of the wok. Add the cabbage and cook for 1 minute, stirring frequently. Incorporate the rest of the vegetables from the sides of the wok with the cabbage. Finally, add the snow peas and bean sprouts and cook for 1 minute longer, continuing to stir. Whisk the reserved sauce and add it to the wok. Cook the vegetables for 1 minute longer, tossing with the sauce, and remove from the heat. Stir in the hot sesame oil, if desired, and serve immediately over bowls of steamed rice.

4 servings

FIERY BEEF CELLOPHANE NOODLE SALAD

Have you ever walked down the noodle aisle in an Asian market? Talk about fun! There must be a thousand varieties of noodles in all shapes and sizes, made from things like potato starch, tapioca, rice, mung beans—you name it. This recipe calls for cellophane noodles, which can also be found in the international aisle of your grocery store and have little flavor on their own but are great for soaking up a flavorful, beefy sauce.

1 teaspoon salt, plus more for the pasta water

12 ounces cellophane noodles

1/4 cup freshly squeezed lime juice

1 tablespoon minced fresh red Thai bird chiles

1 tablespoon toasted sesame oil

1 tablespoon chopped fresh mint leaves

1/2 cup water

1/4 cup plus 1 tablespoon fish sauce (see page 213)

2 tablespoons plus 2 teaspoons palm sugar or light brown sugar

2 tablespoons minced garlic

2 tablespoons soy sauce

1 teaspoon hot sesame oil

1 teaspoon chili garlic sauce

1 pound beef top sirloin, sliced into 1/4-inch-thick strips across the grain

1/4 cup plus 2 tablespoons peanut oil

3 shallots, thinly sliced crosswise into rings

1/2 teaspoon freshly ground black pepper

1 tablespoon peeled and minced fresh ginger

1 cup 2-inch sliced green beans or long beans, blanched

1 cup julienned red bell pepper

Lettuce leaves, for serving

1 cup peeled, seeded, and julienned cucumber, for garnish

1/4 cup chopped fresh basil leaves, for garnish

1/4 cup chopped fresh cilantro leaves, for garnish

1/4 cup crushed roasted unsalted peanuts, for garnish

1.   Bring a large pot of salted water to a boil. Add the cellophane noodles and cook according to the package directions, usually 6 to 8 minutes. Drain the noodles in a colander and rinse under cold running water until the noodles are cool to the touch. Place the noodles in a medium mixing bowl and set aside.

2.   Make the dressing: In a small mixing bowl, combine the lime juice, chiles, toasted sesame oil, mint, water, 1/4 cup of the fish sauce, 2 tablespoons of the

palm sugar, and 2 teaspoons of the garlic. Pour half the mixture over the drained noodles and toss well to mix. Reserve the remaining half until ready to serve.

3. In a medium mixing bowl, combine the soy sauce, hot sesame oil, chili garlic sauce, 1 teaspoon of the remaining garlic, and the remaining 1 tablespoon fish sauce and 2 teaspoons palm sugar. Add the beef and toss well to combine. Let stand at room temperature for 30 minutes or refrigerate for 1 to 2 hours.

4. Heat the wok over medium-high heat and, when hot, add ¼ cup of the peanut oil. Add the shallots and fry until they just begin to turn golden brown, 1 to 2 minutes. Pay particular attention and do not let the shallots burn. Remove the shallots from the pan with a slotted spoon and set aside on a paper towel–lined plate.

5. Remove the beef from the marinade and season with ½ teaspoon of the salt and ¼ teaspoon of the black pepper. Heat 1 tablespoon of the remaining peanut oil in a wok over high heat and stir-fry the beef until it is browned and cooked through, 3 to 4 minutes. Transfer the beef to a medium mixing bowl.

6. Add the remaining 1 tablespoon peanut oil to the wok and reduce the heat to medium-high. Add the ginger and the remaining 1 tablespoon garlic and stir-fry for 30 seconds, until fragrant. Add the green beans, bell pepper, and remaining ½ teaspoon salt and ¼ teaspoon black pepper and stir-fry for 3 to 4 minutes, until the vegetables are crisp-tender. Transfer the vegetables to the same bowl as the beef.

7. To serve, line a platter with the lettuce leaves. Top with the noodles, then the vegetables and the beef. Drizzle the remaining dressing over the beef and vegetables and garnish with the cucumber, basil, cilantro, crushed peanuts, and fried shallots. Serve immediately.

4 servings

STIR-FRIED SQUID WITH CHILI SAUCE

Squid is a versatile and economical ingredient. It is relatively easy to cook as long as you follow a few simple rules. One way to keep it tender is to cook it very quickly; if it's overcooked, it will become rubbery and chewy.

2 tablespoons rice vinegar

1 tablespoon Sriracha chili sauce

1 tablespoon peeled and grated fresh ginger

1 teaspoon light brown sugar

1 teaspoon toasted sesame oil

1 teaspoon sesame seeds

½ teaspoon salt

1 pound squid tentacles and bodies

1 ½ teaspoons Korean ground chili powder (see page 230)

3 tablespoons vegetable oil

2 cups Savoy or Napa cabbage, cut into ¾-inch squares

2 fresh red Thai bird chiles, minced

2 green onions, thinly sliced on the bias

1 jalapeño chile, minced

1 clove garlic, minced

1. In a small mixing bowl, combine the vinegar, chili sauce, ginger, brown sugar, sesame oil, sesame seeds, and salt. Set aside.

2. Cut the squid bodies into ¼-inch rings. Season both the squid bodies and tentacles with the chili powder.

3. Heat 2 tablespoons of the vegetable oil in a wok over medium-high heat. When hot, add the squid and stir-fry for 2 minutes. Using a slotted spoon, transfer the squid to a paper towel–lined plate and set aside.

4. Over medium-high heat, add the remaining 1 tablespoon vegetable oil to the wok. Add the cabbage, Thai bird chiles, green onions, jalapeño, and garlic and cook, stirring, just until the cabbage begins to wilt slightly, about 3 minutes. Add the vinegar mixture and the seared squid and cook until the squid is heated through and the vegetables are tender, 1 to 2 minutes longer. Serve immediately.

4 servings

PAD THAI WITH SHRIMP AND TOFU

Pad Thai literally means "stir-fried noodles." It is one of the myriad of dishes served by street vendors, in noodle shops, and in small restaurants throughout Thailand. Pad Thai differs from region to region throughout the country, and my version is no exception. Here I incorporate fresh and dried shrimp, tofu, eggs, bean sprouts, and noodles with an unmistakable sauce.

8 ounces banh pho or dried Thai rice noodles

3 tablespoons fish sauce (see Note 1), or more to taste

2 tablespoons palm sugar

1 ½ tablespoons tamarind concentrate, or more to taste

¼ cup vegetable oil

3 eggs, lightly beaten

1 ½ pounds medium shrimp, peeled and deveined

6 ounces fried tofu (see Note 2), cut into small dice

⅓ cup minced shallot

1 tablespoon minced garlic

1 tablespoon minced dried shrimp

2 teaspoons minced fresh red Thai bird chile

2 cups bean sprouts

½ cup crushed roasted unsalted peanuts, for garnish

¼ cup chopped fresh cilantro, for garnish

2 green onions, thinly sliced on the diagonal, for garnish

2 limes, cut into wedges, for garnish

1. Soak the rice noodles in warm water for 40 minutes, or until the noodles have softened. Drain in a colander and set aside.

2. In a small bowl, combine the fish sauce, palm sugar, and tamarind concentrate; set aside.

3. Heat a wok over medium heat. When hot, add 1 tablespoon of the vegetable oil and the beaten eggs. Cook, gently swirling the pan, until the eggs have set into a thin omelet, 2 to 3 minutes. Transfer the eggs to a small plate and set aside to cool. Julienne the eggs and set aside.

4. Increase the heat to medium-high, add 2 tablespoons of the remaining vegetable oil, and cook the fresh shrimp, in batches, until just cooked through, about 2 minutes. Remove the shrimp from the wok and set aside.

5. Add the remaining 1 tablespoon vegetable oil to the wok, then add the tofu, shallot, garlic, dried

shrimp, and red chiles. Cook, stirring, over medium heat, until the tofu is heated through and the shallot begins to wilt, about 2 minutes. Add the noodles, egg, and shrimp back to the wok and toss to combine. Add the fish sauce mixture to the pan and stir until everything is well coated with the sauce. If necessary, adjust the flavor to taste by adding more fish sauce or tamarind.

6. When the noodles are heated through, add the bean sprouts. Toss to combine, then remove from the heat and top with the crushed peanuts, cilantro, and green onions. Serve immediately, garnished with the lime wedges.

4 to 6 servings

Note 1: Also known as *nam pla* in Thailand, or *nuoc nam* in Vietnam, fish sauce is a basic ingredient in Southeast Asian cooking. It is used to make marinades and sauces and is often served as a condiment. Fish sauce is derived from fish that has been salted and allowed to ferment. Fish sauce can be found in Asian markets and sometimes in the international aisle of the grocery store. There are many brands of fish sauce, but we prefer Three Crabs, Golden Boy, and Tiparos brands.

Note 2: Fried tofu is available in vacuum-sealed packages in the refrigerator section of many health food stores and Asian markets.

WHOLE FRIED FISH VERACRUZ STYLE

This dish is a collision of cultures. We fried a whole fish Chinese style in a wok, but the sauce is influenced by the town of Veracruz, Mexico, an area known for its fresh seafood. I think you'll find this to be a delicious marriage! This recipe makes a generous amount of sauce—if you're a sauce lover, it'll be just right. Alternatively, if you want to fry two fish to increase the yield to four servings, you'll have just enough sauce for both.

1 whole fish such as speckled trout, drum, or snapper, head on, scaled and gutted (1 to 1 ½ pounds)

1 ½ teaspoons salt

½ teaspoon freshly ground black pepper

½ cup rice flour

2 cups peanut oil

1 cup thinly sliced onion

1 tablespoon minced garlic

½ teaspoon dried Mexican or regular oregano, crumbled between your fingers

1 bay leaf

1 cinnamon stick

One 14.5-ounce can diced tomatoes, with juice

½ cup chicken stock or canned low-sodium chicken broth

2 tablespoons drained capers

¼ cup sliced pitted green olives

¼ cup sliced pickled jalapeño chiles, drained

2 tablespoons chopped fresh cilantro leaves

1. Using a sharp knife, make several deep diagonal slits into the flesh of the fish on both sides. Pat the fish dry with paper towels, then place it in a nonreactive baking dish and rub well on both sides with 1 teaspoon of the salt and the pepper. Dust the fish with the rice flour, shaking to remove any excess.

2. Heat the oil in a wok over high heat until it reaches 375°F. Add the fish, taking care not to splatter the oil, and cook until golden brown and completely cooked through, 12 to 15 minutes, ladling the oil over the fish continuously as it cooks. Transfer the fish to a wire rack set over paper towels to drain briefly before transferring it to a serving plate.

3. While the fish is draining, remove all but 1 tablespoon of the oil from the wok. Return the wok to high heat and add the onion. Cook, stirring, until soft and lightly caramelized, about 2 minutes. Add the garlic, oregano, bay leaf, and cinnamon stick and cook until fragrant, about 10 seconds. Add the tomatoes and stock and bring to a boil. Stir in the capers, olives, and jalapeños and cook until the sauce reduces and thickens slightly, about 10 minutes. Stir in the remaining ½ teaspoon salt. Remove the bay leaf and cinnamon stick. Spoon some of the sauce over the fish, garnish with the cilantro, and serve immediately. Pass the remaining sauce at the table for guests to use to their liking.

2 servings

PORK AND EGGPLANT STIR-FRY

Fermented black bean sauce is an intensely flavorful condiment commonly used in Chinese cuisine. It forms the backbone of this dish, which also gets a nice little kick from beloved Sriracha sauce. Tip: Boston butt is a flavorful, inexpensive cut of pork that is a bit fatty and sinewy, so you'll have to take care to trim it well. Should you prefer to use a leaner cut of pork here, substitute strips of pork loin or tenderloin and take special care not to overcook, since these cuts cook very quickly.

---

1 1/2 pounds eggplant, cut into 1/2-inch dice (6 generous cups)

Salt

2 1/2 pounds boneless Boston butt pork roast, trimmed and cut into 1/4-inch-thick strips (see Note)

1 tablespoon premium dark soy sauce

1 1/2 teaspoons cornstarch

2 tablespoons fermented black bean sauce with garlic

1 tablespoon rice vinegar

2 teaspoons Sriracha or other chili-garlic sauce

1/2 cup plus 2 tablespoons canned low-sodium chicken broth

1/4 cup plus 1 tablespoon vegetable oil

1/4 cup minced shallot

1 tablespoon minced garlic

1 pound baby bok choy, ends trimmed, stems thinly sliced, and leaves roughly chopped, reserved separately (about 4 generous cups)

2 tablespoons chopped fresh cilantro leaves

Toasted sesame oil, for garnish

Steamed jasmine rice, for serving

1.   Place the eggplant in a large mixing bowl and sprinkle lightly with salt. Toss well to coat, then spread the eggplant in a single layer on a baking sheet. Set aside for 30 minutes to drain. In a separate mixing bowl, toss the pork, dark soy sauce, and 1/2 teaspoon of the cornstarch until well coated. Set aside to marinate for 30 minutes.

2.   Combine the black bean sauce, vinegar, Sriracha, and 1/2 cup of the broth and whisk well to combine. Set the sauce aside.

3.   Combine the remaining 2 tablespoons broth in another small bowl with the remaining 1 teaspoon cornstarch and whisk to mix well. Set the thickener aside.

4. When ready to cook the stir-fry, pat the eggplant dry with paper towels.

5. Heat a wok over high heat, then add ¼ cup of the vegetable oil. When the oil is hot, add the shallot and garlic and cook, stirring constantly, for 2 to 3 seconds. Add the eggplant and cook, stirring frequently, until the eggplant is almost cooked through, about 6 minutes. Add the remaining 1 tablespoon vegetable oil along with the pork and cook, stirring, for 1 to 2 minutes. Add the bok choy stems and cook until soft, about 1 minute. Add the bok choy leaves and cook until wilted, about 1 minute longer. Add the sauce and stir to coat the ingredients well. Bring to a boil and add the cornstarch thickener. Cook until the sauce begins to thicken, about 1 minute. Sprinkle with the chopped cilantro, drizzle with a bit of sesame oil, and serve with jasmine rice.

4 servings

Note: You should have just a little over 1 pound of meat after trimming and discarding fat and sinew.

JAP CHAE

Korean vermicelli noodles are the key to this dish—and though you might never guess it, these noodles are made from sweet potato starch. Once cooked, the noodles are clear, but uncooked they have an opaque, slightly gray tint. In Korea, this basic stir-fry is often served hot off the griddle by street vendors, and it's a staple at most Korean restaurants throughout the United States. It's meant to be part of a shared meal, but personally, I want the whole thing for myself!

12 ounces Korean sweet-potato-starch noodles

8 ounces beef rib-eye steak, cut into thin strips

2 teaspoons toasted sesame oil

½ teaspoon Korean ground chili powder (see page 230)

¼ cup plus 1 tablespoon soy sauce

1 tablespoon plus 1 teaspoon sugar

3 green onions, minced

2 tablespoons minced garlic

1 tablespoon toasted sesame seeds

½ teaspoon hot sesame oil

¼ cup plus 2 tablespoons vegetable oil

1 cup stemmed and thinly sliced shiitake mushrooms

1 cup finely julienned red bell pepper

1 yellow onion, thinly sliced

1 cup julienned Napa cabbage

8 ounces spinach or tat soi (Asian greens)

½ cup julienned carrot

1. Bring a large pot of water to a boil over high heat. Add the noodles and cook for 5 minutes. Drain in a colander, reserving ¼ cup of the cooking liquid. Rinse the noodles under cool water and set the drained noodles aside.

2. In a small bowl, combine the meat, toasted sesame oil, Korean ground chili powder, 1 tablespoon of the soy sauce, 2 teaspoons of the sugar, and 1 minced green onion and set aside.

3. In a separate small bowl, make the sauce for the noodles by combining the reserved cooking liquid, garlic, sesame seeds, hot sesame oil, and the remaining ¼ cup of soy sauce and 2 teaspoons sugar. Set aside.

4. Heat 2 tablespoons of the vegetable oil in a wok over medium-high heat. Add the shiitake mushrooms and cook until golden brown, about 2 minutes. Push the mushrooms to one side of the wok and add the bell pepper, onion, cabbage, spinach, and carrot and continue to cook, stirring, until the vegetables are wilted, 3 to 4 minutes. Transfer the vegetables to a large bowl and set aside.

5.   Heat 2 tablespoons of the remaining vegetable oil in the wok, add the meat along with its marinade, and stir-fry until just cooked through, 1 to 2 minutes. Transfer the meat from the wok to the bowl with the vegetables.

6.   Heat the remaining 2 tablespoons vegetable oil, add the noodles, and stir-fry for 1 minute before adding the sauce for the noodles. Toss the noodles with the sauce to coat them evenly. Add the vegetables and the beef back to the wok and toss to combine. Serve immediately.

4 servings

KUNG PAO CHICKEN

This dish really puts the PAO in chicken! The authentic Chinese version includes a handful of Szechuan peppercorns to give it a distinctively spicy flavor, but until recently there has been a ban on importing them into the United States. Though they are finally back, they're not so easy to find. My recipe here uses crushed red pepper and Sriracha sauce in the marinade to pack a punch.

1 pound boneless, skinless chicken breast, cut crosswise into ¼-inch-thick strips

¼ cup rice vinegar

¼ cup peanut or vegetable oil

4½ tablespoons soy sauce

3 tablespoons hoisin sauce

3 tablespoons cornstarch

1 teaspoon Sriracha chili sauce

½ teaspoon salt

¼ cup plus 1 tablespoon low-sodium chicken broth

2 teaspoons sugar

One ½-inch piece fresh ginger, peeled, cut into ⅛-inch-thick slices, and smashed

1½ teaspoons minced garlic

½ teaspoon crushed red pepper

3 green onions, sliced diagonally, white and green parts reserved separately

One 8-ounce can bamboo shoots, drained

1 small red bell pepper, julienned

⅓ cup roasted unsalted cashews or peanuts

Steamed white rice, for serving

1. In a medium bowl, combine the chicken with 2 tablespoons of the vinegar, 2 tablespoons of the oil, 2 tablespoons of the soy sauce, 2 tablespoons of the hoisin sauce, 2 tablespoons of the cornstarch, the Sriracha sauce, and the salt. Cover with plastic wrap and marinate, refrigerated, for 20 to 30 minutes. Remove the chicken and discard the marinade. Reserve the chicken until ready to cook the stir-fry.

2. To make the sauce, combine 3 tablespoons of the chicken broth, the remaining 2½ tablespoons soy sauce and 2 tablespoons vinegar, the sugar, and the remaining 1 tablespoon hoisin sauce in a small mixing bowl. Set the sauce aside.

3. Whisk the remaining 2 tablespoons chicken broth and 1 tablespoon cornstarch in another small mixing bowl until combined. Set the cornstarch thickener aside.

4. Heat the remaining 2 tablespoons oil in a wok over high heat. Add the ginger and garlic and cook,

stirring constantly, for 5 seconds. (The oil should be very hot, but not quite smoking. Take care when stirring so that the oil does not splash out of the wok.) Add the chicken and the crushed red pepper to the hot wok and cook, stirring, for 2 to 3 minutes. Add the white parts of the green onion, the bamboo shoots, and the red bell pepper. Cook for 1 minute, stirring constantly.

5. Stir in the sauce and bring to a boil. Stir the cornstarch thickener and add it to the wok. Cook, stirring, until the sauce boils and thickens. Add the cashews and stir to coat.

6. Remove from the heat and garnish with the green parts of the green onion. Serve hot over steamed rice.

4 to 6 servings

MUSSELS IN A GREEN CURRY BROTH

What's not to love about coconut milk and curry paste? This is an easy one! Steam your mussels in this intense broth, toss with chopped fresh herbs, and enjoy with hearty bread.

2 tablespoons peanut or other vegetable oil

1 cup chopped onion

2 tablespoons minced shallot

1 tablespoon minced garlic

1 small dried hot red chile

1 1/2 teaspoons salt

3 tablespoons green curry paste (see Note)

1 1/2 cups peeled, seeded, and diced tomato

1/2 cup dry white wine

One 14-ounce can unsweetened coconut milk

4 pounds mussels, scrubbed well and debearded

1/4 cup chopped fresh cilantro leaves

1/4 cup chopped fresh mint leaves

1/4 cup chopped fresh basil leaves

Hot crusty bread, for serving

1. Heat a large wok over high heat until smoking. Add the oil and, when hot, add the onion, shallot, garlic, chile, salt, and curry paste. Cook, stirring continuously, for 2 minutes. Add the tomatoes and white wine and cook for 2 minutes longer. Pour in the coconut milk and bring to a rolling boil. Add the mussels and cover the wok with a lid or an inverted large metal bowl. Cook until the mussels just open, about 7 minutes. Uncover the wok and discard any unopened mussels. Add the fresh herbs and stir well to combine.

2. Serve the mussels in shallow bowls, with the hot broth ladled over all. Pass crusty bread at the table.

Note: Green curry paste can be found in Asian markets or in the international aisles of most grocery stores. It is sold in packets, jars, and cans.

4 servings

SALT AND PEPPER SHRIMP

We make this dish the way it's traditionally made in China, cooked quickly with the shrimp shells still on. It makes for some interesting, crispy eating, let me tell you. If you happen to be someone who just can't get used to the idea, simply peel the shrimp before eating . . . you'll still find them delicious.

2 pounds large shell-on shrimp

4 cups peanut oil, or as needed

1 red bell pepper, cut into thin strips

1 green bell pepper, cut into thin strips

2 tablespoons very thinly sliced garlic

2 tablespoons thinly sliced green onion, white part only

1 tablespoon peeled and minced fresh ginger

1 tablespoon plus 1 teaspoon fine sea salt

1 tablespoon plus 1 teaspoon coarsely ground mixed peppercorns

½ teaspoon freshly ground black pepper

¼ teaspoon cayenne

2 tablespoons chopped fresh cilantro leaves

1 lime, cut into wedges, for serving

Steamed jasmine rice, for serving

1. Using cooking shears, cut the shrimp shells lengthwise along the back, leaving the last segment intact. Cut off the legs and the pointy end on top of the tail but keep the rest of the shells on. Remove the vein. Rinse, drain, and pat dry.

2. Add the peanut oil to a large wok (the oil should be 3 to 4 inches deep) and heat until it reaches 400°F. Working in batches, cook the shrimp until they turn pink and the shells have curled, 45 to 60 seconds (the shrimp will not be fully cooked through). Transfer to a paper towel–lined plate. Transfer all but 1 tablespoon of the oil to a heatproof bowl to cool; discard when cooled.

3. Heat the wok with the remaining tablespoon of oil over high heat. When hot, add the bell peppers and sauté, stirring, for 1 minute. Add the garlic, green onion, and ginger and cook until fragrant, 10 to 15 seconds. Add the shrimp, sea salt, mixed peppercorns, black pepper, and cayenne; toss to coat well and cook until the shrimp are just cooked through, about 10 seconds.

4. Sprinkle with the cilantro and transfer to a serving plate. Serve, garnished with the lime wedges, over jasmine rice.

4 servings

KARAHI CHICKEN

A karahi is an East Indian version of a wok—hence the name of this quick Indian-inspired stir-fry—but feel free to use a traditional Chinese wok to make this delicious curried dish. The recipe calls for moong dal—dal (also spelled *dahl* or *dhall*) being the Hindi term for the seeds of dried legumes and moong dal referring to the hulled and split mung bean—which can be found in most Asian or East Indian specialty markets and in some health food stores. The dal adds body to the sauce here and makes this a satisfying and nutritionally well-rounded dish.

3 tablespoons ghee (see page 69)

1 pound boneless, skinless chicken breast, sliced crosswise into 1/4-inch strips

2 teaspoons salt

1 tablespoon freshly squeezed lemon juice

One 3-inch cinnamon stick

4 cardamom pods

3 whole cloves

3 dried hot red chiles

1 cup small-diced onion

1 tablespoon minced garlic

1 teaspoon ground turmeric

1 teaspoon ground cumin

1/2 teaspoon garam masala

1/2 cup moong dal

2 1/2 cups chicken stock or canned low-sodium chicken broth

1/2 cup unsweetened coconut milk

1 1/2 cups frozen lima beans, thawed

1 1/2 cups halved cherry tomatoes

1/4 cup chopped fresh cilantro leaves, for garnish

Steamed basmati rice, for serving

1. Heat 1 tablespoon of the ghee in a wok over high heat. Add the chicken and 1/2 teaspoon of salt and cook, stirring, until the chicken is opaque, 2 to 3 minutes. Transfer the chicken from the wok to a plate. Working quickly, drizzle the lemon juice over the chicken, toss to coat well, and set aside.

2. Melt 1 tablespoon of the remaining ghee in the wok and add the cinnamon, cardamom, cloves, and red chiles. Cook, stirring, until toasted and fragrant, about 10 seconds. Remove with a spoon and place in a piece of cheesecloth. Secure the cheesecloth with twine and set aside.

3. Melt the remaining 1 tablespoon ghee in the wok, then add the onion and 1/2 teaspoon of the remaining salt. Cook until the onion is soft and lightly caramelized, about 2 minutes. Add the garlic and cook until fragrant, about 15 seconds. Add the turmeric, cumin, and garam masala and stir to mix well, 30 seconds.

Add the moong dal and cook, stirring, until toasted, about 30 seconds. Add the cheesecloth bundle, the stock, coconut milk, and the remaining 1 teaspoon salt and bring to a boil. Cover the wok with a lid, reduce the heat to a simmer, and cook, undisturbed, until the moong dal is almost tender, about 12 minutes. Add the lima beans and cook until tender, about 10 minutes. Uncover and add the chicken and the tomatoes, cooking until the chicken is just cooked through, about 2 minutes.

4.   Remove the cheesecloth bundle. Stir in the cilantro and serve with a side of basmati rice.

4 servings

UDON NOODLE STIR-FRY
WITH VEGETABLES

Udon is a thick-cut Japanese noodle that has great texture. The noodles soak up the flavor of the broth that they are cooked in and are a wonderful addition to a stir-fry. We loaded this one up with lots of veggies—shiitake mushrooms, carrots, and watercress, to name a few. Enjoy!

1/4 cup chicken stock or canned low-sodium chicken broth

3 tablespoons soy sauce

2 tablespoons sake

1 tablespoon oyster sauce

1 teaspoon ponzu sauce

1 teaspoon red miso

1/2 teaspoon palm sugar or light brown sugar

1/4 cup plus 1 tablespoon vegetable oil

6 ounces oyster mushrooms, chopped

Salt

5 ounces shiitake mushrooms, stemmed and thinly sliced

1 large red bell pepper, julienned

1/2 cup julienned carrot

1/2 cup thinly sliced red onion

1 tablespoon plus 1 teaspoon minced garlic

2 green onions, white part minced, green part sliced on the bias, reserved separately

1 1/2 teaspoons peeled and minced fresh ginger

12 ounces baby watercress, ends trimmed

2 1/4 pounds frozen udon noodles, cooked according to the package directions and drained

1 tablespoon hot sesame oil

2 tablespoons chopped fresh cilantro leaves

1.   In a small bowl, combine the stock, soy sauce, sake, oyster sauce, ponzu, miso, and palm sugar and whisk well to combine. Set the sauce aside.

2.   Heat 1/4 cup of the vegetable oil in a wok over high heat. When hot, add the oyster mushrooms and a pinch of salt and cook until the mushrooms begin to brown and wilt, about 2 minutes. Add the shiitake mushrooms and another pinch of salt and continue to cook until all the mushrooms are nicely browned, 2 to 3 minutes longer.

3.   Add the remaining 1 tablespoon vegetable oil, the bell pepper, carrot, and red onion and cook until the vegetables just begin to soften, about 2 minutes. Add

the garlic, minced green onion, and ginger and cook until fragrant, about 30 seconds. Add the watercress and cook for another 30 seconds. Add the noodles and the reserved sauce and toss to combine. Cook until heated through, 1 to 2 minutes. Remove from the heat.

4. Drizzle with the hot sesame oil and toss quickly to combine, then serve immediately, garnished with the sliced green onion and chopped cilantro.

4 to 6 servings

KIMCHI-FRIED RICE

Kimchi is a pungent, often spicy mixture of fermented vegetables. In Korea the versions of kimchi vary depending on both the season and the cook. A lighter, more vinegary version is made in spring and summer, while a spicy, heartier version is prepared in large batches for the fall and winter seasons. Traditionally, kimchi was always prepared in the home, but today it is more often made commercially. Kimchi is sold in the refrigerated section of most health food stores or your local Asian market and is also available online.

1 cup short-grain rice, such as sushi rice

1 1/2 cups water

1/4 cup vegetable oil

2 eggs, lightly beaten

1 pound beef top sirloin, sliced across the grain into 1/4-inch-thick strips

1 clove garlic, minced

3 tablespoons toasted sesame oil, plus more for serving

1/4 cup plus 1 tablespoon soy sauce

2 tablespoons lightly toasted sesame seeds

1 teaspoon Korean ground chili powder (see Note)

4 ounces shiitake mushrooms, stemmed and thinly sliced

4 green onions, julienned

2 carrots, julienned

1 medium zucchini, cut into 1/4-inch-thick half-moons

1 cup spinach, with tough stems removed

3 cups kimchi (about 1 1/2 pounds), roughly chopped

1 to 2 sheets seasoned roasted nori, torn or cut into small pieces, for garnish (optional)

1. Place the rice in a fine-mesh sieve and rinse gently under cold running water until the water begins to run clear. Combine the drained rice and the water in a medium saucepan over high heat and bring to a boil, uncovered. Once it begins to boil, reduce the heat to the lowest setting, stir the rice, cover, and cook for 15 minutes. Remove from the heat and let stand, covered and undisturbed, for 5 minutes.

2. Place the hot rice in a mixing bowl and cover with cool water. Swirl the rice in the water, pour the water off, and then repeat two to three more times, or until the water remains clear. Drain the rice in a colander, spread it out on a baking sheet, and refrigerate, uncovered, for at least 2 hours and up to overnight. This will allow the rice to dry out.

3. Heat 1 tablespoon of the vegetable oil in a wok over medium-low heat, then add the eggs. Cook until

they are just set, swirling the pan to make a thin omelet. Transfer the eggs to a platter to cool. Once cool, slice the eggs into thin strips and set aside.

4.   In a small mixing bowl, combine the sirloin strips with the garlic, 1 tablespoon of the sesame oil, 2 tablespoons of the soy sauce, and 1 tablespoon of the sesame seeds. Set aside. In another small mixing bowl, combine the Korean chili powder, 2 tablespoons of the remaining soy sauce, and the remaining 2 tablespoons sesame oil and 1 tablespoon sesame seeds.

5.   Place the mushrooms in a medium mixing bowl. Combine the green onions, carrots, and zucchini in a separate bowl. Divide the chili-soy mixture evenly between the two bowls of vegetables.

6.   Place a wok over medium-high heat and, when hot, add 1 tablespoon of the remaining vegetable oil. Add the mushrooms and sauté until the mushrooms are golden brown on all sides, about 2 minutes. Return the mushrooms to the medium bowl and set aside. Add the green onions, carrots, and zucchini and stir-fry until the vegetables are crisp-tender, 3 to 4 minutes. Add the spinach and cook until it is just wilted, about 2 minutes. Transfer the vegetables to the bowl with the mushrooms and set aside.

7.   Add half of the beef to the hot wok and cook until it is browned and just cooked through, 3 to 5 minutes. Transfer the beef to the bowl with the vegetables. Add the remaining beef to the wok and repeat. Transfer the beef to the bowl and set aside.

8.   Add 1 tablespoon of the remaining vegetable oil to the wok. When hot, add the chopped kimchi and its juices. Cook the kimchi, stirring frequently, for 3 to 4 minutes, or until the liquid has concentrated and the kimchi is heated through. Transfer the kimchi to the bowl with the beef and vegetables and set aside.

9. Reduce the heat to medium and add the remaining 1 tablespoon vegetable oil and the rice. Cook, stirring gently, until the rice is heated through, 2 to 3 minutes. Add the beef-vegetable-kimchi mixture and continue cooking and stirring for another 2 minutes. Add the egg and cook for 1 minute longer.

10. Drizzle the remaining 1 tablespoon soy sauce over the top, garnish with the roasted nori, the toasted sesame oil, and serve immediately.

4 to 6 servings

Note: Korean ground chili powder, also known as *gochu galu,* is made from small red chiles that are dried and ground. It's not as finely ground as cayenne, but finer than our crushed red pepper, and it carries quite a bit of heat. While you can find it in Asian markets and online, crushed red pepper pulsed in a spice mill or in a food processor can be substituted in a pinch.

MISO-GLAZED SCALLOPS WITH SOBA NOODLES

Miso is a fermented bean paste made from soybeans. It is generally used as a base for soups, sauces, and dressings and comes in a variety of colors ranging from a light yellow to a dark red; the darker the miso, the deeper the flavor. Miso has a salty, earthy flavor that, when used in conjunction with sake, provides the perfect balance for a simple and subtle sauce for scallops.

8 ounces soba noodles

¼ cup plus 2 tablespoons red miso

¼ cup sake

3 tablespoons peanut oil

2 tablespoons rice vinegar

1 teaspoon peeled and minced fresh ginger

1 teaspoon minced garlic

12 large (U-10) sea scallops, cut in half crosswise and patted dry with a paper towel

4 cups chopped bok choy

1 ½ cups diced red bell pepper

1 ½ tablespoons minced green onion

1 tablespoon minced shallot

1 fresh red Thai bird chile, minced

½ cup vegetable or chicken stock or canned low-sodium vegetable or chicken broth

1. Bring a large pot of water to a boil. Cook the noodles according to the package directions, stirring occasionally, until tender, 6 to 8 minutes. Drain the noodles in a colander, transfer to a bowl, and set aside.

2. In a medium bowl, whisk together the miso, sake, 2 tablespoons of the oil, the vinegar, ginger, and garlic. Transfer half the marinade to a resealable plastic food storage bag and reserve the marinade remaining in the bowl. Add the scallops to the bag, seal it, and set aside to marinate for 10 minutes. Remove the scallops from the bag, discard the marinade, and pat them dry.

3. Heat a wok over medium-high heat and add the remaining 1 tablespoon oil. When very hot, add half the scallops and cook until golden brown and just cooked through, 2 to 3 minutes per side. Transfer to a plate and cover to keep warm. Repeat with the remaining scallops. Add the bok choy, bell pepper, green onion, shallot, chile, and stock to the wok and cook until the stock has evaporated, 4 to 5 minutes. Transfer to a platter; set aside. Add the noodles to the wok along with the reserved marinade and cook until heated through, 2 minutes.

4. Place the noodles on a platter and top with the bok choy and the scallops. Serve immediately.

6 servings

WOK-SEARED DUCK SALAD

This recipe was inspired by a Thai dish called *laap*, which is made with minced or ground chicken, fish, pork, or duck and seasoned with the wonderful flavors of chiles, ginger, fish sauce, and citrus. I decided to use the same flavors with a seared duck breast and make it into more of a main-course salad. This is a refreshing take on northern Thai street food.

2 tablespoons uncooked jasmine rice

1 tablespoon minced fresh red Thai bird chile

2 magret duck breasts (about 12 ounces each) or 1 ½ pounds other domestic duck breasts

⅓ cup minced shallot

1 ½ tablespoons peeled and minced fresh ginger

¼ cup fish sauce (see page 213)

¼ cup freshly squeezed lime juice

¼ cup freshly squeezed orange juice

1 ½ teaspoons palm sugar or light brown sugar

½ cup fresh cilantro leaves

½ cup fresh mint leaves

½ cup fresh basil leaves

1 medium head of red leaf lettuce, washed and torn into bite-sized pieces

2 cups bean sprouts

1 cup julienned red bell pepper

1. Heat a wok over medium-high heat and add the rice. Toast the rice, shaking the wok constantly, until all the grains have turned golden brown, 3 to 4 minutes. Transfer the rice to a mortar and set aside to cool. Once the rice has cooled, grind it using a pestle until it reaches a sandy consistency. Alternatively, grind the toasted rice in a clean spice grinder. Place the rice in a large mixing bowl and set aside.

2. Place the chile in the wok over medium-high heat and cook, shaking the wok, until lightly colored and fragrant, 30 to 60 seconds. Remove the chile from the pan and add to the bowl with the rice.

3. Using a paring knife, score the fatty side of the duck breasts by making shallow cuts in a diamond pattern; this allows the fat to render more easily. Place the duck breasts in the wok, fatty side down, and cook over medium heat until the skin is golden brown and slightly crisp, 4 to 5 minutes. Transfer the duck breasts to a cutting board, slice them into thin strips, and return the strips to the wok. Add the shallot and ginger and stir-fry over medium-high heat until the duck is just cooked through, about 2 minutes. Transfer the duck from the wok to the bowl with the rice and chile and set aside.

4.   In a small bowl, combine the fish sauce, lime juice, orange juice, and palm sugar and mix well. Pour the mixture over the duck and toss until well coated. Add the cilantro, mint, basil, lettuce, bean sprouts, and julienned red pepper and toss to combine.

5.   Serve the salad immediately.

4 servings

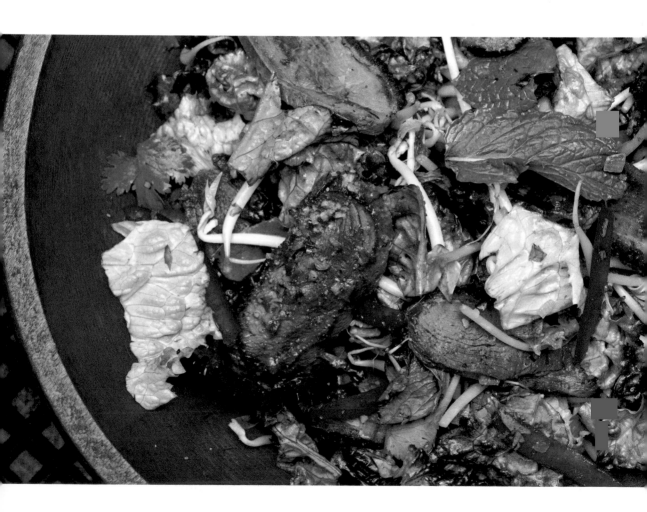

TEMPURA "FISH AND CHIPS"

Try my Japanese twist on the classic "fish and chips": here we use sweet potatoes and a tempura batter to really kick things up. The tempura batter makes for an extra-light and crispy coating, and, oh man, the simple ponzu sauce is great drizzled over everything!

½ cup ponzu sauce

2 tablespoons finely shredded radish

½ cup water

5 cups peanut oil or enough to come 2 to 3 inches up the sides of a wok

2 egg yolks, beaten

1½ cups cold seltzer water

1 cup all-purpose flour

½ cup cornstarch

¼ cup rice flour

2 teaspoons salt

1 pound sweet potatoes, peeled and cut into ⅛-inch-thick slices

1½ pounds skinless firm-fleshed white fish fillets (such as grouper), cut into 3×1½-inch pieces

½ teaspoon freshly ground black pepper

1. Combine the ponzu sauce, shredded radish, and water in a dipping bowl. Stir to mix well and set aside until ready to serve.

2. Add the oil to a large wok and heat over high heat until it reaches 375°F.

3. While the oil is heating, combine the egg yolks and seltzer in a medium mixing bowl and whisk to mix well. In another bowl, sift together the all-purpose flour, cornstarch, rice flour, and 1 teaspoon of the salt. Add the flour mixture to the egg mixture and stir quickly to combine, taking care not to over-work the batter (lumps are okay). Working in batches, dip the sweet potato slices into the batter, allowing excess to drain off, and place them in the hot oil. Cook, working in small batches so as not to overcrowd the pan, until golden brown and crisp, about 2 minutes. Remove from the oil with a slotted spoon and transfer to a paper towel–lined baking sheet to drain. Season lightly with salt. When all the sweet potatoes have been fried, set them aside while you fry the fish.

4. Pat the fish dry with paper towels and season on both sides with the pepper and remaining 1 teaspoon salt. Working in batches, dip the fish in the batter and add it to the hot oil. Cook, taking care not to

overcrowd the pan, until the fish flakes easily and the batter is crisp and golden brown, turning as necessary, 5 to 6 minutes. Remove from the oil and transfer to a paper towel–lined tray to drain briefly before serving.

5. Serve the "fish and chips" with the ponzu dipping sauce.

4 to 6 servings

BEEF AND BROCCOLI

Here's an at-home version of a favorite dish from your local Chinese cuisine hot spot. The family will go crazy over this one—talk about a fun way to get the kids to eat their broccoli!

½ cup oyster sauce

¼ cup low-sodium soy sauce

2 tablespoons plus 2 teaspoons rice vinegar

2 tablespoons orange blossom honey or your favorite local honey

2 teaspoons toasted sesame oil

1 teaspoon crushed red pepper

2 pounds beef flank steak, thinly sliced across the grain (freeze slightly for easier slicing)

¼ cup cornstarch

6 tablespoons peanut oil

1 bunch green onions, cut into 2-inch pieces on the diagonal (about 1 cup)

1 red bell pepper, cut into 1-inch dice (about 1 ½ cups)

2 tablespoons minced garlic

2 tablespoons peeled and minced fresh ginger

2 large heads of broccoli, cut into florets

2 teaspoons sesame seeds

Steamed rice, for serving

1. Combine the oyster sauce, soy sauce, vinegar, honey, sesame oil, and crushed red pepper. Mix well and set aside.

2. Toss the beef in the cornstarch, shake to remove any excess, and set aside.

3. Heat a wok or large skillet over high heat. Add 2 tablespoons of the peanut oil. Once it begins to smoke, add the green onions, bell pepper, garlic, and ginger and cook for 1 minute. Add the broccoli and cook, stirring frequently, for 3 minutes. Transfer the broccoli and peppers to a small platter and set aside.

4. Add 2 tablespoons of the remaining peanut oil to the wok. Add half of the beef and sauté, stirring frequently, until browned, about 1 minute. Transfer the beef to the platter with the broccoli. Add the remaining 2 tablespoons peanut oil to the pan and cook the remaining beef.

5. Return the reserved broccoli and beef mixture to the wok. Add the sauce and cook, stirring to coat the beef and broccoli evenly, until warmed through, about 2 minutes. Add the sesame seeds, stir to combine, and serve immediately with steamed rice.

4 to 6 servings

BANH XEO: VIETNAMESE CRÊPE

There is a thriving Vietnamese community in New Orleans, so you don't have to go far to find amazing Vietnamese restaurants, bakeries, and markets. Perhaps one of my favorite Vietnamese dishes is banh xeo, a thin and crispy crêpe filled with shrimp, pork, and bean sprouts. The best way to eat it is to tear off a piece of the crêpe, place it in a lettuce leaf, top with the pickled vegetables and herb leaves, and dip the whole thing in the Spicy Vietnamese Dipping Sauce. Yum!

½ cup peeled and split mung beans (moong dal; see page 224)

2 cups unsweetened coconut milk

1 cup rice flour

¾ teaspoon sugar

½ teaspoon ground turmeric

½ teaspoon salt

12 ounces boneless pork loin, thinly sliced crosswise and cut into ¼-inch strips

1 pound medium shrimp, peeled, deveined, and halved lengthwise

1 ½ tablespoons Vietnamese fish sauce (nuoc nam)

2 cloves garlic, minced

¼ teaspoon freshly ground black pepper

4 green onions, thinly sliced

2 cups bean sprouts

Vegetable oil, for frying

Red leaf lettuce leaves, for serving

Fresh mint, cilantro, and basil leaves, for serving

Pickled Cucumber, Carrot, and Daikon (recipe follows), for serving

Spicy Vietnamese Dipping Sauce (recipe follows), for serving

1. In a small bowl, soak the mung beans in warm water until softened, about 30 minutes. Drain the beans and transfer them to a blender. Add the coconut milk and puree until very smooth. Transfer to a bowl and whisk in the rice flour, ½ teaspoon of the sugar, and the turmeric; season with the salt. Refrigerate the crêpe batter for 1 hour.

2. In a large bowl, combine the pork, shrimp, fish sauce, garlic, the remaining ¼ teaspoon sugar, and black pepper. Let stand for 15 to 20 minutes.

3. In a separate bowl, combine the green onions and bean sprouts. Divide the mixture into 6 small, separate mounds and place them on a clean work surface.

4. Heat 1 tablespoon vegetable oil in a wok. When hot, add the pork and shrimp mixture and sauté until nearly cooked through, about 2 minutes. Transfer to a platter and set aside.

5. Preheat the oven to 200°F. In a wok or a 10-inch nonstick omelet pan, heat 2 tablespoons vegetable oil over medium heat. When the oil is very hot, swirl to coat the pan. Stir the crêpe batter well and then pour ½ cup of the batter into the hot pan; tilt and swirl the pan to coat with a thin layer of batter on the bottom and partially up the sides. Scatter the crêpe with 1 of the vegetable mounds, 4 slices of the pork, and 4 pieces of shrimp. Reduce the heat and cook until the bottom of the crêpe is golden and crispy, 2 to 3 minutes. Using a spatula, loosen the crêpe from the bottom of the pan and gently fold in half. Slide the crêpe onto an ovenproof plate or platter and transfer to the oven to keep warm. Repeat with the remaining ingredients, adding oil between crêpes as needed.

6. To serve, place 1 crêpe onto a plate and serve with bowls of the lettuce, herbs, and pickled vegetables for guests to use to their liking. Each guest should receive a small dipping bowl with some of the Spicy Vietnamese Dipping Sauce, for drizzling.

6 crêpes

PICKLED CUCUMBER, CARROT, AND DAIKON

1 ¼ cups rice vinegar
3 tablespoons sugar
¼ teaspoon crushed red pepper
¼ teaspoon salt
2 carrots, julienned
1 cucumber, julienned
1 cup julienned daikon

In a small nonreactive saucepan, combine the vinegar, sugar, crushed red pepper, and salt and bring to a boil, stirring until the sugar is dissolved. Remove from the heat and allow to cool slightly. Transfer to a nonreactive mixing bowl and add the carrots, cucumber, and daikon. Stir to combine, then refrigerate for at least 30 minutes and up to overnight.

About 3 cups

SPICY VIETNAMESE DIPPING
SAUCE (NUOC CHAM)

2 teaspoons sugar

2 teaspoons red chili paste or 1 finely chopped red chile

2 to 3 tablespoons Vietnamese fish sauce (nuoc nam),
    to taste

1 to 2 tablespoons freshly squeezed lime juice, to taste

1 clove garlic, minced

1 teaspoon peeled and minced fresh ginger

1 teaspoon minced green onion

$\frac{1}{4}$ cup water

Combine all the ingredients in a nonreactive bowl and stir to
blend. Taste and adjust the seasoning if necessary.

1 cup

SLOW

Cookers

For the family on the go, the SLOW COOKER may be the most necessary piece of equipment in the kitchen.

CHICKEN IN THE POT

Here's a delectable country-French-inspired dish you can make in your slow cooker. The only effort involved is in browning the chicken. Though it may be tempting, don't skip this step; there are few things more enticing than a golden chicken, in its own juices, with vegetables. So take your time, add it to your slow cooker, and walk away.

One 4-pound whole chicken, excess fat removed, rinsed and patted dry

1 tablespoon kosher salt

1 teaspoon freshly ground black pepper

1 tablespoon unsalted butter

4 ounces applewood-smoked bacon, cut into 1/2-inch pieces

3 medium carrots, peeled and cut into 4-inch lengths

2 medium onions, chopped into large pieces

1 celery stalk, cut into 1/2-inch pieces

1 3/4 pounds new potatoes (about 12)

4 garlic cloves, smashed and peeled

1 tablespoon dried thyme, crumbled between your fingers

1/2 cup dry white wine

1 tablespoon chopped fresh parsley leaves, for serving

1. Season the chicken inside and out with the salt and pepper. Tuck the wings behind the back and tie the legs together with kitchen twine.

2. In a Dutch oven large enough to hold the chicken, melt the butter over medium heat. Add the bacon and cook, stirring as needed, until the fat is rendered and the bacon is crispy. Transfer the bacon to a paper towel–lined plate and set aside.

3. Place the chicken on its back in the Dutch oven. Cook until nicely browned, 4 to 5 minutes. Carefully turn the chicken onto its breast and brown for 4 to 5 minutes longer. (Stick the handle of a long wooden spoon into the cavity of the chicken to help you maneuver it.) Turn the chicken on its side and cook for 4 to 5 minutes. Repeat on the other side. Transfer the browned chicken to the crock of a 6-quart slow cooker.

4. Add the carrots, onions, celery, potatoes, garlic, and thyme to the Dutch oven. Cook, stirring as needed, until the vegetables are nicely glazed, about 4 minutes. Remove from the heat and transfer the vegetables to the slow cooker, scattered around and under the chicken so that everything will fit. Add the bacon and wine. Cover, set the slow cooker on high,

and cook until the chicken and vegetables are very tender, about 4 hours. Remove the chicken from the slow cooker and set aside to rest for 15 minutes before serving.

5. Using a large metal spoon, divide the vegetables and broth among serving bowls. You will be able to portion the chicken easily with the spoon. Lay the chicken pieces over the vegetables. Sprinkle with the parsley and serve immediately.

4 to 6 servings

MUSHROOM AND FALL SQUASH
BARLEY RISOTTO

Barley's chewy texture offers a nice alternative to the typical Arborio rice used in most risotto and also happens to offer more nutritional value. Here sautéed baby bella mushrooms and acorn squash enhance barley's wonderful, earthy flavor.

5 tablespoons unsalted butter

2 tablespoons grapeseed or canola oil

½ cup finely chopped shallot

1 ½ cups pearled barley

1 ½ teaspoons salt

½ teaspoon freshly ground black pepper

¼ cup dry white wine

¾ pound baby bella mushrooms, stems trimmed, sliced ⅛ inch thick

12 ounces acorn squash, peeled, seeded, and diced

4 cups chicken stock or canned low-sodium chicken broth

2 tablespoons chopped fresh parsley

1 tablespoon chopped fresh sage

¾ cup finely grated Parmigiano-Reggiano cheese

1. Heat 1 tablespoon of the butter and 1 tablespoon of the oil in a 12-inch sauté pan over medium-high heat. When hot, add the shallot and cook, stirring, until tender, 1 to 2 minutes. Add the barley, salt, and pepper and cook for 1 minute. Pour in the wine and cook, stirring, until the wine is evaporated, 1 to 2 minutes. Transfer to the crock of a 6-quart slow cooker.

2. Add 2 tablespoons of the remaining butter and the remaining 1 tablespoon oil to the sauté pan over medium-high heat. Add the mushrooms and cook until lightly browned and wilted and the fat has been absorbed, 4 to 5 minutes.

3. Add the mushrooms, squash, and stock to the slow cooker. Stir gently to combine. Set the slow cooker to low and cook until the liquid is absorbed and the barley and squash are tender, 2½ to 3 hours, stirring occasionally to ensure that all the grains are evenly cooked. Remove the lid and stir in the parsley, sage, ½ cup of the Parmesan, and the remaining 2 tablespoons butter. Serve the risotto hot, garnished with the remaining cheese and additional pepper if desired.

4 to 6 servings

BRAISED PORK CHOPS WITH APPLES AND ONIONS

These pork chops are as tender as can be. Cooked with sweet apples and onions, everything mingles to make a delicious gravy that would be wonderful over rice, buttered noodles, or even mashed potatoes.

2 teaspoons kosher salt

1 teaspoon paprika

½ teaspoon cayenne

6 center-cut pork chops, ½ inch thick (about 2 ½ pounds)

¼ cup plus 2 tablespoons all-purpose flour

¼ cup plus 2½ tablespoons olive oil

2 medium onions, cut into ¼-inch slices

⅓ cup Calvados or other brandy

1 ½ cups chicken stock or canned low-sodium chicken broth

½ teaspoon caraway seeds

2 bay leaves

2 teaspoons salt

1 teaspoon freshly ground black pepper

1 teaspoon chopped fresh thyme

1 teaspoon chopped fresh marjoram

2 Granny Smith apples, cored and cut into ¼-inch slices, sprinkled with lemon juice to prevent browning if sliced ahead

1. Combine the kosher salt, paprika, and cayenne and mix well. Using paper towels, lightly pat the pork chops dry, then season the chops on both sides with the salt mixture. Lightly dredge the pork chops in ¼ cup of the flour.

2. Heat 1½ tablespoons of the olive oil in a 12-inch sauté pan over medium-high heat. Add the pork chops, 2 at a time, and cook until lightly browned, about 2 minutes per side. Transfer the pork chops to the crock of a 6-quart slow cooker. Repeat with the remaining pork chops, adding a tablespoon of the olive oil to the pan with each batch.

3. Add 1 tablespoon of the remaining oil to the pan along with the onions and season with a pinch of salt. Sauté, stirring, for 30 seconds, then add the Calvados, scraping to remove any browned bits from the bottom of the pan. Cook until most of the alcohol has evaporated, about 30 seconds. Transfer to a plate and set aside.

4. Turn the heat down to medium. Add the remaining 2 tablespoons oil and 2 tablespoons flour. Cook, stirring constantly, until the flour is lightly browned and smells nutty. Whisk in the stock, bring to a boil, and cook until the mixture has thickened, about 1 minute. Pour over the pork chops and add the cara-

way seeds, bay leaves, 2 teaspoons salt, pepper, and half of the herbs. Top with the onions, then cover the slow cooker.

5. Set the temperature to high and cook until the pork chops are very tender, about 4 hours. Check the pork chops once or twice during cooking, gently shifting them around in the crock so that they are evenly submerged in the cooking liquid to promote even cooking. During the last 45 minutes, push the onions aside and layer with the apples. Cover the apples with the onions and finish cooking. Remove the bay leaves. Sprinkle with the remaining herbs and serve hot with a side of your choice.

4 to 6 servings

MINESTRONE

Minestrone is an Italian vegetable soup made with the best vegetables you can find. Don't panic when you see the lengthy ingredient list here—this dish is easily adapted to use whichever veggies you have in your pantry or fridge. Minestrone often contains pasta, beans, and sometimes meat—tailor it to suit your taste!

5 tablespoons extra-virgin olive oil

½ cup small-diced pancetta or thick-cut bacon

1 cup diced yellow onion

½ cup half-moon or quarter-cut carrot

½ cup diced celery

½ cup diced fennel

4 cloves garlic, minced

¾ cup diced peeled celery root

½ cup diced peeled turnip

½ cup half-moon or quarter-cut peeled parsnip

½ cup stemmed and diced shiitake mushrooms

½ cup diced yellow bell pepper

½ cup diced red bell pepper

½ cup diced orange bell pepper

One 14.5-ounce can diced tomatoes, with juice

¾ cup tubetti or other small soup pasta

One 1×3-inch Parmigiano-Reggiano cheese rind

10 cups beef or chicken stock or canned low-sodium beef or chicken broth

1 tablespoon salt

1 teaspoon freshly ground black pepper

1 bunch lacinato kale, other kale, or spinach, cut into bite-sized pieces

½ cup diced zucchini

½ cup diced yellow squash

½ cup ½-inch sliced green beans

¼ cup thinly sliced fresh basil

2 tablespoons chopped fresh parsley

½ cup freshly grated Parmigiano-Reggiano cheese, plus more for serving

Warm crusty bread, for serving

1. Heat 2 tablespoons of the olive oil in a medium skillet over medium heat. When hot, add the pancetta, reduce the heat to medium-low, and cook the pancetta until it is crispy and golden brown and most of the fat has rendered. Using a slotted spoon, transfer the pancetta to a paper towel–lined plate and set aside. Add the onion, carrot, celery, fennel, and garlic and cook, stirring occasionally, until the vegetables begin to wilt, 6 to 8 minutes.

2. Transfer the vegetables to the crock of a 6-quart slow cooker. Add the celery root, turnip, parsnip, and shiitake mushrooms to the same pan with 1 tablespoon of the remaining olive oil and cook over medium-high heat for 5 to 6 minutes, or until the vegetables begin to caramelize. Add the caramelized vegetables, bell peppers, diced tomatoes, pasta, Parmesan rind, and stock to the slow cooker. Season with the salt and pepper and stir to combine. Cover and cook on high for 3 hours, stirring occasionally. Add the kale, zucchini, squash, and green beans and cook for 30 minutes longer.

3. Stir in the remaining 2 tablespoons olive oil, the basil, parsley, and Parmesan. Taste and adjust the seasoning if necessary. Remove the Parmesan rind. Serve garnished with the crispy pancetta, with more cheese on the side and a loaf of warm crusty bread.

4 quarts, 6 to 8 servings

PORTUGUESE PORK AND CLAMS

This classic dish is a specialty of the Alentejo region in Portugal. Cork oaks are grown there, and in the late summer and fall local farmers allow their famous black pigs to gorge themselves on acorns that have fallen from the oaks, encouraging them to fatten up before the winter harvest. The meat from these special pigs is considered a delicacy because it is meltingly tender from the fat. The fatty pork is paired with briny clams and hot paprika, providing the perfect balance. Here in the United States, Berkshire pork is a wonderful substitute—it is available online and at local specialty butchers—but regular Boston butt works just fine! Note that the pork marinates overnight for exquisite flavor; then the next day it gets browned quickly and added to the slow cooker for stress-free cooking.

3 pounds boneless Boston butt pork roast, cut into 1-inch cubes

2 ½ teaspoons hot pimentón (smoked Spanish paprika)

1 teaspoon freshly ground black pepper

½ teaspoon cayenne

2 teaspoons salt

¼ cup extra-virgin olive oil

1 tablespoon tomato paste

2 ½ cups diced yellow onion

2 tablespoons minced garlic

2 bay leaves

½ cup dry white wine

½ teaspoon crushed red pepper

Three 14.5-ounce cans diced tomatoes, with juice

2 pounds littleneck clams, scrubbed and purged (see page 32)

2 teaspoons chopped fresh thyme

2 teaspoons chopped fresh oregano

½ cup chopped fresh flat-leaf parsley

1 loaf ciabatta bread, for serving

Good-quality extra-virgin olive oil, for drizzling

1.   Season the pork with the pimentón, black pepper, and cayenne. Transfer the pork to a 1-gallon resealable plastic food storage bag and refrigerate overnight.

2.   Remove the pork from the refrigerator and allow the meat to come to room temperature for at least 1 hour.

3.   Season the pork with the salt. Heat a large sauté pan over medium-high heat. When hot, add 2 tablespoons of the olive oil. Place half of the pork in the pan and brown on all sides, 3 to 4 minutes per side.

Once the pork has browned, add it to the crock of a 6-quart slow cooker. Repeat with the remaining pork and olive oil.

4.   Reduce the heat to medium, add the tomato paste to the pan, and cook, stirring, for 2 minutes. Add the onion and cook until tender, 3 to 4 minutes. Add the garlic, bay leaves, wine, and crushed red pepper and cook for 3 minutes, or until the wine has completely evaporated. Add the tomatoes, increase the heat to high, and bring the sauce to a boil. Reduce the heat to a simmer and cook until the sauce begins to thicken, 10 to 12 minutes. Pour the hot tomato sauce over the pork, cover the slow cooker, set the temperature to high, and cook until the pork is very tender, about 5½ hours.

5.   Once the pork is tender, add the clams, arranging them around the outer edges of the crock and tucking them into the tomato sauce. They will open more readily if they are submerged in the hot sauce. Add the thyme and oregano, replace the cover, and cook until all the clams have opened, about 30 minutes. Once all of the clams have opened, remove the bay leaves and add the parsley and stir. (Discard any clams that do not open.)

6.   Serve the pork and clams with wedges of warm ciabatta bread, drizzled with a good-quality extra-virgin olive oil.

8 servings

SIMPLE CHOUCROUTE

We love making this simplified choucroute with at least two types of sausages—one smoked and one garlic or other fresh sausage—but feel free to use your favorite sausages here. A coarse-grain mustard and a loaf of crusty bread are all you need to elevate this to full meal status.

2 pounds jarred sauerkraut, drained

2 tablespoons olive oil

3 ounces thick-sliced bacon, diced

1 large smoked ham hock (14 to 16 ounces), skin scored

4 cups sliced yellow onion

1 teaspoon coarsely ground black pepper

½ teaspoon salt

2 tablespoons minced garlic

1 tablespoon chopped fresh thyme

One 12-ounce bottle amber beer, such as Abita amber

½ cup chicken stock or canned low-sodium chicken broth

3 bay leaves

1 pound smoked sausage, cut into 3-inch lengths

1 pound bratwurst, garlic, or other fresh sausage, cut into 3-inch lengths

1 pound new potatoes (about 2 inches in diameter), halved (quartered if large)

Coarse-grain mustard, for serving (optional)

Crusty bread, for serving (optional)

1.   Taste the drained sauerkraut; if it is excessively salty, rinse briefly under cool running water and drain. Transfer to the crock of a 6-quart slow cooker.

2.   Heat 1 tablespoon of the olive oil in a 12-inch skillet and add the bacon and ham hock. Cook until the bacon is crisp and the fat has rendered, about 4 minutes. Add the onion, pepper, and salt to the hot skillet and cook, stirring the onion and turning the hock occasionally, until the slits in the hock have opened up and the onion is golden around the edges, 4 to 6 minutes. Add the garlic and thyme and cook, stirring, for 1 minute. Transfer the hock and bacon-onion mixture to the slow cooker, nestling the hock down into the sauerkraut. Return the hot skillet to the heat and deglaze the pan with the beer, scraping to release any browned bits from the bottom of the pan. Pour the beer and any browned bits over the sauerkraut-onion mixture in the slow cooker. Add the stock and bay leaves, cover the slow cooker, set the temperature to high, and cook, undisturbed, for 1½ hours.

3. While the sauerkraut is cooking, return the same skillet to the heat and add the remaining 1 tablespoon oil to the pan. Using a sharp knife, lightly score the casings of the sausages on both sides. When the oil is hot, brown the sausages, on both sides, in batches if necessary, 3 to 5 minutes. Transfer to a bowl, cover lightly, and set aside until ready to use.

4. When the sauerkraut has cooked for 1½ hours, remove the lid and stir briefly, then add the potatoes and nestle them down into the sauerkraut. Top with the browned sausages, cover, and cook, undisturbed, for 2½ hours longer, or until the ham hock and potatoes are fork-tender and the sauerkraut is flavorful. Adjust the seasoning if necessary.

5. Transfer the sausages and hock to a serving platter. (Pull the meat off the hock for serving if desired.) Remove the bay leaves. Serve the sauerkraut and sausages together, with a dollop of coarse-grain mustard and pieces of crusty bread.

6 to 8 servings

BRAISED MEATBALL AND CHICKPEA PITA WITH YOGURT-GARLIC SAUCE

A sandwich from a slow cooker? Now that's different! Assemble and brown the meatballs, toss them in the slow cooker, and go run your errands. It's a perfect no-work weekend meal in a snap. And I don't have to tell you how good this is.

1/4 cup vegetable oil

One 10-ounce bag prewashed spinach

1/2 teaspoon freshly ground black pepper

2 teaspoons salt

1/4 cup chicken stock or canned low-sodium chicken broth

2 slices white bread

1/2 cup whole milk

1/3 cup minced onion

1/4 cup chopped fresh flat-leaf parsley leaves

2 teaspoons ground coriander

1 1/2 teaspoons chopped garlic

1 1/2 teaspoons freshly grated lemon zest

1/4 teaspoon cayenne

2 pounds lean ground beef or lamb

Two 14-ounce cans chickpeas, drained

6 pita breads, warmed, for serving

Thinly sliced red onion, for serving

Yogurt-Garlic Sauce (recipe follows), for serving

1. Heat 2 tablespoons of the vegetable oil in a 12-inch sauté pan over medium-high heat. Add the spinach, black pepper, and 1/2 teaspoon of the salt and cook for 1 1/2 minutes (the spinach should not be fully cooked). Remove the pan from the heat and continue to stir the spinach for 30 seconds longer, until nicely wilted. Set the spinach and the juices in a strainer set over a bowl and allow the spinach to drain. When the spinach is cool enough to handle, chop it and set it aside. Add the reserved juices and stock to the crock of a 6-quart slow cooker. Clean the skillet and set it aside.

2. Place the bread in a large mixing bowl and add the milk. Allow it to sit for 10 minutes. Use your hands to squeeze the bread together, then tear the bread into small pieces. Add the remaining 1 1/2 teaspoons salt, the minced onion, parsley, coriander, garlic, lemon zest, cayenne, and spinach to the bowl. Mix well. Add the ground beef and mix gently but thoroughly until combined. This is best done with your hands, but you can use a rubber spatula if you prefer. Portion the meatball mixture using a 1/3-cup measure and place on a parchment paper–lined baking sheet or platter. Rub the meat portions between the palms of your hands to form smooth, large meatballs. You will have about thirteen 3-ounce balls.

3. Return the skillet to the stove and heat the remaining 2 tablespoons vegetable oil over medium heat. Add enough meatballs to fill the pan without crowding and cook until nicely browned on all sides, turning as needed, 3 to 5 minutes. Add the browned meatballs to the slow cooker and repeat with the remaining meatballs.

4. Add the chickpeas to the slow cooker. Cover and cook on high, undisturbed, for 2 hours.

5. To serve, remove the chickpeas and meatballs with a slotted spoon. Cut the edge off one side of each pita and gently pry it open to form a pocket. Fill each pita with 2 meatballs, halved if desired, and some of the chickpeas. Garnish with the red onion slices and generous spoonfuls of the yogurt-garlic sauce.

6 servings

YOGURT-GARLIC SAUCE

---

2 cups Greek yogurt (or plain low-fat yogurt drained for
    10 minutes through a fine-mesh strainer)
2 tablespoons extra-virgin olive oil
2 tablespoons chopped fresh mint
1 1/2 teaspoons minced garlic
1 1/2 teaspoons finely grated lemon zest
1/2 teaspoon salt

Combine all the ingredients and whisk until smooth and creamy. Cover and refrigerate until ready to use, up to 1 week.

2 cups

VEGETARIAN CHILI

Chili is one of those dishes that people have strong feelings about. There are chili cook-offs and contests around the country, and great debates have been launched over whether or not chili should contain beans. I've included a recipe in this book for a traditional chuck wagon chili (page 278), but here's my favorite vegetarian version for those folks who don't eat meat.

2 cups du Puy lentils

1 cup dried pink or pinto beans, soaked overnight

1 cup dried cream peas or small white beans, such as navy beans or crowder peas, picked over, rinsed, and soaked overnight

2 tablespoons chili powder

1 1/2 teaspoons ground cumin

1 1/4 teaspoons hot paprika

1 teaspoon cayenne

3/4 teaspoon dried Mexican or regular oregano, crumbled between your fingers

1/4 teaspoon ground cinnamon

1 head of garlic, minced

2 cups small-diced yellow onion

1 cup small-diced red bell pepper

1 cup small-diced yellow bell pepper

1 cup small-diced poblano chile

One 14.5-ounce can petite diced tomatoes, with juice

1/4 cup dry red wine

2 tablespoons tomato paste

1 tablespoon chipotle sauce (see page 39)

8 cups vegetable stock or canned low-sodium vegetable broth

1 tablespoon kosher salt

1 teaspoon hot sauce, or to taste

1/4 teaspoon crushed red pepper

Grated cheddar cheese, for serving

Sour cream or yogurt, for serving

Sliced green onion, for serving

Chopped fresh cilantro leaves, for serving

1. Add the lentils, pink beans, cream peas, chili powder, cumin, paprika, cayenne, oregano, cinnamon, garlic, onion, bell peppers, poblano, tomatoes, wine, tomato paste, chipotle sauce, stock, and salt to the crock of a 6-quart slow cooker. Cover and cook on high for 3 hours. Continue to cook for 2 hours longer, or until the beans are tender and almost creamy. Season the chili with the hot sauce and crushed red pepper before serving.

2. Serve the chili in bowls, garnished with grated cheddar, sour cream, green onion, and cilantro.

4 quarts, 6 to 8 servings

NEW ENGLAND-STYLE FISH AND SHELLFISH CHOWDER

The success of this simple, foolproof chowder relies on the freshness of the seafood that goes into it. The shellfish will open more quickly if the cover is left on the slow cooker; stir very quickly during cooking to maintain the heat necessary to open the shellfish. Remember that any shellfish that do not open should be discarded before serving.

1 pound Yukon Gold potatoes, diced

3/4 cup chopped celery

1/2 cup chopped red bell pepper

4 ounces thick-sliced bacon, diced

1 1/2 cups chopped onion

2 tablespoons minced garlic

1 tablespoon fresh thyme leaves

1 3/4 teaspoons kosher salt, or to taste

1 teaspoon freshly ground black pepper

2 tablespoons all-purpose flour

4 cups clam juice, clam stock, or light fish stock

4 cups heavy cream

1 pound littleneck clams, scrubbed well and purged (see page 32)

1 pound mussels, scrubbed and debearded

1 pound skinless cod, halibut, or other firm white fish, cut into 1-inch cubes

1/4 cup sliced green onion

1. Place the diced potatoes in the bottom of the crock of a 6-quart slow cooker and sprinkle with the celery and bell pepper.

2. In a medium sauté pan, cook the bacon until it is crisp and most of the fat has rendered, 4 to 6 minutes. Add the onion, garlic, thyme, 1½ teaspoons of the salt, and ¾ teaspoon of the pepper and cook until the onion is softened and the garlic is fragrant, 2 to 3 minutes. Add the flour and cook, stirring, for 2 minutes. Add the clam juice and cook, stirring, until the liquid comes to a boil and thickens, 2 to 3 minutes. Pour the hot bacon-stock mixture over the potatoes in the slow cooker.

3. Add the cream to the hot pan and bring to a simmer. Pour the hot cream into the slow cooker, cover, and cook, undisturbed, on high until the potatoes are tender, about 2½ hours. Add the clams and cook until they have opened, about 30 minutes, stirring once

midway. Add the mussels and cook until they have opened, about 15 minutes. Season the fish with the remaining ¼ teaspoon salt and ¼ teaspoon pepper and add to the slow cooker along with the green onion. Cook just until the fish is cooked through and flakes easily, about 15 minutes longer. Serve the chowder hot in shallow bowls.

4 quarts, 6 to 8 servings

SLOW-COOKED PULLED PORK

This simple recipe serves a crowd and will make folks think you slaved over a smoker all day long. The meat is slathered with delicious spices and seasonings and kept overnight in the fridge. The next day, it gets transferred to the slow cooker, and that's it! It is not even necessary to add any liquid to the slow cooker—the pork will exude the most delicious juices as it cooks.

One 6- to 7-pound Boston butt pork roast, bone in or boneless

8 large cloves garlic, peeled and halved lengthwise

2½ tablespoons light brown sugar

1½ tablespoons kosher salt

1 tablespoon sweet pimentón (smoked Spanish paprika)

2 teaspoons Mexican or regular chili powder

1½ teaspoons Mexican or regular oregano, crumbled between your fingers

1½ teaspoons ground cumin

1 teaspoon crushed red pepper

1 teaspoon cayenne

½ teaspoon ground coriander

12 to 14 soft buns or rolls, for serving

Your favorite barbecue sauce, for serving

1. Place the pork in a shallow baking dish. Using the tip of a paring knife, make 16 narrow but deep slits in the meat, evenly spaced and on all sides, and insert a piece of the garlic into each slit. In a small bowl, combine the brown sugar, salt, pimentón, chili powder, oregano, cumin, crushed red pepper, cayenne, and coriander and stir to combine. Using your hands, rub the spice blend evenly over the entire surface of all sides of the meat. Cover loosely and refrigerate overnight.

2. Remove the pork from the refrigerator and allow to come to room temperature for 1 hour.

3. Place the pork in the crock of a 6-quart slow cooker, fat side up, and cook on high until tender and falling apart, about 8 hours. (As the meat becomes tender, break the roast into several smaller pieces.)

4. Remove the meat from the crock and transfer to a large heatproof bowl or platter. Remove any excess fat and/or bones and discard. Using two forks, pull the meat into shreds. Ladle on enough of the accumulated cooking juices from the slow cooker to keep the meat moist. Taste and adjust the seasoning if necessary.

5. Serve the meat hot, on toasted buns or rolls, with your favorite barbecue sauce. (Alternatively, adjust the setting on the slow cooker to the "keep warm" setting and remove about half of the cooking juices from the crock. Return the pulled pork to the remaining juices in the slow cooker and allow guests to serve themselves from the slow cooker. This is especially useful for parties or tailgating. The extra cooking juices make a great addition to soups, stews, or posole.)

12 to 14 sandwich servings

RED BEAN AND RICE SOUP

This throw-it-all-in-the-pot soup is heartwarming and satisfying...try it on a chilly winter's day when you need something to warm you through and through. If you make it ahead of time, the flavor will only improve, but keep in mind that you'll likely need to thin it with a bit of water or stock, as it will thicken as it sits.

1 pound dried kidney beans, rinsed and picked over

6 cups water

2 cups chopped yellow onion

1 cup chopped celery

1 cup chopped green bell pepper

¼ cup chopped fresh cilantro stems

1 to 2 jalapeño chiles, to taste, seeded and minced

2 bay leaves

One 14.5-ounce can petite diced tomatoes, with juice

½ cup tomato puree

1 teaspoon dried Mexican or regular oregano, crumbled between your fingers

1 ¼ pounds fresh chorizo or other fresh hot sausage, removed from the casings and broken into bite-sized pieces

2 tablespoons extra-virgin olive oil

¼ teaspoon cayenne

3 cups chicken stock or canned low-sodium chicken broth, heated

½ cup converted rice

3 ¼ teaspoons salt

2 cloves garlic, minced

¼ cup chopped fresh cilantro leaves

Louisiana hot sauce, to taste (optional)

1. Place the kidney beans in a large pot with the water. Bring to a simmer over medium-high heat, cover, and remove from the heat. Set the beans aside to soak while you assemble and prepare the remaining ingredients.

2. Place the onion, celery, bell pepper, cilantro stems, jalapeño(s), bay leaves, tomatoes, tomato puree, oregano, chorizo, olive oil, and cayenne in the crock of a 6-quart slow cooker. Pour the hot beans and their soaking liquid into the slow cooker and stir gently to combine. Cover and cook on high until the beans are very tender but still hold their shape, about 4 hours, stirring once after 2 hours. Add the hot stock, rice, and 3 teaspoons of the salt and continue cooking, stirring once midway, until the rice is just tender, 20 to 30 minutes longer.

3. While the rice is cooking, mash the garlic to a paste using the side of a chef's knife and the remaining ¼ teaspoon salt. Once the rice is cooked, add the

garlic paste and the cilantro leaves to the soup. Stir well; taste and adjust the seasoning if necessary. Remove the bay leaves from the soup and discard. Serve the soup hot, with hot sauce to taste if desired.

4¹/₂ quarts, 8 to 10 servings

CHICKEN SAUCE PIQUANTE

Here's a traditional New Orleans dish for the slow cooker in all its peppery glory. Hence, piquante. You'll enjoy its pungency, tempered with tomatoes and herbs and spooned over white rice.

1 whole chicken (about 4 pounds), cut into 8 pieces

1 tablespoon Emeril's Original Essence or Creole Seasoning (page 3)

1/2 cup all-purpose flour

3 tablespoons vegetable oil

1 medium onion, chopped

1 medium green bell pepper, chopped

3/4 cup chopped celery

1/2 jalapeño chile, minced

1 1/2 teaspoons chopped garlic

1/2 teaspoon crushed red pepper

1/2 teaspoon dried thyme

1/4 teaspoon cayenne

2 bay leaves

One 28-ounce can whole tomatoes, drained and juice reserved

1/4 cup tomato paste

1 tablespoon Worcestershire sauce

1 teaspoon sugar

1 teaspoon salt

Steamed white rice, for serving

1/4 cup chopped fresh flat-leaf parsley

1. Add the chicken pieces to a large mixing bowl and season all over with the Essence. Add the flour and mix well until the chicken is evenly coated. Shake the chicken to remove any excess flour, then set it aside on a plate.

2. Heat the oil in a 12-inch or larger skillet over medium-high heat. Add the chicken pieces to the pan, in batches if necessary, and cook until golden brown on all sides, about 8 minutes. Transfer the browned chicken pieces to the crock of a 6-quart slow cooker.

3. Add the onion, bell pepper, celery, and jalapeño to the skillet and cook for 2 minutes, stirring to incorporate the browned bits from the bottom of the pan. Add the garlic, crushed red pepper, thyme, cayenne, and bay leaves and cook for 1 minute longer. Add the tomatoes, breaking them up into pieces with the spoon, the tomato paste, Worcestershire, sugar, and salt. Add 1/2 cup of the reserved tomato juice and bring to a simmer. Cook for 1 minute, then transfer the hot sauce to the slow cooker. Cover and cook the chicken on low until very tender, about 3 hours. Remove the bay leaves if desired.

4. Serve over steamed rice and garnish with the parsley.

4 servings

BEEF BRISKET PHO

At first glance this may seem an unlikely dish for the slow cooker, but just think—a good pho is all about good stock. Here you simmer brisket with shank and knuckle bones in the slow cooker for a layered beef broth and super-tender meat. Add your noodles, fresh herbs, and condiments and enjoy a popular dish from Vietnam.

4 pounds beef shank soup bones, beef knuckle bones, or a combination

5 ½ quarts water

Two 3-inch cinnamon sticks

2 small dried chiles

1 tablespoon coriander seeds

1 tablespoon fennel seeds

8 whole star anise

4 cardamom pods

12 whole cloves

2 to 2 ½ pounds beef brisket

2 tablespoons kosher salt

1 to 2 tablespoons peanut oil

One 4-inch piece fresh ginger, cut crosswise into ¼-inch-thick slices

1 onion, unpeeled, halved

1 head of garlic, halved crosswise

1 carrot, cut into 3 pieces

¼ cup fish sauce (see page 213), plus more for serving

1 ½ tablespoons sugar

1 ½ teaspoons salt

14 ounces rice stick noodles

Lime wedges, for serving

1 bunch fresh cilantro sprigs, for serving

1 bunch fresh mint sprigs, for serving

1 bunch fresh basil sprigs, preferably Thai basil, for serving

Bean sprouts, for serving

Romaine lettuce leaves, for serving

Sliced jalapeño chiles, for serving

Thinly sliced onion, for serving

Sriracha chili sauce, for serving

Hoisin sauce, for serving

1.   Add the beef bones to a large stockpot and cover with 12 cups of the water. Bring the water to a boil over high heat, reduce the heat to a simmer, and cook for 10 minutes. Using a ladle or large spoon, skim the foam that rises to the top and discard. Remove the bones, rinse them in cool water, and add them to the crock of a 6-quart slow cooker. Discard the broth.

2.   Combine the cinnamon sticks, dried chiles, coriander seeds, fennel seeds, star anise, cardamom pods, and cloves in a small bowl and set aside.

3. Season the brisket all over with the kosher salt. In a 12-inch skillet, heat 1 tablespoon of the oil over medium-high heat. Add the brisket, fat side down first, and brown for 3 to 4 minutes per side. Transfer the brisket to the slow cooker, fat side up. Add the ginger, halved onion, garlic, and carrot to the pan and brown for 1 minute (adding the remaining 1 tablespoon oil if necessary). Add the seasoning mix to the pan and toast for 1 minute. Transfer the contents of the skillet to the slow cooker and add the fish sauce, sugar, 1½ teaspoons salt, and the remaining 10 cups water. Cook on high, undisturbed, for 6 hours.

4. Cook the rice stick noodles according to the package directions and set aside. Arrange the lime wedges, cilantro, mint, basil, bean sprouts, romaine, jalapeños, and sliced onion on a serving platter.

5. Remove the meat from the slow cooker and set aside on a cutting board. Strain the broth through a fine-mesh sieve into a small pot and cover to keep warm. Discard the vegetables and spices. Chop the meat from the soup bones and knuckle bones and set aside. Slice the brisket.

6. To serve, divide the noodles and meat among bowls. Ladle the hot broth over all and serve immediately. Each person should garnish the soup to taste with the ingredients on the serving platter and the condiments.

4 to 6 servings

PORK LOIN WITH DRIED FRUIT AND ORANGE-CIDER SAUCE

This dish is simple and yet impressive . . . and the sauce, oooh, it'll knock you off your feet! It works just as well for a family weeknight dinner as it does for a celebratory holiday meal. I especially like the silky sauce and plumped dried fruit served with mashed sweet potatoes.

1 teaspoon sweet paprika

½ teaspoon cayenne

½ teaspoon freshly ground black pepper

2 ½ teaspoons kosher salt

One 3-pound boneless pork loin roast, trimmed and tied

8 cloves garlic, smashed lightly and peeled

1 ½ tablespoons olive oil

4 cups ¼-inch sliced red onion

2 teaspoons chopped fresh thyme

¾ cup dried apricots

½ cup dried cranberries

½ cup dried cherries

¼ cup golden raisins

¼ cup dried currants

1 cup freshly squeezed orange juice

½ cup apple cider vinegar

4 tablespoons (½ stick) cold unsalted butter, cut into cubes

Mashed sweet potatoes, for serving

1. Combine the paprika, cayenne, black pepper, and 1½ teaspoons of the kosher salt in a small bowl and stir together to mix well. Set aside.

2. With a small knife, make twelve 1½-inch-deep, evenly spaced slits around the outside of the pork loin. Cut 6 of the garlic cloves in half lengthwise and insert ½ clove into each slit. Rub the pork on all sides with the seasoning mixture.

3. In a 12-inch sauté pan, add the olive oil and heat over medium-high heat. When hot, add the pork loin and cook each side until lightly golden brown, about 2 minutes per side. Transfer to the crock of a 6-quart slow cooker. Add the remaining 2 smashed garlic cloves, the onion, and thyme to the same pan and sauté, stirring, for 1 minute. Remove from the heat.

4. Surround the pork with the dried fruit. Top with the onion, then add the remaining teaspoon salt, the orange juice, and vinegar. Cover the slow cooker and cook on low until the pork reaches an internal temperature of 140°F, 2½ to 2¾ hours. Remove the pork from the slow cooker, transfer to a cutting board, and tent with foil to keep warm. Let the pork rest for about 10 minutes before slicing.

5. Gently stir the butter into the hot sauce. Remove the twine from the roast and slice the pork. Arrange on a serving platter and top with the sauce and plumped fruit.

6 servings

INDIAN-INSPIRED BEEF WITH YOGURT SAUCE

This dish is a spin-off of an Indian dish called *rogan josh,* which is traditionally made with lamb. It is characterized by the Indian spices, yogurt, and almonds—and is so delicious that some of the test kitchen team members had a difficult time sharing it with their loved ones at home!

2 tablespoons ground coriander

2 teaspoons ground cumin

1/2 teaspoon freshly ground black pepper

1 tablespoon plus 1/2 teaspoon salt

2 1/2 pounds boneless beef chuck, cut into 1 1/2- to 2-inch cubes

1 cup finely chopped onion, plus 1 cup small-diced onion

2 tablespoons peeled and minced fresh ginger

1/2 cup all-purpose flour

7 tablespoons ghee (see page 69) or clarified butter

2 fresh serrano chiles, seeded and finely chopped

One 3-inch cinnamon stick

1 bay leaf

6 cardamom pods

6 whole cloves

1/2 teaspoon garam masala

2 cups beef stock or canned low-sodium beef broth

1 1/4 cups yogurt, preferably Greek style

2 tablespoons chopped fresh mint leaves

2 tablespoons chopped fresh cilantro leaves

Steamed basmati or jasmine rice, for serving

1/2 cup toasted sliced almonds

1. Combine the coriander, cumin, black pepper, and 1 teaspoon of the salt in a medium mixing bowl and stir to blend. Add the beef, the finely chopped onion, and 1 tablespoon of the minced ginger and toss to coat well. Allow to marinate at room temperature for 1 hour. Remove the beef from the marinade and shake the pieces to remove most of the onion. Add the onion from the beef to the crock of a 6-quart slow cooker. Lightly dredge the beef in the flour.

2. Heat 2 tablespoons of the ghee in a 12-inch sauté pan over medium-high heat. Add one-third of the beef to the pan and cook, turning as necessary, until well browned on all sides, 3 to 4 minutes per side. Transfer the beef to a paper towel–lined plate to drain. Repeat with the remaining beef, adding 2 tablespoons of ghee with each batch of beef. Transfer the browned beef to the slow cooker.

3. Wipe the pan clean with a paper towel, add 1½ teaspoons of the remaining ghee, and melt it over medium-high heat. Add the chiles, cinnamon stick, bay leaf, and remaining 1 tablespoon ginger. Sauté for 30 seconds, then add the diced onion. Sauté for 30 seconds, then add the sautéed spice-onion mixture to the slow cooker. Add the remaining 1½ teaspoons ghee to the pan along with the cardamom and cloves and sauté until aromatic, about 30 seconds. Wrap the cardamom and cloves in a small piece of cheesecloth and secure it with twine. Add the cardamom-clove pouch, garam masala, stock, and the remaining 2½ teaspoons salt to the slow cooker. Cover the slow cooker, set the cooker on high, and cook, stirring once midway, until the beef is tender, 3 to 3½ hours. During the last 10 minutes of cooking, stir in the yogurt. Right before serving, remove the bay leaf, cinnamon stick, and pouch and stir in the herbs. Serve with rice and garnish with the almonds.

6 to 8 servings

BEEF AND KIMCHI STEW

Despite its geographic location, Korean food is noticeably different from its Japanese and Chinese neighbors. The basic Korean seasonings are soy sauce, garlic, ginger, sesame oil, rice vinegar, and sugar as well as chili powders and chili pastes. Savory stews and soups are a mainstay in the Korean diet, and they range from delicate, light broths to hearty, spicy stews. This stew falls in the latter category and makes for a substantial meal when served with rice or noodles. The beef is marinated and cooked in soy sauce, so it doesn't need any extra seasoning. Feel free to use low-sodium soy sauce if you prefer.

1 ½ cups soy sauce

½ cup toasted sesame oil

¼ cup plus 2 tablespoons roughly chopped garlic (about 18 cloves)

¼ cup peeled and minced fresh ginger

¼ cup mirin (rice wine)

2 teaspoons Korean ground chili powder (see page 230) or crushed red pepper

4 ½ pounds boneless chuck roast, cut into 1-inch cubes

¼ cup peanut oil

3 cups beef stock or canned low-sodium beef broth

½ cup light brown sugar

4 small yellow onions, cut into ½-inch wedges

1 ¾ pounds baby bok choy, cut into bite-sized pieces

2 pounds spicy cabbage kimchi (about 2 jars)

4 cups steamed short-grain rice, for serving (see Note)

½ cup thinly sliced green onion, for garnish

3 tablespoons toasted sesame seeds, for garnish

1.   In a medium mixing bowl, make a marinade for the beef by combining 1 cup of the soy sauce, ¼ cup of the sesame oil, ¼ cup of the garlic, 1 tablespoon of the ginger, the mirin, and the Korean ground chili powder. Place the meat in a large resealable plastic food storage bag and pour the marinade over the meat. Refrigerate for at least 1 hour and up to 4 hours. Allow the meat to come to room temperature before cooking.

2.   Remove the meat from the marinade and discard the marinade. Heat a large sauté pan over medium-high heat and add 2 tablespoons of the peanut oil. When the oil is hot, add half of the beef and cook until browned on all sides, turning as needed to ensure even cooking, 8 to 10 minutes per batch.

Transfer the beef to the crock of a 6-quart slow cooker. Add the remaining 2 tablespoons peanut oil to the sauté pan and repeat with the remaining beef.

3.   Add the stock, brown sugar, onions, and remaining ½ cup soy sauce, 2 tablespoons garlic, and 3 tablespoons ginger to the slow cooker, cover, and cook, undisturbed, on high for 3½ hours. Add the bok choy and kimchi, stir to incorporate, and cook until the meat is fork-tender, about 30 minutes longer.

4.   Serve the stew over the cooked rice, garnished with the green onion, toasted sesame seeds, and remaining ¼ cup sesame oil.

6 to 8 servings

Note: Although I recommend serving this dish with rice, I think it would be equally good with almost any type of noodle.

PORK AND RED CHILE POSOLE

Posole, a traditional dish served in Mexico for special occasions, is basically a pork and hominy stew. So what in the heck is hominy? Hominy, very simply, is corn kernels that have the germ and bran removed and are dried and either cooked whole or ground into what southerners call *grits*. This dish has a very distinctive flavor derived from the hominy itself and is usually served with ingredients that enhance this flavor, such as avocado, radishes, chopped onion, lime wedges, and fried corn tortillas.

---

12 ounces dried hominy (see Note 1)

1 head of garlic

4 to 5 pounds bone-in pork shoulder, cut into 3 or 4 equal pieces

1 teaspoon New Mexican or other red chile powder

1 teaspoon freshly ground black pepper

1 tablespoon salt

2 tablespoons olive oil

4 cups chopped yellow onion

One 14.5-ounce can diced tomatoes, with juice

10 cups water

4 cups chicken stock or canned low-sodium chicken broth

1 1/2 teaspoons dried Mexican or regular oregano, crumbled between your fingers

2 ounces ancho chiles, seeded

1 ounce guajillo chiles, seeded

Diced avocado, for serving

Julienned radish, for serving

Chopped red onion, for serving

Chopped fresh cilantro, for serving

Sour cream, for serving

Toasted pumpkin seeds, for serving

Tortilla chips, for serving

Lime wedges, for serving

Crushed red pepper, for serving

1. Soak the hominy in enough cool water to cover by 4 inches while cooking the pork, at least 2 hours and up to overnight.

2. Peel the garlic cloves. Reserve 2 whole cloves for the chile sauce and slice the remaining cloves.

3. Season the pork with the red chile powder, black pepper, and 1 teaspoon of the salt.

4. Heat a large sauté pan over medium-high heat. When hot, add the olive oil and brown the pork on all sides, 8 to 10 minutes. Transfer the browned pork to

the crock of a 6-quart slow cooker. Add the sliced garlic and 3 cups of the chopped yellow onion to the sauté pan and cook for 4 to 5 minutes, or until the onion begins to caramelize. Add the onion, garlic, and tomatoes to the slow cooker, along with the water and 2 cups of the stock. Cover and cook on high for 4 hours.

5. Drain the soaked hominy in a colander. Add the hominy and 1 teaspoon of the oregano to the slow cooker and cook on high until the pork and hominy are tender and the broth is flavorful, about 4 hours longer.

6. While the pork is cooking, toast the ancho and guajillo chiles in a pan over medium-high heat, turning occasionally, until they are pliable and fragrant, 3 to 4 minutes. Add the remaining 2 cups chicken stock; bring to a boil, cover, remove from the heat, and let stand for 20 to 25 minutes.

7. In a blender, combine the chiles and their soaking liquid with the remaining 1 cup chopped yellow onion, the remaining 2 whole cloves garlic, 1 teaspoon of the remaining salt, and the remaining ½ teaspoon oregano and puree until smooth. Strain through a sieve to remove any skins or seeds. Discard the solids. Set the chile sauce aside (see Note 2).

8. Transfer the pork to a cutting board, discard the bones, and shred the meat with two forks. Return the pork to the broth; add ¼ cup of the chile sauce or more to taste and the remaining 1 teaspoon salt.

9. The posole should look hearty but still be brothy enough to be thought of as a soup or brothy stew. Serve the posole buffet style, with bowls of the accompaniments and additional chile sauce for guests to add to their taste.

About 6 quarts, 8 to 10 servings

Note 1: Dried hominy can be found in Mexican specialty markets, at Whole Foods Market, or online.

Note 2: Any leftover chile sauce can be stored in an airtight container in the refrigerator for 2 to 3 weeks and may be stirred into marinades, sauces, soups, or stews or used to flavor meats before grilling or sautéing.

PORK AND BEANS

You may be looking at this recipe and thinking, *That's it?* Yes. This dish can be assembled in the morning to cook while you are away. Just chop your veggies and meat the night before. Better yet, put everything but the stock in the crock and place it in the fridge the night before, pull it out first thing in the morning (remember to add the stock), and flip the switch.

2 pounds country-style pork ribs, bones removed, cut into 1 ½-inch pieces

1 tablespoon Emeril's Original Essence or Creole Seasoning (page 3)

4 ounces salt pork, chopped

1 pound great Northern beans, rinsed well and picked over

2 medium onions, peeled and cut into large pieces

1 celery stalk, chopped, including leaves

2 teaspoons dried thyme leaves

4 bay leaves

¼ cup tomato paste

6 cloves garlic, smashed and peeled

1 teaspoon freshly ground black pepper

6 cups chicken stock or canned low-sodium chicken broth

1 pound smoked bratwurst, cut crosswise into 1-inch slices

1. Add the pork ribs to a medium bowl, season with the Essence, and set aside.

2. Add the salt pork, beans, onions, celery, thyme, bay leaves, tomato paste, garlic, black pepper, stock, and bratwurst to the slow cooker. Top with the pork ribs.

3. Cover and cook on high for 6 hours, stirring once or twice, until the beans are tender. Remove the bay leaves before serving.

14 cups, 4 to 6 servings

EMERIL'S CHUCK WAGON CHILI FOR THE SLOW COOKER

Come and get it! The real-deal chili is right here. Large chunks of beef chuck steeped in spices and cooked slowly in tomatoes, beer, and a bit of chocolate create a succulent mouth feel. Serve this up in bowls garnished generously with sour cream, grated cheddar, and green onions for a true home-on-the-range feeling.

¼ cup chili powder

2 tablespoons whole cumin seeds

1 teaspoon cayenne

¾ teaspoon ground cinnamon

2 teaspoons dried Mexican or regular oregano, crumbled between your fingers

3 bay leaves

2 teaspoons light or dark brown sugar

4 pounds boneless beef chuck, trimmed and cut into 1 ½- to 2-inch cubes

1 teaspoon freshly ground black pepper

2 ½ tablespoons kosher salt

3 tablespoons vegetable oil

3 medium onions, coarsely chopped (about 4 cups)

1 ½ cups chopped celery, including leaves

6 cloves garlic, roughly chopped

2 jalapeño chiles, roughly chopped

One 12-ounce bottle dark Mexican beer, such as Negro Modelo

2 tablespoons tomato paste

One 28-ounce can crushed tomatoes

1 ounce semisweet chocolate, coarsely chopped

3 tablespoons masa harina (corn flour, not cornstarch)

½ cup chopped fresh cilantro leaves

½ cup chopped fresh parley leaves

Grated cheddar cheese, for garnish

Chopped green onion, for garnish

Sour cream, for garnish

1. Combine the chili powder, cumin seeds, cayenne, cinnamon, oregano, bay leaves, and brown sugar in a small bowl; set the spice mixture aside.

2. Add the beef to a medium bowl and season with the pepper and 1 tablespoon of the kosher salt.

3. Heat 2 tablespoons of the vegetable oil in a 12-inch or larger skillet over high heat. Add enough beef to fill the pan and cook until nicely browned on one side, about 2 minutes. Turn the pieces over and cook for another 2 minutes. Transfer the browned beef to

the crock of a 6-quart slow cooker. Repeat with the remaining beef, adding the remaining vegetable oil between batches as necessary.

4. Add the onions, celery, and 1 tablespoon of the remaining salt to the skillet and cook, stirring, until the vegetables begin to soften, about 2 minutes. Add the garlic, jalapeños, and spice mixture and cook for 1 minute longer. Pour in the beer, tomato paste, and crushed tomatoes and simmer for 3 minutes. Stir in the chocolate, masa harina, and remaining 1½ teaspoons salt and cook for 1 minute longer. Transfer this mixture to the slow cooker. Cover and cook the chili on high, undisturbed or stirring only once during cooking, for 6 hours, or until the beef is very tender. Remove the bay leaves and stir in the cilantro and parsley. Serve the chili hot in bowls, topped with grated cheddar, chopped green onion, and sour cream.

Generous 12 cups, 6 servings

Note: Leftover chili may thicken up and need to be reheated with a little low-sodium broth.

Index

Pad Thai with Shrimp and
Tofu, 212–13
Tortilla Española, 28–29
Enchiladas, Cheese, with a Smoky
Red Chile Sauce, 85–86
English Cottage Pie with Root
Vegetables, 59–60

F

Fajitas, Spicy Sirloin Steak,
38–39
Farfalle and Swiss Chard with
Meatballs in Broth, 157–58
Fennel
Coq au Vin Blanc, 128–30, *129*
and Green Olives, Braised
Breast of Veal with, 137–39,
138
Fettuccine with a Crawfish
Cream Sauce, 2–3
Fideuà, 24–27, *25*
Fish. *See also* Shellfish
Bouillabaisse, 172–73, *175*
and Chips, Tempura, 234–35,
235
Potato and Salt Cod au Gratin,
74–75
and Shellfish Chowder, New
England–Style, 258–59, *259*
Whole Fried, Veracruz Style,
214–15
Flap Steak, Ancho-Rubbed, with
a Warm Corn and Black
Bean Relish, 30–31, *31*
Fruit(s). *See also specific fruits*
Dried, and Orange-Cider
Sauce, Pork Loin with,
268–69, *269*
Roasted Pork Chops with
Jeweled Rice Pilaf, 67–69,
68

G

Garlic
Alioli, 27
-Basil Oil, Beef and Barley
Soup with, 198–99
Caper Parsley Aïoli, 169–70
Crispy, 182

Roasted Red Pepper Aïoli,
174–75
-Yogurt Sauce, 256
Gnocchi, Baked Semolina, with
Smoked Ham and Green
Beans, *50*, 51–53
Grains. *See also* Rice
Beef and Barley Soup with
Garlic-Basil Oil, 198–99
Grillades and Stone-Ground
Grits, 126–27
Mushroom and Fall Squash
Barley Risotto, 245
Green Beans
Fiery Beef Cellophane Noodle
Salad, 208–9
Minestrone, 248–49, *249*
and Smoked Ham, Baked
Semolina Gnocchi with, *50*,
51–53
Greens. *See also* Cabbage; Spinach
Arugula Pesto, 185
Meatballs with Swiss Chard
and Farfalle in Broth, 157–58
Minestrone, 248–49, *249*
Pasta e Fagiole, 40
Wok-Seared Duck Salad,
232–33, *233*
Grits, Stone-Ground, and
Grillades, 126–27
Gumbo, Hunter's, 192–94

H

Ham
Simple Choucroute, 252–53
Smoked, and Green Beans,
Baked Semolina Gnocchi
with, *50*, 51–53
Tortilla Española, 28–29
Turkey Club Casserole,
90–91
Herbs. *See also specific herbs*
Wok-Seared Duck Salad,
232–33, *233*
Hominy
Pork and Red Chile Posole,
274–76, *275*

I

Indian-Inspired Beef with Yogurt
Sauce, 270–71

J

Jambalaya, Chicken and
Andouille, 114–15, *115*
Jap Chae, 218–19, *219*
Jumbo Shells Stuffed with
Ricotta, Mushrooms, and
Roasted Red Peppers, 48–49

K

Kale
Minestrone, 248–49, *249*
Pasta e Fagiole, 40
Karahi Chicken, 224–25, *225*
Kimchi and Beef Stew, 272–73
Kimchi-Fried Rice, 228–30, *230*
Kung Pao Chicken, 220–21

L

Lamb
Moussaka, 65–66
Patties with a Mediterranean
Vegetable Ragout, 34–35
and Potato Stew with
Artichokes and Olives,
131–32
Roast Leg of, with Lemon and
Oregano-Scented Potatoes,
70–71
Lasagna, Butternut Squash, with
Italian Sausage and Sage,
76–78, *77*
Leek(s)
and Bacon Quiche in a Potato
Crust, 93–95, *94*
Coq au Vin Blanc, 128–30,
129
Pot-au-Feu, 167–69
Legumes. *See* Bean(s); Lentils;
Moong dal
Lemon(s)
and Oregano-Scented
Potatoes, Roast Leg of Lamb
with, 70–71

Preserved, and Cerignola
Olives, Tagine of Chicken
with, 145
Preserved, Simple, 146, *147*
Lentils
Emeril's Mulligatawny Soup,
186–87
Vegetarian Chili, 257
Linguine with Artichokes,
Shrimp, and Mascarpone,
36, 37

M

Matzoh Ball Soup, 188–89
Meat. *See* Beef; Lamb; Pork;
Rabbit; Veal
Meatball(s)
Big Boy, and Spaghetti, 178–80,
180
Braised, and Chickpea Pita
with Yogurt-Garlic Sauce,
254, 255–56
with Swiss Chard and Farfalle
in Broth, 157–58
Minestrone, 248–49, *249*
Miso-Glazed Scallops with Soba
Noodles, 231
Mojo-Marinated Pork and Black
Bean Stew, 112–13
Moong dal
Banh Xeo: Vietnamese Crêpe,
237–38, *239*
Karahi Chicken, 224–25, *225*
Moussaka, 65–66
Mulligatawny Soup, Emeril's,
186–87
Mushroom(s)
Beef and Barley Soup with
Garlic-Basil Oil, 198–99
Beef Bourguignon, 140–41
Chicken Cacciatore, 110–11
and Fall Squash Barley Risotto,
245
Gorgonzola Sauce, Beefy,
Rigatoni with a, 4–5
Jap Chae, 218–19, *219*
Meat and Veggie Lover's Deep-
Dish Pizza, 61–63, *62*
Ricotta, and Roasted Red
Peppers, Jumbo Shells
Stuffed with, 48–49

Shiitake, Sauce, Creamy, Pork
Schnitzel with, 10–11
10-Vegetable Stir-Fry, 205–7, *207*
Thai Chicken and Coconut
Soup, 190–91, *191*
Udon Noodle Stir-Fry with
Vegetables, 226–27
Veal Marsala, 9
Wonton Soup, 195–97, *196*
Mussels
Bouillabaisse, 172–73, *175*
Emeril's Paella, 17–19, *18*
in a Green Curry Broth, 222
New England–Style Fish and
Shellfish Chowder, 258–59,
259
Steamed, with Toasted Israeli
Couscous, 171

N

Noodle(s)
Beef Brisket Pho, 265–67, *266*
Cellophane, Beef Salad, Fiery,
208–9
Jap Chae, 218–19, *219*
Pad Thai with Shrimp and
Tofu, 212–13
Soba, Miso-Glazed Scallops
with, 231
Udon, Stir-Fry with Vegetables,
226–27
Nuts
Roasted Pork Chops with
Jeweled Rice Pilaf, 67–69, *68*
Spinach and Phyllo Tart,
87–89

O

Olives
and Artichokes, Lamb and
Potato Stew with, 131–32
Cerignola, and Preserved
Lemons, Tagine of Chicken
with, 145
Green, and Fennel, Braised
Breast of Veal with, 137–39,
138
Whole Fried Fish Veracruz
Style, 214–15

Onions
Beef Bourguignon, 140–41
Tortilla Española, 28–29
Oxtails, Caribbean-Style, 118–19,
119
Oysters, Poached, Artichoke
Soup with, 164–66, *165*

P

Pad Thai with Shrimp and Tofu,
212–13
Paella, Emeril's, 17–19, *18*
Pancetta
Cassoulet with Confit and
Garlic Sausage, 133–36
Pasta e Fagiole, 40
Pappardelle, Rabbit Ragout over,
142, 143–44
Parsley Caper Aïoli, 169–70
Pasta. *See also* Couscous;
Noodle(s)
Baked Cavatappi with Chicken
in a Pesto Cream Sauce,
56–58, *57*
Baked Semolina Gnocchi with
Smoked Ham and Green
Beans, 50, *51*–53
Big Boy Meatballs and
Spaghetti, 178–80, *180*
Butternut Squash Lasagna with
Italian Sausage and Sage,
76–78, *77*
e Fagiole, 40
Fettuccine with a Crawfish
Cream Sauce, 2–3
Fideuà, 24–27, *25*
Jumbo Shells Stuffed with
Ricotta, Mushrooms, and
Roasted Red Peppers,
48–49
Linguine with Artichokes,
Shrimp, and Mascarpone,
36, 37
Meatballs with Swiss Chard
and Farfalle in Broth, 157–58
Minestrone, 248–49, *249*
Rabbit Ragout over
Pappardelle, *142,* 143–44
Rigatoni with a Beefy
Mushroom Gorgonzola
Sauce, 4–5